I0198791

Conservative Hurricane

Florida Government and Politics

UNIVERSITY PRESS OF FLORIDA

Florida A&M University, Tallahassee
Florida Atlantic University, Boca Raton
Florida Gulf Coast University, Ft. Myers
Florida International University, Miami
Florida State University, Tallahassee
New College of Florida, Sarasota
University of Central Florida, Orlando
University of Florida, Gainesville
University of North Florida, Jacksonville
University of South Florida, Tampa
University of West Florida, Pensacola

Conservative Hurricane

How Jeb Bush Remade Florida

MATTHEW T. CORRIGAN

Foreword by David R. Colburn and Susan A. MacManus, series editors

University Press of Florida

Gainesville · Tallahassee · Tampa · Boca Raton

Pensacola · Orlando · Miami · Jacksonville · Ft. Myers · Sarasota

VIVA FLORIDA 500
1513-2013
A Florida Quincentennial Book

Copyright 2014 by Matthew T. Corrigan
All rights reserved
Printed in the United States of America on recycled, acid-free paper

This book may be available in an electronic edition.

19 18 17 16 15 14   6 5 4 3 2 1

Library of Congress Control Number: 2014943167
ISBN 978-0-8130-6045-3

The University Press of Florida is the scholarly publishing agency for the State
University System of Florida, comprising Florida A&M University, Florida At-
lantic University, Florida Gulf Coast University, Florida International University,
Florida State University, New College of Florida, University of Central Florida,
University of Florida, University of North Florida, University of South Florida,
and University of West Florida.

University Press of Florida
15 Northwest 15th Street
Gainesville, FL 32611-2079
http://www.upf.com

To John, 12, and Jane, 5

May the Florida of their future meet their dreams and expectations.

Contents

Foreword

Florida has held a unique place in the American mind for more than six decades. For many retirees, its environment has been like a healthy elixir that allows them to live longer and more robust lives; for others, Florida is a place of renewal, where all things are possible; and for immigrants, it is a place of political freedom and opportunity. Historian Gary Mormino describes the state as a "powerful symbol of renewal and regeneration." It has been suggested that, if Florida had not existed in the post–World War II era, Americans would have been the poorer for it. Others who watched the 2000 presidential election wondered if that were so.

During World War II, Americans from all walks of life discovered Florida through military service, and it opened their eyes to the postwar possibilities. With the end of the war in August 1945, Florida veterans returned home, where they were soon joined by hundreds and then thousands of Americans who were ready to pursue a new life in the Sunshine State. In the sixty-five years between 1945 and 2010, millions of people moved into the state, and the population swelled from 2.25 million to 18.8 million.

Florida's population growth, the settlement patterns of new residents, and their diversity had a profound effect on the state's place in the nation, as well as on the image Floridians had of themselves. Prior to 1940, Florida was the least populous state in the South and one of the poorest in the nation. Its society and economy were rural and agricultural, biracial and segregated, and most residents lived within forty miles of the Georgia border. These demographics and the state's history shaped the public's racial and cultural mindset and its politics. Florida was a one-party state, controlled by the Democratic Party since the end of Reconstruction in 1876.

All that changed in the sixty years following World War II. By 2014, in less than an average life span today, Florida became the most populous state in the region, the fourth largest in the nation (soon to be third), a senior haven, and a dynamic multiracial and multiethnic state. Most Floridians now reside closer to the Caribbean than to Georgia, and, for most, their image of themselves and their state has been significantly influenced by this new geographic orientation. By the twenty-first century, demographers viewed Florida as a microcosm of the nation because of its size and population complexity.

As Florida changed, so too did its politics. In 1968 voters threw out the Constitution of 1885 in favor of a new document which would speak to the needs of a new state. They then gradually abandoned the Democratic Party in favor of a dynamic two-party system. By the 1990s, Republicans used an expanding constituency and control of the districting process following the 1990 census to take control of the state legislature and the congressional delegation. These were remarkable developments and reflected the dramatic changes taking place in the state's population and demographic makeup. By 2008, Republicans controlled all state offices that were districted, although Democrats frequently won in statewide races for governor, U.S. senator, and elected cabinet positions, as well as in presidential contests, and they led Republicans by 42 to 36 percent in registered voters.

Such a politically and demographically complex and diverse population has made Florida today something other than a unified whole. The political maxim "All politics is local" is truer of Florida than of most other states. For example, people who reside in North Florida have little in common with those living in Central or South Florida. While those in Southeast Florida see themselves as part of the "new

America," those in North Florida view Miami as a foreign country. Ask a resident what it means to be a Floridian and few, if any, can answer the question. Ask a Floridian about the state's history, and even fewer can tell you that it has operated under five different flags, or that its colonial period is much older than that of New England or Virginia. Perhaps one in ten or twenty residents can tell you who LeRoy Collins was, despite Republican Jeb Bush's recognition of this Democratic governor as the model for all who followed. It is literally a state unknown and indefinable to its people. Such historical ignorance and regional division become major obstacles when state leaders try to find consensus among voters and solutions that address the needs of all citizens.

An essential purpose of the Florida Government and Politics series is to put Floridians in touch with their rich and diverse political history and to enhance their understanding of the political developments that have reshaped the state, region, and nation. This series focuses on the Sunshine State's unique and dynamic political history since 1900 and on public policy issues that have influenced the state and the nation. The University Press of Florida is dedicated to producing high-quality books on these subjects. It welcomes book-length manuscripts and is also committed to publishing in this series shorter essays of 25 to 50 pages that address some of the immediately pressing public policy issues confronting Florida.

In this volume focusing on former governor Jeb Bush (1999–2007), University of North Florida political scientist Matthew Corrigan describes Bush as "the first governor in Florida history to combine a strongly conservative agenda with an activist approach to government." Bush's governance style and free-market, pro-development, pro-growth philosophy became the blueprint for the newly emerging Republican Party in Florida and for Republican governors across the United States. Corrigan asserts that by the time Bush left office at the end of his second term, he had become "the most powerful governor in Florida history."

Utilizing detailed historical chronologies, Corrigan reveals how the timing was right for the emergence of a strong Republican governor. Bush's rise to power was aided by significant population and economic growth, the growing presence and clout of Republican voters and officeholders, major changes in the structure of Florida government, especially the constitutional amendments reducing the size of the cabinet and imposing legislative term limits, and the rise of the conservative movement nationally and in Florida. His initial victory as the first Republican governor in more than a decade, coupled with a Republican-controlled Florida legislature—the first united Republican government since Reconstruction—enabled Jeb Bush to win legislative approval of his proposals more easily than his predecessors. His forceful personality and his extraordinary leadership skills were also invaluable assets.

The governor's leadership and communication skills were on full display in 2004 when the state was hit with four major hurricanes in a single year. His constant radio and television appearances, speaking in both English and Spanish and calmly describing what was going to happen and advising citizens how to prepare, got high marks from the public and the media. So, too, did his coordination of state and local emergency centers and the securing of logistical support from key industries in the state. Corrigan cites polling data showing how closely Floridians' evaluations of Bush's gubernatorial performance were intertwined with his crisis management skills.

No chief executive, including Jeb Bush, goes without criticism or fully escapes controversy. Among the several high-profile rough spots he had to navigate was the 2000 presidential election, which exposed major flaws in Florida's election system and prompted many Gore supporters to blame him personally for the fiasco that ended up in a U.S. Supreme Court decision placing his brother George W. Bush in the presidency. Another was a sit-in by two African American legislators, followed by a large-scale protest by many minority students against his One Florida initiative ending affirmative action in college admissions. Then there was the heart-wrenching Terri Schiavo case, which became a national test of what government should or should not do when individuals confront end-of-life issues. The Schiavo case embroiled the governor in fierce battles involving all three branches of government at the state and national levels before he finally bowed out of the controversy. The episode led some to label him a (religious) "culture warrior." For Corrigan, Bush's repeated efforts to prevent the removal of Schiavo's feeding tube "showcased Bush's stubbornness, his belief in executive branch supremacy, and his wariness of the judicial system." Throughout his tenure, Bush repeatedly sparred with and lost tussles with the Florida Supreme Court over various school reforms, most notably vouchers. But, as Corrigan notes, through all of these controversies, Bush never abandoned his conservative principles.

Overall, the most compelling support for the author's major thesis—that Bush effectively expanded the power of the governor's office and changed the ideological direction of the state—comes from a very thorough and engaging examination of state policies in three key areas: 1) education (school choice, student testing, teacher accountability, grading of schools based on student performance, ending affirmative-action-based college admissions), 2) social and religious issues (abortion, gun rights, faith-based prison rehabilitation), and 3) management of state government (tax cuts, privatization, personnel reduction, economic development incentives to the Scripps Institute and others). Corrigan's analysis of the impact of major reforms based on before-and-after statistics concludes that the results have been mixed. At the same time, many of these policy redirections have had far longer-lasting consequences than critics initially predicted.

In sum, this book offers invaluable insights into the governing philosophy and leadership skills of Florida's powerful forty-third governor, which both his political allies and his adversaries will find fascinating. In the words of the author, in spite of some of his more moderate stances on the environment and immigration reform, Jeb Bush "was a solid conservative leader. . . . Bush made Florida into a laboratory of conservative governance at the state level, and its effects are still being felt today in the state and around the nation."

Corrigan concludes by raising the interesting question of whether Bush's brand of conservatism is conservative enough for the vocal Tea Party component of the Republican Party should he seek higher office in the future.

David R. Colburn and Susan A. MacManus
Series editors

1

Introduction

"Florida has just wobbled into Weirdsville." These words from CBS anchor Dan Rather at three a.m. on the presidential election night/morning of November 7–8, 2000, aptly described the chaos that was occurring in the state of Florida. Earlier in the night the state had been called for Vice President Al Gore and then called for George W. Bush and then finally called for no one.

In a scenario worthy of Shakespeare, the election to become the leader of the free world had come down to a single state—Florida, the strange mix of conservative southern history and diverse multiethnic population; Florida, where Jeb Bush, brother of the Republican nominee George W. Bush, was governor. The Bush family, including former president George H. W. Bush and Jeb Bush, had gathered in a Texas hotel to watch the results with George W. Thus the governor of

Florida was sitting next to his brother when the confusion in Florida unfolded. After the election night of November 2000, the election system in Florida would literally be put on trial, and it would not hold up well. George W. Bush would be declared the winner of Florida and the next president by the U.S. Supreme Court when it decided *Bush v. Gore*. The Court basically concluded there was no fair way to do a complete recount, so Bush was the winner. Voters had been purged from registration lists, different Florida counties had different standards for counting votes, and few officials at the state and local levels had an understanding of how to conduct a recount. While Florida counties, and not the state government, have most of the responsibility for holding elections, the fact that the disputed election came out in favor of the brother of the sitting governor stained both the state of Florida and its governor.

Such is the mental association that many observers outside Florida make when the name Jeb Bush is mentioned. This is an unfortunate consequence of history. A better example of Jeb Bush's career as Florida's governor came during the terrible hurricane season of 2004. The number and the ferocity of the hurricanes named Charley, Frances, Ivan, and Jeanne was unprecedented in recent Florida history. Every section of the state was impacted by one of these hurricanes. Before every storm, Governor Bush mobilized the Emergency Operations Center in Tallahassee. From the Operations Center, Bush would appear on television and calmly describe what was going to happen and how best to prepare. His appearances were televised throughout the state, and he spoke in English and in Spanish. The ability to communicate fluently in Spanish helped to assure Spanish-speaking Floridians that the state government was there for them as well. This was critical in a state where Hispanic Americans were nearing 20 percent of the population. One newspaper columnist wrote about Bush's outreach to all citizens: "when they write the history of the storm-tossed Summer and Fall it should note that these were the days when the governor showed just how much he was worried about us and I do mean all."[1]

Bush led the coordination of the state emergency center with all of the local emergency centers in the sixty-seven counties of Florida. The cooperation between the state and the local emergency operators was constructive. This was a stark contrast to the performance of the state government at the time of Hurricane Andrew in 1992. Democratic governor Lawton Chiles's administration was severely criticized for its response to the hurricane that killed sixty-five Florida citizens and cost billions. The federal response to the hurricane under Bush's father, President George H. W. Bush, was also severely criticized.

Governor Bush's leadership involving the hurricanes just happened to occur during the 2004 presidential election season. After the controversy over the election outcome of *Bush v. Gore* in Florida in 2000, many observers believed that the state would be very close again. However, with his brother George W. Bush running for reelection, Governor Jeb Bush had left a strong positive impression of the Bush name in Florida. Less than one month before the presidential election in 2004, a public opinion poll by the firm Mason-Dixon found that a majority of Florida voters judged Governor Bush's handling of the disasters as "excellent" or "good."[2] On election night in 2004, George W. Bush surprised observers by winning the state of Florida with a comfortable 5 percent margin. In 2000, Governor Jeb Bush had received criticism for the close presidential race in Florida that his brother barely won. In 2004, it can be argued, the governor delivered the critical state of Florida for his brother with his leadership during the hurricanes. Ironically, the empathy and efficiency and attention to detail that earned Governor Jeb Bush praise for with his handling of the hurricanes in Florida in 2004 was completely different from the perception of how his brother George W. Bush handled the devastation of New Orleans by Hurricane Katrina in 2005. The most famous image of President Bush in that crisis has him looking down on the massive destruction from an airplane high above. This conveyed the terrible impression that President George W. Bush was not involved or really concerned about the victims of Hurricane Katrina. He should have consulted his brother, because Governor Jeb Bush understood that citizens want responsive leaders during a time of crisis.

The hurricanes are an example of how Jeb Bush took control in a state that was grounded in a tradition of having weak governors, as were most southern states after the Civil War. The hurricane is also an appropriate metaphor for the way Jeb Bush changed the politics and policy of the state of Florida. The conservative Southern Democratic period of Florida politics from the end of the Civil War to the 1960s was marked by government inaction on a host of issues facing the state. Since the early 1970s, Florida had been mostly governed on the state level with the moderate to progressive policies of a series of Democratic governors and legislatures. A brief interlude occasioned by the election of a Republican governor in 1986 did not last, as Republican Bob Martinez lost his reelection bid in 1990 to a Democrat, former U.S. senator Lawton Chiles.

Jeb Bush's real legacy is that he completely changed Florida's politics and policy during his time as governor of the state from 1999 to 2007. Unlike what his brother George W. Bush was able to accomplish as president, Jeb Bush was able to pass and implement a comprehensive conservative domestic policy agenda. As chapters 2 and 3 will show, conservatism is not new to Florida. However, Jeb Bush was a politician who was able to shepherd sweeping conservative changes through the state legislature. Jeb Bush implemented conservative *action*. For example, in 2003 Governor Bush got the Florida legislature to pass a law to bypass the Florida courts in the case of Terri Schiavo, a woman in a vegetative state whose husband was seeking to remove her artificial nutrition so she could die. The case became a national spectacle and almost a constitutional showdown between Bush and the United States Supreme Court. In the *same week*, Bush secured from the Florida legislature the largest incentive package for an industry in Florida history, totaling more than half a billion dollars, after Bush made the case that the Scripps Research Institute would substantially remake Florida's economy.

Throughout Florida history, even when Democratic governors shared power with Democratic legislatures, the state legislature had usually held the upper hand. The Florida Constitutions of 1885 and 1968 had created a weak-governor system, and the Florida legislature was usually slow to act. Moreover, legislators built up institutional power because there were no term limits on their positions until the 1990s. Even by the year 1999, Florida was ranked thirty-fifth among the fifty states in gubernatorial institutional power.[3]

With adroit use of timing, changes in government structure, and his personality, Jeb Bush turned a weak-governor state that moved incrementally in public policy into an executive-driven conservative public-policy showcase. He also put forth a governing blueprint for other conservative Republican governors to follow. As detailed in these pages, the unique combination of Florida history, major changes in the structure of Florida government, and the rise of the conservative movement in the nation had come together to make Governor Jeb Bush the most powerful governor in Florida history. Power here is defined as having clear policy preferences and being able to pass and implement these policies. This book does not make judgments on whether Bush was the best or most important governor. Those words are more subjective, those qualities harder to analyze. Florida has had several remarkable governors including Democrats LeRoy Collins and Reubin Askew, but none managed to get his policy preferences enacted and implemented to the extent that Jeb Bush did. Bush not only advocated and campaigned on large, bold themes, he was able to get the legislature to pass a large part of his agenda. Many of the policies he championed and carried out in Florida have become templates for other conservative governors around the nation since the earliest years of the new century. In late 2006 before he left the governor's office, he talked about his greatest accomplishment: "I believe a weak form of governorship is not appropriate for a dynamic state like Florida. . . . My gift perhaps is that with this office now, we've shown that governors can be activist, they can be reformers if they want to. If they want to create the agenda and work as a team with the Legislature, things can be accomplished."[4] If it was a team, Jeb Bush was clearly in charge and calling the plays. Even though he won his office four years after his brother George W. was elected governor of Texas, Jeb, armed with a compliant Republican majority in the legislature, passed a broader conservative agenda than his brother did in Texas.

This book is not a biography. The plan is to focus on the historical and legal factors that helped Jeb Bush gain such power, how his policies passed, and what impact these polices have had on the state. The book does not examine in great detail Governor Bush's political campaigns and does not chronicle every minute of his time as governor. Instead it focuses on major policy changes he proposed, got passed into law, and implemented. The title of the book represents the fact that Jeb Bush turned Florida in a new direction. The book details how a number of important factors came together to allow Jeb Bush to become the most powerful governor in Florida history, and how he used this power to make real changes in the political and policy direction of the state. The results of these policies are clearly mixed. Yet, agree or disagree with his policy direction, the bottom line for the Bush years is that Jeb Bush changed the state of Florida and the nation by setting an example of conservative action at the state level.

Accordingly, the book examines Florida history to put Bush's time in office in perspective. The historical chapters are not meant to be definitive studies of Florida political history. Instead, they are included to help readers who are not versed in Florida history to put Bush's years in context. Changes in Florida's gubernatorial powers and the conservative movement in America came together at the same time to give Jeb Bush unprecedented power in the state. Journalistic accounts of his time in office are reviewed to detail how Bush got his agenda passed. Where possible, the impact of his policies is evaluated by examining public polling, measurable outcomes, and whether these policies are still in place today.

The book differs in its approach from other analyses of Bush's time as governor. Award-winning journalist S. V. Dáte's *Jeb: America's Next Bush* is a searing indictment of Bush's gubernatorial record. That book was told from the insider perspective of someone who covered him as a journalist, and had a difficult relationship with him during his time in office, especially after Dáte reported on deficiencies in Bush's school choice program. Professor Robert Crew's book *Jeb Bush: Aggressive Conservatism in Florida* is a detailed and exhaustive account of almost all of Governor Bush's executive actions. Crew's well-researched book concludes that Bush's tenure did not leave a lasting impact on the state. In contrast, this book concludes that historical and political factors made Jeb Bush the most powerful governor in Florida history and that the impacts of his agenda have been long-lasting and important. Told from the (hopefully) objective viewpoint of a Florida political scientist and observer, it is written for both political analysts and the general reader with an interest in Florida politics and Jeb Bush and his future as a possible presidential candidate.

Chapter 2 explores how Florida's gubernatorial office became so weak and how Jeb Bush's time as governor was such a departure from this trend. Chapter 3 focuses on the conservative movement in the nation and how Jeb Bush represents different strains of this movement, with various conservative ideas appearing time and time again in his tenure as governor. Bush was able to use changes in the governing structure of the state along with a conservative ideology to begin a strong shift away from the moderate-to-progressive policies that Florida had followed since the governorship of Reubin Askew in 1970. Yet even with his solidly conservative record, Jeb Bush presently has a mixed relationship with the Tea Party movement that has gained strong influence in the Republican Party since 2010—a relationship that is examined in the last chapter.

In chapters 4, 5, and 6, three major policy areas are examined to show the extent of changes to Florida's politics and policy. Chapter 4 looks at cultural and moral issues. For those national observers who question Governor Bush's conservative credentials, a look at his record on issues such as abortion, gun rights, faith-based prisons, and the Terri Schiavo case show that Jeb Bush had an active and comprehensive approach to legislating cultural issues. Chapter 5 examines how Governor Bush completely changed K–12 education in the state, enacting controversial and comprehensive accountability measures that would fundamentally impact every school in the state. Chapter 6 focuses on Bush's efforts to manage state government by reducing taxes, encouraging massive privatization, and using government funds to attract businesses to the state. The final chapter provides a summary and an update of both Jeb Bush's political standing and his policy initiatives in the state, as well as a discussion of how he would use his record as governor of Florida as the centerpiece of a possible presidential run in 2016.

The results of these efforts in conservative policymaking have been unpredictable and mixed, and some are not clear even now, seven years after he left office. However, what is not up for dispute is the breadth of change Jeb Bush brought to Florida's public sector. Whether Governor Bush ultimately decides to run for president of the United States, become secretary of education in the next Republican administration, or remain an elder statesman in the Republican Party, his time as Florida governor is the best indicator of his governing philosophy and style and what he can offer the nation as a policy and/or political leader.

2

Gubernatorial Power
in Florida History

For nearly a decade in the early 1800s, United States Army general Andrew Jackson worked to conquer Spanish Florida. Andrew Jackson suffered no fools. He pursued the battle in Florida beyond the mandate given to him by President James Monroe. Jackson waged two military campaigns, including the First Seminole War, to induce Spain to sign the territory over to the United States.[1] By 1821 General Andrew Jackson was the governor of the Florida Territory. He had the power to appoint all local and state officials. He was America's most effective general and the undisputed leader of the unsettled and unpredictable Florida Territory.

Given Florida's geography, political structure, and constantly changing demographics, it would be 177 years before the state again had a governor with both national stature and unquestioned political power.[2] To understand why Jeb Bush stands out as a political leader, his governorship must be placed in the context of the political and social history of Florida. Because of its history, a conservative southern political tradition collides with an ever-changing diverse population in the state of Florida to produce a unique political makeup. This history would forge a governing structure that limited strong executive leadership. Vigorous government leadership relied too often on the personal background and characteristics of its leaders. According to scholars Richard Scher and David Colburn, three factors—changing demographics, a weak constitutional structure, and the personal characteristics of the governors—combined to produce a distinctive political culture that often blocked fundamental political and policy changes.[3] Aided by timing, strategy, and good fortune, Governor Jeb Bush completely jolted Florida's political culture and turned these limiting factors on their collective heads. He also moved Florida politics strongly to the right and away from the moderate policies of the late twentieth century under Democratic governors Reubin Askew, Bob Graham, and Lawton Chiles. In many respects, Jeb Bush used important changes in the governing structure of the state to vigorously implement conservative policies that had roots in Florida political history. These changes include a shrinking of the Florida cabinet, with whom the Florida governor shares power, and the imposition of term limits for Florida legislators in the 1990s. In order to understand the unusual nature of Bush's time as governor, the historical underpinnings of the office need to be examined.

The territory that Andrew Jackson conquered in 1821 evolved into a state with a shifting political power structure that would allow only a few governors to truly make a significant impact on the state's future. The time between the founding of the territory in 1821 and the Civil War in 1861 would exhibit the challenges of governing Florida that have persisted to the present day.

The biggest hurdle to making Florida part of the United States was finding Americans who wanted to live there. Unlike the tourist mecca and high-growth state it became in the twentieth century, the Florida of the 1820s was a harsh place. The stifling heat, the lack of good trails, and the hostile relations between whites and Seminole Indians made Florida a tough sell.

The economic and population center was in the northern part of the territory. Central and southern Florida were still largely inaccessible and, apart from the port city of Key West at the very southern tip, mostly uninhabited by white settlers. The middle part of the Panhandle was the most promising area to begin farming and a plantation way of life. The city of Tallahassee in the Panhandle would become the first state capital because it was about equidistant between northern Florida's two main cities, Pensacola and St. Augustine. These geographic facts strongly influenced Florida's political culture. The northern part of the state, being attached to other southern states, absorbed their traditional conservative way of life. And the northern part of the state would retain its political primacy even when Florida's wealth and growth eventually became centered in the lower part.

In order to spur population and economic growth, the federal government passed the Armed Occupation Act of 1842, targeted at increasing white settlement in the central and southern parts of the state. White citizens were given 160 acres of land at no cost, and 1,200 citizens took part in the government-supported land giveaway. This action set a precedent that was repeated over and over during Florida's history. A pro-development and pro-growth philosophy would remain part of Florida's political and social culture. Several wars with Native Americans in the state made it difficult to attract new white settlers. Accordingly, incentives often were used. This would not be the first time that Florida residents failed to see the value of their own state and, as a result, gave away its resources for little or nothing. Tax and other monetary incentives would be continuously offered to outside business interests to attract more employment to the state.

The Florida Territory achieved statehood in 1845 because it received support in Congress as a new slave state to balance the addition of the "free" state of Iowa in 1846. Race and the condition of African Americans in the state would continue to be a major factor in the state's politics and development for decades to come.[4]

With its small and transient population, uncertain political leadership, and continually shifting demographics, the new state struggled to form its own identity. From the beginning, Florida found itself in a political battle between banking interests and Jacksonian populists. Andrew Jackson's populist message and military profile finally won him the presidency in 1828. Part of his political appeal was a visceral dislike for banks and other concentrations of financial power.[5] Jackson believed that political power should belong to white landowners, businessmen, and laborers. He also believed that slavery was a vital economic necessity for America in the 1820s. His presidency along with the expansion of the vote to most white male Americans fostered a powerful political force in the United States. As Florida was becoming a state in the 1840s, the leading politicians of the territory adopted most of Jackson's ideals. This political affiliation was the beginning of the Florida Conservative Democratic Party that would form after the Civil War (Conservative was part of its original name).[6] These early conservative Democrats made sure that economic and political power was not concentrated in the hands of bankers and other northern interests. They wanted political power for landowners who were making the new state their permanent home. Their democratic impulse did not translate into concern about the human rights of black residents, whether free or slave. Moreover, after two wars and decades of abuse, the Seminole Indians were also ignored by the state's political leaders. Slavery was seen as a lynchpin of the economy in the developing state. In sum, the time from the founding of the territory to the beginning of the Civil War helped to form the major factors in the state's political culture that would impact political leadership for decades to follow. These factors included a frontier mentality concerning land and development, no clear lines of authority within the political leadership, changing demographics, and a strong aversion to the national government and outsiders. The circumstances that led Florida into the Civil War would serve to solidify these factors even further and would continue to limit executive leadership well into the next century.

The Jacksonian Democratic Party in Florida provided a platform for secessionist views right from the founding of the state in 1845. Among the first governors and most of the leaders of the new state, there was an intense dislike of abolitionists and northerners. The 1860 presidential election in Florida highlighted these sentiments. The Democratic presidential candidate John Breckenridge received the most votes in the state (just 8,543—by way of comparison, nearly 6 million votes were cast in Florida in the controversial 2000 presidential election). The newly formed Republican Party's candidate, Abraham Lincoln, was not even on the ballot in the state.

As soon as Lincoln's national victory became apparent, Florida's course was set in regard to secession. Representatives to a Florida state convention that had formed to respond to Lincoln's victory voted 62 to 7 in favor of joining the revolt. There were Unionists, especially from Duval County, who argued that civil war would be disastrous for the state, but they were in the clear minority. The state with a small population and vast tracts of unsettled land endorsed a civil war against its own national government even though it lacked the militia to defend its own territory. The Civil War and its aftermath would shape the political and social future of the state until the present day. Most southern states did not recover for many years after the economic and social hardships brought on by the war.

Civil War and Reconstruction

The impact of the Civil War and the failed attempt at Reconstruction had a major impact on Florida's political future. Joining ten other states in rebellion against the national government made native Floridians sworn enemies of leaders in Washington and citizens in the North. The resentments that built up over the loss of slavery and the defeat in the war would permeate the attitudes of native white Floridians for generations. As white conservative Floridians struggled to regain power after the Civil War, they remembered the military defeats and the postwar political humiliation. These visceral feelings among Florida citizens resulted in a Redemption constitution in 1885 that would emasculate strong political leadership in the state for decades to come.

Florida was no particular bargain for the Confederacy. The state possessed important ports, but from a military standpoint it was difficult to defend. The low population density ensured that the Confederacy would not expend tremendous resources to defend the southernmost state. At the beginning of the Civil War, the state averaged only three people per square mile. What the Confederacy needed from Florida was its fighting men and its food production. Early in the war, the Confederacy left only 2,500 soldiers to defend Florida's 54,000 square miles of land. Florida governor John Milton declared that leaving such a small force in the state effectively ceded the state to the "Lincoln government." The population that remained in Florida dealt with the harsh impacts of the Civil War. The port cities of Pensacola, Panama Beach, and Jacksonville were invaded and plundered by Union troops. Poverty was widespread as the Confederate economic system never fully developed. A series of taxes imposed by a Confederate government desperate for revenue added even more to the economic burden of Floridians trying to survive. As the war dragged on and more taxes were imposed, resentment toward the Confederate government grew. Even in the midst of a secession the state had supported, Floridians did not want to pay higher taxes, and this antitax sentiment has remained a central part of its politics until the present day. More than a century later, Jeb Bush's legislative program would include some of the largest tax cuts in Florida history.

In 1864 as the war was winding down, the Confederates won a major battle in the town of Olustee near Lake City, Florida. This victory was short-lived, as the depleted Confederate army basically abandoned Florida to the Union. After Lee's surrender to Grant in April of 1865, the small number of Confederate troops in Florida surrendered to William Tecumseh Sherman's army a few days later.[7] The depth of some Floridians' revulsion at the Union victory was highlighted by the suicide of the sitting Confederate governor of Florida, John Milton, during the last weeks of the war. Before his suicide, Milton said that "death would be preferable to reunion."[8] Many native Floridians did not enter the postwar period looking for reconciliation but instead carried their contempt of northern Republicans with them as an essential part of their psyche. For a century these feelings would make it difficult for the Republican Party to become an accepted political power in the state. Until the 1960s the conservative political party in the South was the Democratic Party. It was thus a monumental achievement when Jeb Bush brought in the first unified Republican government in

Florida since Reconstruction and fundamentally changed politics in the state.

Reconstruction in Florida

After a war that had killed the most Americans in its history and divided a nation, Floridians and other Southerners had an opportunity to constructively reengage with the Union. This reengagement did not occur for numerous reasons. Many white Floridians simply could not fathom that American slaves were now full American citizens. Moreover, the destitution brought on by the war did not foster a spirit of cooperation. Because of its small population, Florida was also an ideal place for northern carpetbaggers to seek riches and influence. These carpetbaggers came to fill the void of economic capital and opportunity. Native Floridians saw these new residents as plunderers and con artists. After a brief period of more moderate presidential Reconstruction, congressional Reconstruction was imposed in 1866. Military law was reinstated along with a federal guarantee of civil rights for black males. Several state conventions in Florida produced a Reconstruction government composed of Union loyalists, carpetbaggers, and some native white Floridians. Even though the government in 1868 in Florida had a strong Republican bent, this did not produce complete equality of rights for the newly freed slaves. A small number of blacks were elected to public office during this period, but comprehensive political and economic freedoms were not granted.[9] The Reconstruction governments in the state of Florida were marred by corruption and a lack of focus. In the 1870s, both native and newly arrived Floridians were growing disenchanted with the Republican government.

An example of the political tensions of the time was the 1874 assassination of a Republican state legislator, which gave the Conservative Democrats a majority in the state senate. Republicans were losing control of Florida politics. Even if the Republicans had governed wisely, it would have been difficult to retain political power as native white Floridians reasserted themselves. An economic crisis across the nation in the early 1870s hit Florida particularly hard. The economic dislocation caused Republican officeholders to ignore the difficult realities that many new black citizens were encountering. Democratic clubs and vigilantes in the rural areas of the state made sure that the newly freed slaves would not be integrated fully into society.

In the midst of all this turmoil came the important presidential election of 1876. Not unlike the year 2000, the fate of the presidency rested on the outcome in Florida. The race between Democrat Samuel Tilden and Republican Rutherford B. Hayes came down to a few of the southern states. National Republicans let it be known to state and local officials in these disputed states that support for Hayes would translate into the end of military occupation and Reconstruction. The vote count was disputed in Florida, and the Florida Supreme Court ordered a recount.[10] The recount showed that Hayes was the winner on the presidential level in Florida but that the Conservative Democrats had won enough votes to regain the governor's mansion. After three months a congressional commission agreed with the results of the recount. Florida Democrats had the best of all worlds. The national government would no longer interfere in the state's affairs because of Hayes's victory. Moreover, the state government again belonged to the Conservative Democrats. This election started a period known as Redemption when white conservative southerners reestablished their political power. Over the next couple of decades, the Redeemers would put in place legal and cultural norms that made black Americans second-class citizens in their own country once again. In many ways, Conservative Democrats in Florida had lost the war but won the peace. In the view of many Floridians, a large national government had invaded the state, installed former slaves in political positions, and stolen their property and their taxes. Government could not be trusted and powerful executives should not be encouraged. These antigovernment and anti-executive sentiments would direct state leaders to call a constitutional convention to rewrite the 1868 Constitution, which was seen by many as Yankee dominated.

The convention that produced the 1885 Constitution had a profound effect on leadership in Florida for the next eighty years. At that time Florida remained an unsettled frontier state. Hard agricultural work for minimal pay was the norm for most Floridians, along with a lack of both societal and political opportunities.

Into this political vacuum Conservative Democrats inserted themselves. One major thrust of the constitutional convention was to deny blacks the franchise. In disregard of the Fourteenth and Fifteenth Amendments to the U.S. Constitution, a poll tax was approved. This provision would require any potential voter to pay a fee in order to vote—a fee beyond the means of most of the black male adult population—and would thus severely curtail black political participation in Florida. The other major theme of the 1885 Constitution was a complete aversion to executive authority. Strong executive leadership was equated with northern Republicans, not native Floridians. Accordingly, the 1885 Constitution put in place strict limits on the power of the governor. Colburn and Scher in their research highlighted the constraints on the office:

1. The governor could not succeed himself. Limited to one term, he was a lame duck as soon as he was elected.
2. The office of lieutenant governor was eliminated, so the governor would not have a clear successor.
3. The convention delegates created six other executive officers, who comprised a cabinet to work with the governor. The governor would have to share power in areas such as agriculture and education. These other executives could run for reelection and simply wait out a governor they did not like.
4. The governor would no longer appoint local officials; the constitution favored home rule for local governments.
5. The constitution provided for numerous boards and commissions that implemented public policy in important areas such as education and road construction. These boards and commissions would sometimes be in conflict with the governor.
6. With all of these restrictions, the governor still retained the title of chief executive. This title made governors responsible in the eyes of the public, but they had little authority to meet this responsibility.[11]

The Constitution of 1885 put in place a system of governance that would make activist government a real challenge. The Conservative Democrats were much more concerned about preventing a Republican resurgence than attending to the needs of Floridians.[12] The constitution took firm aim at the civil liberties and the voting power of black citizens. In 1902 the Democratic Party in Florida declared itself to be a private entity. This "private club" could exclude any prospective members for any reason, and black citizens were not allowed to join. The Democratic primary elections would now be shut to black voters completely. Black voters who could work their way around local election registrars could only register as Republicans. Since any real competition for political seats occurred in the Democratic primary, voting as a Republican was almost useless.[13]

A prominent Florida journalist, Martin Dyckman, describes the real impact of the 1885 Constitution and its emphasis on racial control: "The existence of a voteless, powerless, and despised underclass would provide cover, the distraction and pretext for nearly a century of misgovernment."[14] Black citizens served as an outlet for the frustrations of both upper-class and lower-class whites. Dyckman's "distraction" aptly describes how the race question was used to keep the Conservative Democrats in power. This distraction also helped to divert the attention of Florida citizens away from the mounting problems that the state faced. Its vast territory had little in the way of basic infrastructure, even by the standards of the late nineteenth century. Schools, transportation, and basic health services were lacking. The challenge of providing these services with a voting population wary of government power and the taxes that would make government action possible remained a major issue for Florida leadership, as the governmental structure put in place by the Constitution of 1885 left little room for strong leadership and government action and no room for racial reconciliation.

The focus on race concealed other political divisions in the state. The unsettled and shifting nature of leadership left the conservative Democrats (no longer named Conservative Democrats but ideologically unchanged) with possible vulnerabilities. Two approaches to Florida government emerged after the 1885 Constitution. One approach reflected the majority conservative Democrats who were centered in the rural counties of the state. These conservative Democrats would remain wary of strong executive leadership and any sense of a return to Republican government. Some historians have labeled these Democrats the Bourbon Democrats because their economic policies focused on the economic elite and—unlike the Democrats before the Civil War—on out-of-state interests such as railroads and land developers.[15] The Bourbon Democrats had a vested interest in seeing that Florida's agricultural system remained based upon cheap sharecropping labor. Accordingly, they moved aggressively against any efforts that might increase the civil rights of blacks—many of whom worked the land for little in return. At the same time these Democratic leaders also were open to the development of the state's natural resources by outside investors. Since Democratic leaders and citizens were not willing to pay the taxes to develop their own state, they had to turn to outsiders for development assistance in exchange for land. This policy approach led to minimalist government with little social progress and very few restrictions on outside business interests.

Progressive and populist issues were not totally gone from the Florida scene. To be sure, these issues would not be taken up by establishing a new party. Starting new political organizations became much more difficult after 1902 when the Democrats established themselves as the only real political party, with a private status that made the Democratic primary the only locus of competition. Instead a progressive movement would emerge and reemerge within the Democratic Party itself. Thus politics in Florida experienced tension throughout the twentieth century. Conservative elements that sought to keep the status quo and limit new political movements (especially civil rights) vied with social and economic reformers who believed that the state had to address the basic needs of its citizens in a more fundamental way. This tension took place within a conservative box, but progressive elements were present in Florida politics throughout the twentieth century, most notably in the LeRoy Collins gubernatorial administration in the 1950s. These progressive elements would help set the stage for a moderate Democratic leadership in the late twentieth century in the state. Jeb Bush effectively stopped progressive leadership in the governor's office when he won in 1998.

Political Leadership in the Twentieth Century

To understand why Jeb Bush's two terms as governor were such a historical departure, the background of other twentieth-century governors needs to be explored. In their seminal work on Florida's governors, Colburn and Scher take a multipronged approach that combines examining the demographic makeup of the state with an examination of the structure and processes of state government along with the personal characteristics of the men who have held the office of governor. With this framework, the authors conclude that, historically, most Florida governors have been constrained in their office.

The governors for most of the twentieth century in Florida could be labeled as cautious in their approach because the citizens and elected officials did not seek or demand much from the office. The factors outlined above worked together to limit their power and effectiveness. An examination of these factors will point up how greatly Jeb Bush's administration differed from many of his predecessors'.

In 1880 Florida was the least populous southern state. By 1970 it would be second only to Texas. The massive migration and immigration into the state that has occurred throughout the twentieth century has left a destabilizing political structure in its wake. Jeb Bush as a young adult would be one of Florida's incoming migrants.

Even though the population comprised citizens from different parts of United States and the world, Florida politics remained dominated by rural interests in the northern part of the state. The demographic profile of Florida's governors in the twentieth century reflects this regional bias. Of the twenty-three Florida governors who served between 1900 and 1998, the vast majority came from the northern and central parts of the state.[16] The malapportionment of legislative districts until the late 1960s guaranteed that political power in the legislature remained in the northern agricultural section of the state. Two-thirds of Florida governors in the twentieth century came from a rural background, and three-quarters were lawyers, although many of these men also had other business interests. Pointing a clear path for future office seekers, 75 percent of the twentieth-century governors served first in the Florida House or Senate. In short, Florida's governors generally have been lawyers who became state legislators representing the northern and central parts of the state.

These characteristics have made it difficult for Florida's governors to assert their independence from the Florida state legislature. Since most governors came from the legislature, they were accustomed to the governor deferring to the legislature on policy issues. Since they had a strong regional bias, they generally did not seek momentous change. Of course, there were important exceptions to this trend. Democratic governor David Scholz implemented extensive New Deal economic policies in the 1930s. Even though most of the other southern state governors fought racial integration vigorously, LeRoy Collins guided a moderate course for the state during the civil rights movement in the 1950s. Reubin Askew fought for the imposition of a corporate income tax to fund the emerging needs of a state in the midst of a population boom in the 1970s. From 1950 onwards, Florida's population would grow an average of 40 percent per decade. State government would continually struggle to provide the infrastructure to meet this growth. Democratic governors Bob Graham and Lawton Chiles attempted to follow in Askew's footsteps. Yet most Florida governors followed a path of small reforms and limited government.

With the substantive restrictions placed on gubernatorial power by the 1885 and 1968 Florida Constitutions, the leadership style of Florida governors became even more important. Since the office's effectiveness depends upon the governor's ability to persuade the legislature, the personal characteristics and appeal of governors are crucial. Colburn and Scher examined the styles of all Florida governors up to Reubin Askew and found that more than half had "reserved personalities."[17] Only five had truly "charismatic" personalities and style. While such traits did not guarantee governing success, this analysis is revealing. Florida governors who found themselves in a structurally limiting system had "reserved" personalities that complemented an office that was reserved in its own powers. Jeb Bush could never be called reserved. His forceful personality would translate into a powerful executive—underscoring the importance of individual characteristics in the job.

The influences on gubernatorial power in the twentieth century, then, were limiting. The constraints of southern history and a structurally weak office combined with governors who came from similar backgrounds and who had reserved personalities. All of these factors led to a less than vibrant gubernatorial office. Scholars Larry Sabato and Thad Beyle have written about how governors across the country became more important in the second half of the twentieth century as executives.[18] Because of the historical strength of the Florida legislature, this power shift to the governor's office was not linear in Florida. Governor Reubin Askew in the early 1970s exhibited strong executive leadership. Yet even he was limited by a legislature (of his own political party) that had amassed institutional power and would not leave public office. Askew's immediate successors all had difficulty dealing with the Florida legislature and an executive bureaucracy slow to react to the state's mounting challenges. Jeb Bush was not limited by many of these factors and as a result became the most powerful Florida governor since Reconstruction. Jeb Bush would be the first governor in Florida history to combine a strongly conservative agenda with an activist approach to government.

To evaluate the historical potential and limits of Florida's governorship, and to draw an informed contrast with Jeb Bush's eight years in office beginning in 1999, three important periods in the twentieth century need to be examined: the land boom of the 1920s and its aftermath in the Depression era; the post–World War II and civil rights period; and the post-civil-rights years.

The Land Boom (1920s)

The state of Florida emerged from World War I as a state transformed. The federal government had provided infrastructure improvements with military bases throughout Florida. Important advances in transportation were making Florida more easily accessible by train and by mass-produced automobiles. The Henry Flagler railroad system now connected most parts of the state with the rest of the nation.[19] At the beginning of the twentieth century, Florida had a small population with lots of cheap land. It also had a mild climate that would give visitors a welcome break from the winters of the North.

These enticements led to a major land boom from 1920 to 1926. Landowners in South Florida led the way into this period of wild real estate speculation accompanied by a large population increase. Developers like Carl Fisher in Miami would send photographs to northern newspapers depicting the tropical luxury of South Florida.[20] In truth, most beach communities in South Florida were underdeveloped and had little supporting infrastructure. But these harsh realities did not slow the land boom. During the decade of the 1920s, the state increased in population by 50 percent, and thirteen new counties were created to handle the incoming population.[21]

However, much of the economic activity around the real estate boom was built upon faulty economics. Real estate brokers would purchase vast amounts of property (including swampland) with 10 percent binders, allowing them first right to purchase the land. The brokers would then sell these binders to other investors, and those investors in turn would sell their newly acquired binders. The Miami newspapers carried thousands of advertisements offering the opportunity for individuals to purchase tracts of land in Florida.[22] Two pro-business governors, Carey Hardee and John Martin, made little attempt to manage or regulate these fundamental changes. To further attract businesses and investors, the legislature passed a proposed prohibition on state income and inheritance taxes, and this constitutional amendment was approved by the voters.[23]

This was a watershed moment in Florida governance. The leaders of the state sent a message to Florida citizens and outside investors: the state would not rely on the wealth of its own citizens to fund its future. The property tax and gas tax could not provide enough funds for the schools and roads that would be needed as Florida's population continued to grow. This dynamic between providing a welcoming environment for outside businesses and funding the needed infrastructure would continually be a major factor in Florida politics. Moreover, much like the real estate boom and bust of the first decade of the twenty-first century in Florida, real estate would be a crucial but speculative part of the economy. Jeb Bush attempted to diversify Florida's economy, but it still remained too reliant on housing and tourism. The leaders of the 1920s made it very clear: taxes in Florida were going to remain low even in the face of a rapidly increasing population. Jeb Bush would build on the same philosophy more than seventy years later.

This bargain with land investors came to a hard end. When a hurricane hit the state in the mid-1920s, investors began to recognize the risk of buying land in Florida. Since most of the land purchases involved undeveloped parcels, they had become extremely overvalued. The land boom quickly became the land bust. Before the Great Depression started nationwide in 1929, Florida showed the nation the economic calamities that were approaching. A series of bank failures crippled the business climate, and the state entered the Depression in worse shape than many others. Moreover, because of Florida's minimalist approach to government, no structure was in place to provide a safety net for its citizens.

The Depression (1930s)

By the early 1930s, Florida government was feeling the real impact of economic crisis. In the 1920s, many cities and counties had issued various bond instruments to fund improvements necessitated by population growth.[24] When the economy soured, local governments could not pay their obligations. This in turn hurt not only Florida banks but other banks that invested in the state. When the banks failed, many Florida residents lost both their liquid assets and any access to credit at the same time. This lack of spending money and available credit crippled Florida's economy. State and local attempts at assistance did not meet the tremendous need. With the state facing the greatest economic catastrophe since the Civil War, Democratic governor Doyle Carlton said that the Depression was being overhyped by "anarchists and communists."[25] He was a conservative Southern Democrat who had campaigned on the theme of lower spending and efficient government. Like other conservative Florida governors, he would have to balance his ideological belief in smaller government with the real needs of the citizens. By the start of the 1931 legislative session, Governor

Carlton realized the depth of the challenges that the state faced. He asked for a major reduction in state expenditures but did ask for new resources for the state's public schools. These resources were desperately needed, because counties could no longer afford to finance a majority of their public school systems. The legislature attempted to meet the governor's request by finding new revenue in taxing gambling activities and increasing the gas tax.[26] While agreeing to help localities keep the schools open, the legislature did nothing to aid the unemployed residents. During this time the millionaire industrialist Alfred I. duPont took a large interest in Florida. After the land bust in the late 1920s, duPont bought thousands of acres of land in northwest Florida at bargain rates. These land purchases caught the eye of Florida politicians and allowed Alfred's brother-in-law and personal representative Ed Ball to become a major figure in Florida's politics and economy. DuPont personally contributed to welfare efforts in the city of Jacksonville when thousands of unemployed men were looking for assistance and no other relief was in sight.[27]

However, the kindness of a few wealthy individuals was hardly enough to address the economic devastation that was occurring in the state. In 1932 Democratic governor David Scholz was elected, again on a promise to cut expenditures and taxes. Even in the midst of this crisis, the conservatism of Florida's leaders still was deeply embedded. State leaders and citizens had a difficult decision to make. Even if residents agreed to be taxed more, they simply did not have the resources to confront the Depression. Since Reconstruction, Floridians, like other southerners, harbored a serious distrust of the federal government. On the national level Franklin Roosevelt had been elected and offered aggressive federal assistance to the states to combat their economic problems. New Deal programs such as the Works Progress Administration could provide direct relief to the cities and counties in Florida. The Federal Deposit Insurance Corporation was created to help ensure the solvency of the banking system—assistance that Florida banks desperately needed. Accordingly, Governor Scholz changed his entire perspective. He would work aggressively to get all the funds that he could from Washington. He demanded that Florida pass the Social Welfare Act of 1935, which established the State Department of Social Welfare, an agency that would work closely with the federal government. This legislative action was so significant that Roosevelt's government hailed it as a model for other states to follow. It also affirmed that Florida's leaders supported the huge transfer of resources from the federal government to the state during this economic crisis.

Still, the state's conservative political culture could bend only so far. The state government became masterful at winning federal funds, but the legislature made little attempt to establish state programs that could address the state's grinding poverty. State leaders and citizens showed that they were willing to accept millions of dollars from the federal government, but they were not willing to pay higher taxes. In 1934 the nation's first homestead exemption law was passed in Florida. This law would exempt taxes on the first $5,000 of valuation for property owners. For a state that relied so heavily on property taxes to fund its operations, this law would impact state revenues for decades to come and widen the gap between demand for services and the revenues to pay for them. The New Deal years showed that Florida citizens were in favor of government benefits but balked at finding revenues to pay for these services—not unlike the majority of the American populace today.

Governor Scholz had come a long way in his political progression. He ran for office as a Florida conservative and left office as a strong liberal New Deal Democrat. In his last report as Florida's governor, he warned his successor, Democrat Fred Cone, that the job "isn't all that it was cracked up to be." When he took office in the middle of the Depression, his own conservative approach to state activism had encountered the equally conservative political cultural and governance structure inherited from the Constitution of 1885. However, when he realized the depth of the economic problems that the state faced, he advocated strong government action.[28] The legislature did not act with the same urgency that Scholz demanded, and the citizens of the state voted to lower their taxes in 1934. Even when the governor wanted to be an activist governor in the midst of a national emergency, Florida's legislature and citizens put a limit on just how far he could go. Governor Cone returned to a more traditional model of Florida leadership. He would be reserved and deferential to the legislature. In 1937 he did not even submit a legislative program. He supported Roosevelt's programs, but he made little effort to improve state government. The structure of Florida's government, the personality of its governor, and the unsettled nature of its population combined to produce a government that was passive and unresponsive. Florida's government would not get another serious push for reform until the leadership of LeRoy Collins in the 1950s.

Post–World War II and the Civil Rights Period

As it had with the previous war, Florida emerged from World War II as a different place. The Depression had made this poor, isolated state even more isolated and poor. The political establishment was solidly conservative even while accepting New Deal aid from the federal government. World War II brought drastic changes. More than two million military personnel came to Florida for training at the state's new military bases. These men and women remembered the state after the war and saw it as a land of opportunity. Air-conditioning for buildings and better transportation also made it a more attractive place for living and working.[29] Florida's population increased by 25 percent during the 1940s. Many of these new residents headed to South and Central Florida. They also brought different political views with them. They were not as socially conservative as the conservative Democrats in Tallahassee, and they were looking for a dynamic environment to grow their families and their businesses. This population shift to the south of the state would divide the state politically and socially.

In this period of dramatic change, a state senator from Tallahassee named LeRoy Collins would become the most consequential governor since the Civil War. Collins began his service in the state legislature in the 1930s, and by 1954, when Governor Dan McCarty died in office, he was ready to run for governor.

Segregation and racial politics were at the forefront of the political scene in Florida in the early 1950s. Strom Thurmond, a U.S. senator from South Carolina, had started a political earthquake in the South in 1948 by running as a Dixiecrat independent candidate espousing states' rights—which was a clear code for retaining segregation. With support from the new Floridians in the southern part of the state, Florida rejected Thurmond in 1948 and went for Harry Truman. However, Thurmond received thousands of votes in the northern part of the state—the very part that held the legislative power in Florida.

LeRoy Collins took a cue from Truman and attempted to find a moderate path on the segregation issue in the 1954 governor's race. He knew that the thousands of new Florida residents in the South were less concerned about the segregation issue than about developing the state economically. Collins did not call for the end of segregation, but he did denounce the extremists on the race issue. In fact, he used his more moderate position on segregation as a major campaign issue. His opponent was the acting governor, Charlie Johns, who had refused to support legislation that would limit the Ku Klux Klan in Florida. Johns epitomized everything conservative about Southern Democrats. He was from a small rural county and a strong supporter of segregation.

Many of the new residents in Florida could not be called progressive on the race issue, but they were not as conservative as their fellow citizens in North Florida. Collins slammed Johns as being part of the old Democratic establishment that had not moved the state forward for decades.[30] His strategy paid off when he won the Democratic runoff with 55 percent of the vote. Collins had lost 44 counties out of 67, but he won all of the populous counties in South Florida. Collins's victory in 1956 was a precursor to the political trends in the late twentieth century in Florida. As the Republican Party grew in strength and won over former conservative Democrats, most Democratic strength in the state became confined to a few large counties in the southeastern part of the state.

The state was divided politically, but Collins's victory was important. Since he was completing the term of the previous governor, he served for two years and then could run again in 1956. If he won reelection, he would be governor for more consecutive years than any other governor since Reconstruction. Collins's view of state government was strongly activist. In his first speech to the Florida legislature, he told the conservative legislators: "So much to be done, so little time."[31] He believed that Florida was in need of fundamental reform. To exemplify how far the state needed to progress, the state legislature in 1949 seriously debated whether to remove cows and horses from the state's highways to allow for better transportation.

Collins came into office with a full agenda. His major initiatives included revising the 1885 state constitution, putting together a reapportionment of state legislative seats, and establishing a junior college system of higher education, while attempting to avoid the cultural conflict brought on by the fledgling civil rights movement throughout the South. Any one of these initiatives would have been a lot to ask of Florida state government. Reforming the Constitution and revising the way state legislative seats were apportioned was taking power away from well-entrenched political leaders. Moreover, Florida's cabinet executive system continually blocked fundamental changes. Two of Governor Collins's cabinet officers had served for 25 years or more, and a third served for 21 years. It did not matter that they all shared the same political party. As in many southern states at the time, the only viable party on the state level was a conservative Democratic Party. These old-time conservative Democrats were not excited about Collins's ideas for fundamental reform. The 1885 Constitution, while creating a weak governor's office, had given considerable latitude to the legislature. Since there were no term limits on state legislative offices until the 1990s, legislators could serve for decades. The advantages of being an incumbent made it extremely difficult for legislators to lose reelection. In the 1880s, when the Constitution was created, the northern part of the state had the population and the political power. Even with the tremendous growth of the state in the 1940s, northern candidates still occupied a majority of the legislative seats. This disconnect between population and representation became so egregious in the 1950s that less than 20 percent of Florida's voting population elected a majority of the House and the Senate.[32]

These rural county legislators from northern Florida became known as the Pork Chop Gang. They were culturally conservative and strong supporters of segregation. They wanted to take care of their constituents but did not want to pay for improvements in other parts of the state. They received financial support from business interests that advocated for low taxes and less regulation.[33] Unconcerned about the rest of the state, the Pork Choppers were able to block meaningful regulation of business and development. One version or another of this northern Florida coalition had ruled Florida since the beginning of the state; they were not about to let Governor Collins take away their power without a fight.

The northern-county legislators received a political boost when, just before the state election in 1954, the U.S. Supreme Court made the fundamental ruling that outlawed racial segregation in public schools in *Brown v. Board of Education*. This ruling was a major victory for the civil rights movement, but it created a strident and passionate mobilization of southern whites opposed to integration. Collins privately told his aides and his friends that he wanted to take a stronger position on his opposition to segregation.

Yet in the mid-1950s as the importance of the *Brown* decision began to be realized, Collins knew he could only go so far.[34] In his 1956 campaign, Collins concentrated more on economic development than the race issue, but his opponents in the Democratic primary made it clear that they thought he was soft on the segregation issue. A little-known candidate who was a strict segregationist finished second in the Democratic primary in 1956. This was an omen for Collins that, despite the other issues he wanted to address, segregation and racial justice would dominate his term of office from 1956 to 1960. Jeb Bush would learn about the difficulties of dealing with race in Florida politics when he attempted to change affirmative action policies early in his administration.

In 1957, after the highly publicized struggles in Little Rock, Arkansas, to enforce integration, race dominated politics in the South. Massive resistance, a strategy that advocated openly defying the Supreme Court decision, was invoked throughout the Deep South. Collins bravely stepped up to refute the rhetoric of segregationists. This was not the easy political position to take in the South in the mid-1950s. Many southern politicians who were moderate on the segregation issue became strict segregationists as the political winds shifted. During the 1950s a state legislator from Alabama named George Wallace was known as a progressive judge who was fair to black citizens. By the early 1960s he became the leading voice for segregation in the South.[35]

In order to block the possible integration of Florida schools, a majority of the state legislators wanted to close Florida's public schools. Collins refused, saying, "I will never approve any plan to abolish any public school anywhere." The legislature also passed a resolution supporting interposition—a controversial legal doctrine that argues that states do not have to follow the dictates of the federal government, in direct violation of the Supremacy Clause of the U.S. Constitution. During the late 1950s, Collins had to veto several bills that attempted to close Florida public schools. He would not sacrifice the education of Florida's children to further the agenda of segregationists. Collins grew more decisive in his opposition to segregation and also pleaded with his fellow citizens that massive resistance would lead to economic catastrophe. Southern states that vigorously opposed segregation suffered economically in the late 1950s. Florida depended upon attracting businesses and residents to the state. Businesses did not like social controversies, and Collins was concerned that the struggle over segregation would discourage business relocation to the state. He encouraged fellow southern governors not to wrap themselves in a "Confederate blanket"—an extraordinarily courageous statement at the time. During the last year of his governorship in 1960, sit-ins at lunch counters and other demonstrations were sweeping the South. Cities in Florida like Tallahassee and Jacksonville were no exception. Collins again reminded his fellow citizens about the importance of the rule of law and their moral duty to confront the issue of segregation.[36]

The limitations of the office of governor of Florida made it difficult for Collins to implement his ambitious agenda. However, he deftly found ways to mitigate the racial crisis of the 1950s. He used his veto pen aggressively and was a master of the new medium of television. Since the Pork Chop Gang in the state legislature would not follow his lead, he used TV to go directly to the electorate. In political science terms this is known as "going public," and it was an effective tool for Collins because he was fighting against rumors and exaggerations.[37] He ended his time as governor with considerable accomplishments. He had led the way on merit-based public employment, several important education initiatives, and economic development. However, he knew his office was limited, and he pushed hard for reform of state government. His push for reapportionment and constitutional revision were blocked by the state legislature again. Jeb Bush would not have these obstacles when he pursued his agenda more than fifty years later. Bush had Collins's leadership acumen, but he also had a legislature that submitted to his will.

Still, by the end of the next decade, some of the reforms that Collins advocated finally became reality. Collins took on the political culture of Florida and its antiquated constitution. He did not always succeed, but he showed that even in a place like the state of Florida, activist government was possible. More important, the example he set was followed by future Democratic governors Askew, Graham, and Chiles and in some ways by Republican Jeb Bush.

Askew and the Emergence of a New Democratic Party

The 1960s were a strange decade for Florida politics. While the state continued to undergo amazing transformations, including nearly doubling its population, its politics remained embroiled in a conflict over civil rights and cultural values. Democrat Farris Bryant succeeded LeRoy Collins as governor, but he did not share his moderation on racial issues. A riot in St. Augustine was allowed to get out of control, and Governor Bryant refused any state action to alleviate the unrest. Democratic governor Haydon Burns succeeded Bryant in 1965 after defeating a candidate from South Florida whom Burns called an "integrationist." The Democratic Party in Florida was still split between southern Floridians (more moderate) and northern Floridians (more conservative) on the issue of civil rights.

This split manifested itself in the 1966 gubernatorial election. Miami mayor Robert King High was able to defeat Haydon Burns in the Democratic primary. This was noteworthy because a Democratic candidate from South Florida had won.

High was more liberal on social issues and had been identified with Presidents Kennedy and Lyndon Johnson. He offered a vision of a new Florida focused on development of the economy and the infrastructure.[38] But a cultural backlash was occurring throughout the South. After the passage of the Civil Rights Act of 1964 and the Voting Rights Act of 1965, public opinion shifted sharply against the Democrats.

Race riots in several large cities helped to turn whites who were moderate on race relations against Democrats who supported civil rights. Moreover, the prevalence of more liberal social mores in the nation regarding personal behaviors impacted Florida voters in a negative way. Protests on college campuses across the country impelled social conservatives to speak out. When Jeb Bush became governor, he would be a leading conservative voice in the so-called "culture wars."

Barry Goldwater, the Republican presidential nominee of 1964, had begun to pick up on this backlash. While he was trounced by Lyndon Johnson nationwide in the 1964 presidential election, he won five southern states and was competitive in most states of the South. Claude Kirk, a Republican with an outlandish campaign style, used Goldwater's message in the 1966 Florida gubernatorial race to attack his Democratic opponent. He made sure that Florida voters knew that Robert High was not only a liberal but an "ultraliberal."[39] Even moderate Florida Democrats were tired of the social unrest and upheaval of the 1960s and were looking for new political options. Accordingly, they went with Republican Claude Kirk in overwhelming numbers. Kirk shocked the Democratic establishment by winning 58 counties and most of the state. He would have to deal with a Democratic legislature, but his election was a real triumph that showed the state's Republicans what was possible. For the first time since Reconstruction, a Republican was governor of Florida.

However, Kirk governed in a wildly unpredictable manner. He quarreled with the state legislature, and he started a political fundraising group whose sole purpose was to support him financially. Instead of relying upon the state's law enforcement officers, he hired a private security company to formulate a crime-fighting strategy.[40] Kirk's unusual leadership set the stage for Democrat Reubin Askew to challenge the policies of Kirk and reestablish Democratic dominance in the state. If Kirk had governed successfully as a Republican, Jeb Bush's state government revolution in 1999 might never have happened.

While Florida experienced uneven governance in the 1960s, two critical reforms took place in the decade. With pressure coming from South Florida representatives and citizenry, the state finally addressed some of the weaknesses of the antiquated Constitution of 1885. The new Constitution of 1968 would allow the governor to succeed himself and serve a total of two consecutive four-year terms. The term of office was important because, under the one-term system, legislators and bureaucrats could simply wait out the sitting governor. With two possible terms, the governor would be a stronger political force. The governor would still have to share power with the cabinet, but the office was given clearer lines of authority within the executive branch. The governor was also given the duty of presenting the budget to the legislature, replacing a budget commission that was made up of the entire cabinet. This budget power would allow the governor to write the first draft for the state's fiscal priorities—a critical tool for implementing a political agenda. Finally, the office of lieutenant governor was created, so a clear line of succession would be in place. In sum, the Constitution of 1968 clearly gave more power and authority to the governor, but it did not completely erase the limiting structure placed upon Florida's governors in the century since Reconstruction.[41] The cabinet would still have a share of the executive power, and the legislature would still maintain its role as a powerful counterweight to the governor.

The second major reform was the redrawing of state legislative districts. In the case *Swann v. Adams* in 1967, the United States Supreme Court declared that Florida's system of drawing district borders was unconstitutional. The infamous Pork Chop Gang had blocked progress on this question for years. Citizens from Central and South Florida were not receiving equal representation in the legislature. The *Swann* case now would force the state to effect a redistricting based upon the principle of one person, one vote.[42] This decision would shift power in the legislature to the central and southern parts of the state. It also would allow for more progressive policies, because the conservative northern lawmakers would no longer be able to block legislation.

Into these changed circumstances, Reubin Askew came to rescue the Democratic Party in Florida and to reinvigorate the office of governor. Askew was from the Panhandle, so he understood conservative politics, but he was a progressive reformer at heart. He sought to reestablish the moderate social positions of LeRoy Collins with a pragmatic approach to governing after the lost decade of Florida politics. In the 1970 gubernatorial election, Republican Claude Kirk remained entangled with the politics of race. Kirk refused to enforce a federal court order mandating busing in a Florida county. He fired the school board and the school superintendent and put the system directly under the authority of his office.[43] He also threatened violence if anyone attempted to override his authority.

Because of his bizarre actions, Kirk was challenged in the Republican primary for governor, and four Democrats were waiting to get at him in the general election. Askew won a very competitive Democratic race in a runoff. When the mercurial Kirk faced Askew in the general election, he called Askew names, while Askew concentrated on issues of concern to voters, including education and environmental regulation. Kirk tried to label Askew a liberal, but Askew's military service and his strong Christian faith helped to shield him from these attacks. After Kirk's antics, the people of Florida were ready for a more serious approach to governance. The additional powers granted by the 1968 revision of the constitution would allow for a more activist approach to the office.

Askew's time as governor bore out the importance of the three factors that Colburn and Scher have emphasized—population growth, government structure, and personality—to the ability of a governor to lead the state of Florida. His progressive and moderate policies also present a starkly different model from Jeb Bush's gubernatorial record. From 1950 to 1970, Florida experienced massive population growth. Growth itself became its own economic industry. As more people moved to Florida, houses needed to be built, consumer services needed to be offered, and demands on government would be drastically increased. In the early 1970s the central part of the state became home to the tourism powerhouse of Disney World. The advent of Disney World accelerated a trend that was already seeing huge growth in the central part of the state, especially in the cities of Tampa and Orlando. These central Florida communities would become the political bellwethers of the nation in the 1990s and 2000s because of their ethnic and political diversity. Meanwhile the southern part of the state continued to grow dramatically with a large migration of citizens from the northeastern United States and immigrants from Cuba and other places in Latin America. Florida needed a government that could respond to these changes. Not only had the changes in Florida's constitution given more power to the governor's office than it had had since the end of the Civil War, but Reubin Askew had the personal skills to make determined, persuasive appeals to both citizens and the legislature. The melding of these three major factors helped Askew to become one of the most effective governors of the twentieth century.

David Colburn submitted that Askew represented the reestablishment of the Collins era.[44] Availing himself of the greater opportunities that constitutional reforms afforded to impact the policy process, Askew deftly handled the turbulent racial politics of the time. In 1972 both the Florida legislature and voters were concerned about the implementation of busing in the state's public school systems. Busing was a controversial remedy imposed by federal courts to further the racial integration of public schools. Responding to the concerns of their constituents, Florida legislators voted to put an advisory referendum on the state ballot in 1972 that would allow voters to vote against busing in Florida. Askew negotiated with the legislature and offered a companion referendum that would ask the citizens of Florida whether they supported equal educational opportunities for students from all racial and economic backgrounds. Not surprisingly, voters voted against busing but supported the idea of equal education for all. The passage of the second proposition helped to cool the heated racial politics of the time and reminded Florida voters from all backgrounds that they did agree on an equal educational opportunity.[45]

This would not be the first instance that Askew used the ballot to put pressure on the Florida legislature. Even with the constitutional reforms of 1968, the Florida legislature still held tremendous structural power in Florida's constitutional system.

With no term limits, some legislators built up seniority and dominated the key legislative committees. These committees could scuttle the most important legislation. Askew, seeing that the state of Florida would need more revenue to meet the challenges of growth, boldly advocated for the establishment of a corporate income tax. This proposal marked an abrupt change to Florida's political culture. Since the establishment of the Reconstruction constitution in 1885, most of Florida's political leadership sought to keep taxes as low as possible. However, this low-tax tradition kept colliding with the realities of the growing state. Askew persuaded the legislature that the corporate tax proposal should be decided by the electorate. The legislators finally agreed, and the issue was put to Florida voters in the form of a referendum. The main business interests in the state mounted a determined campaign against the ballot measure. However, Askew and other business leaders in the state including agricultural leader Ben Hill Griffin campaigned for the proposal. Askew was able to cast large corporations as freeloaders in the state. He argued that they did not contribute enough to the state's coffers while ordinary citizens paid their fair share of taxes. In November 1971 the initiative passed overwhelmingly. Florida's residents trusted Askew when he said that more state revenue was needed. Askew's integrity and personal appeal had won the day.

After this considerable achievement, Askew was not finished. During his time as governor, he reformed funding for public school education, he established meaningful environmental regulations, and he threw his support behind a constitutional initiative for more open government. The "Sunshine Amendment" established ethics procedures and standards for state and local officials. This initiative passed overwhelmingly.

Considering Florida's traditions and political culture, Askew's accomplishments are historic. In the post-Collins era, Reubin Askew and Jeb Bush stand out as the most powerful and effective governors. Biographer Martin Dyckman called Askew's mix of progressive policies and ambitious personal agenda "the Golden Age of Florida's Politics."[46] Along with a fellow governor at the time, Jimmy Carter of Georgia, Askew represented the new Democratic Party in the South. Askew's accomplishments also put into perspective how much political attitudes and policies have changed in Florida since Jeb Bush was elected as governor in 1998.

One of Askew's far-reaching achievements was to pave the way for two other moderate Democratic governors—Bob Graham and Lawton Chiles. State senator Bob Graham succeeded Askew in 1979. Graham had difficulty following the large legacy of Reubin Askew. The state's population continued to grow tremendously, which put more and more demands on state government. Graham also had to deal with an international crisis when Cuban leader Fidel Castro released prisoners and mental patients in the Mariel Boatlift. Floating on ill-constructed rafts and boats, more than 100,000 Cuban immigrants were added to the already growing South Florida population. The federal government did not offer much assistance in meeting this humanitarian challenge.[47] Graham also dealt with a resurgent Florida legislature led by legislative legends like Dempsey Barron, the longtime Democratic state senator from Panama City. Barron was chairman of the powerful Rules Committee and could block almost any piece of legislation from a vote if he desired. In his second term Graham found his way, with an emphasis on education in Florida's environment. The state economy along with the national economy was recovering from a recession. Graham finished his governorship with notable reforms in higher and K–12 education. In particular, he established groundbreaking legislation to make growth management policies in the state more environmentally friendly. He became a U.S. senator, admired for his civility and his expertise on national security. As governor, he continually faced the stark demographic issue that affected most of Florida's governors since the 1920s: more people moving to the state and not enough revenue to provide government services for them.

The end of Graham's tenure offered Republicans a real chance to regain the governorship. They took advantage of a divided Democratic Party that nominated a liberal candidate, Steve Pajcic, to carry its message forward. The Republican mayor of Tampa, Bob Martinez, shocked the political establishment by winning the governor's office by nearly 10 percent over Pajcic. Martinez came into office promising to cut back on government, but he soon realized that the needs of citizens in the state would demand more revenue. He proposed a tax on such services as accounting, legal representation, and lawn care. The services tax was extremely unpopular, and although it was repealed soon after its passage, the tax reversal tainted Martinez, allowing former Democratic U.S. senator Lawton Chiles to beat him easily in 1990 in his reelection bid.

Chiles would reestablish the moderate Democratic legacy of LeRoy Collins and Reubin Askew. However, he had a difficult time dealing with such circumstances as recession in the early 1990s and a devastating hurricane in South Florida. Hurricane Andrew was one of the most destructive in Florida history. It left more than 300,000 residents homeless and more than a million without power. Some estimates had the winds reaching a speed of 170 miles per hour at their height. No state was ready for such a powerful storm. The state of Florida and the federal government struggled to meet the needs of all those who were impacted. Chiles took political damage from the response to the storm. Two years later he barely won reelection over a first-time candidate by the name of Jeb Bush, showing that the Republican Party was rising in the state. Chiles's second term would be stymied by a legislature that was growing more Republican with every election. By 1996 both houses of the state legislature were in Republican hands for the first time since Reconstruction. Chiles was able to pass legislation that allowed the state to sue the tobacco companies for money the state had spent on health care for smokers. Yet for most of his governorship, it seemed Lawton Chiles was trying to catch up with events that were speeding ahead of Florida government.

Reubin Askew versus Jeb Bush

Altogether, in the years since 1960, Reubin Askew and Jeb Bush had more meaningful impacts on Florida's government and society than any of their fellow governors. However, their approaches to Florida government could not have been more different. Askew believed that Florida needed more revenue to responsibly offer services to its growing population. Bush believed that state government had become too big, and he sought to reduce taxes at every opportunity. Askew especially believed that the public education system needed more resources. Bush also added resources to the system, but his educational reform focused on teacher and school accountability as opposed to large increases in state support. Askew fought for environmental regulations that he believed were central to keeping Florida's natural resources intact. Bush supported Everglades restoration but thought most environmental regulations were hampering business development. Askew believed that state government had a particular responsibility to ensure racial justice; Bush drastically altered affirmative-action policies in the state. Askew believed in a strong, independent judiciary with merit retention; Bush demanded more authority over the nomination process for the state courts and publicly criticized court decisions.

Both Bush and Askew were activist governors, but their governing philosophies brought them to starkly different results. One of Askew's major accomplishments was the establishment of the corporate tax. Bush and his successors have worked to reduce the tax, and it narrowly escaped repeal in 2011 by Republican governor Rick Scott. Bush has moved the ideological pendulum in Florida politics in the conservative direction. In his two victorious elections, Democrats essentially were isolated in the large counties of Broward and Palm Beach and did not have much of a political base outside these two counties. This conservative trend has held up in gubernatorial (off-year) elections but, interestingly, not on the presidential level. Bush has accomplished his conservative shift at the state level, but when Florida was part of national presidential elections in 2008 and 2012, Democrat Barack Obama won the state with strong turnout from African Americans.

Even with a state legislature that did not always follow his lead, and in a conservative political culture, Reubin Askew increased the scope and power of state government in many areas that mattered to the people of Florida. Jeb Bush used his power to reverse many of Askew's policies, because he believed that state government was too bureaucratic and wasteful. Bush's sharp change in direction led Florida to the establishment of activist conservative government that would fundamentally change the state. To understand Bush's governing philosophy, it is important to examine the conservative movement in the United States during the last part of the twentieth century and find Jeb Bush's place in this movement.

3

The Conservative Movement
and Jeb Bush

In 1995, after his defeat in Florida's 1994 gubernatorial election by Democrat Lawton Chiles, Jeb Bush wrote a book called *Profiles in Character* where he makes it clear that American society needs a fundamental transformation, a "renewal of character and virtue." As a conservative in the mid-1990s, Bush was apparently trying to "conserve" traditional values. Yet at the same time he was advocating for large-scale changes in the way state government operates. In some ways his ideas could be judged to be a revolution in state-level public administration, because he was attempting a massive overhaul of Florida government. It is a paradox that many modern-day conservatives face: are they attempting to restore American government or to radically change it? This contradiction plays such an important part in Jeb

Bush's time as Florida's governor that it needs to be placed in historical context. Without the momentum that the conservative movement of the late twentieth century provided, it would have been impossible for Governor Bush to implement his governing agenda in Florida. The maturation of the conservative movement came at the same time that changes in Florida state government made a strong-governor model possible for the first time in Florida history. This combination gave Jeb Bush the opportunity to put into play the ideas of both a conservative and a policy reformer.

The history of the Bush family itself reflects the maturation of the conservative movement. Nowhere is this progression more evident than with the children and grandchildren of Prescott Bush (1895–1972), U.S. senator from Connecticut (1952–63); the choices they made would help define the nation's politics. The fact that George W. Bush and Jeb Bush became two of the South's most prominent governors in the 1990s would have been hard to imagine seventy years earlier. The Bush family gained its influence in American society as northeast-erners. George H. W. Bush's grandfather Samuel Bush was originally a Democrat; however, as Samuel Bush became involved as a business leader in the railroad industry, he foreshadowed the future political leanings of his family.[1] Samuel Bush's son Prescott became a success-ful broker on Wall Street in the 1920s and 1930s. Franklin Roosevelt's attempt to regulate Wall Street motivated Prescott Bush to become a Republican. While the Bushes of the 1930s were northeastern Re-publicans, Prescott's son George H. W. Bush moved to Texas in the 1950s and tried to become a southern conservative. George W. Bush grew up in Texas and Jeb Bush moved to Florida as a young adult and they became Reagan conservatives—a far cry from their grandfather's politics. This evolution continues in the present decade, with Jeb's son George Prescott Bush winning the Republican nomination for the of-fice of Texas Land Commissioner in the spring of 2014 running as a Texas Tea Party conservative. To understand the conservative move-ment in United States politics and Jeb Bush's place in that conserva-tive movement, its origins need to be examined.

The Executive Conservatives

Scholars generally agree that no one movement labeled "conservative" existed in the United States before the mid-twentieth century. This does not mean that conservatism was not present, simply that the term "conservative" was not used to a great extent in American politics until after World War II.[2] In truth, most of the policies of the American government prior to the New Deal could be viewed as one form of conservatism or another. Since the United States emerged from open rebellion against an established monarchy, it is not natural to label the founders as conservatives. However, the lauded founding fathers of the nation were not all democratic revolutionaries. Instead many of them came from merchant elites or plantation families in the South. They chafed at the control Great Britain attempted to exert over the colonies, but most of the signers of the Declaration of Independence were not seeking an open political process for all. Whites who did not own property were excluded, along with slaves, Native Americans, and women. Moreover, there were no provisions for the direct election of the president of the United States or of U.S. senators by the relatively few citizens who were eligible voters. In short, most of the leaders of the new nation were tremendously wary of putting too much power in the hands of all the American people.

Furthermore, at the founding of the nation, the word "liberal" was used in the classic sense to emphasize the rights of individuals. This understanding of the word came from the Enlightenment movement that swept Europe in the 1700s. In this context the word "liberal" was used to contest the power of the state in controlling the lives of its citizens and to emphasize individual worth and freedom. It bears little resemblance to the term used today that emphasizes the large role of government in attempting to ensure the safety and well-being of citizens through strong state action.

Yet it was very soon after the American Revolution that a form of conservatism emerged. The Articles of Confederation—the loose arrangement that was the original governing document of the United States—was a failure at providing stability and structure for the new nation. A stronger central government was needed that could raise revenue and enforce economic regulations across state borders. As the Constitutional Convention was convened in 1787, a real debate was emerging in the United States about centralized national power versus individual state power and authority. With the failings of the Articles of Confederation as a stark reminder, the delegates to the convention created a much stronger federal government in the United States Constitution. However, to placate those delegates who were concerned about too much federal authority, a vigorous system of separation of powers with checks and balances was put in place. To ensure that the individual citizen would not be at the whim of unchecked federal authority, a Bill of Rights was added to the Constitution as the first ten amendments.[3]

Accordingly, at the founding of the nation, a real separation existed between two basic political ideas. One group, the Federalists, advocated for a stronger central government in order to create a national bank, build a system of national defense, and guard against too much political participation by uneducated citizens. This group, led by Secretary of the Treasury Alexander Hamilton and Vice President John Adams, was protective of the merchant class, which had financial interests located mostly in the cities of the North. The Federalists had a real fear of expanding democracy among the vast majority of American citizens. The French Revolution that began in 1789 and intensified in the early 1790s showed how "democratic" mobs could go after the monied elite.

The anti-Federalists led by Thomas Jefferson were wary of this increased centralization of power in the federal government. Jefferson's attempts to broaden the political class to include more agricultural interests were again seen as a direct threat to the Federalists. When, as president, Jefferson approved the Louisiana Purchase, some Federalists called it a strategy to overwhelm the new nation with uneducated backwoodsmen to take on the monied interests of the North. While Jefferson and other Jeffersonian Republicans of the time wanted to extend voting rights to all white men, their expanded definition of democracy did not include free blacks, slaves, and women. Yet even the idea of giving all white men the franchise was seen as a real threat by the conservative Federalists. While the Federalists would never win the presidency again, the remnants of the movement attempted to slow down the expansion of democracy led by Andrew Jackson in the late 1820s and 1830s. While his issues were very different, Jeb Bush believed in strong executive authority in the governor's office to advance conservative ideals. His vision of strong gubernatorial power often clashed with his professed adherence to the principle that localities and communities knew best how to govern themselves.

States' Rights Conservatives

When Jackson was sworn in as president in 1829, his inauguration was open to all. Many in Washington were appalled at the large crowds of planters, backwoodsmen, and everyday citizens that rushed to the capital. With Jackson's victory being seen as a strong statement against the merchants and bankers of the North, and Jackson himself seen as representing the common man, historians have tabbed his election as an important event in the expansion of democracy in the United States. Yet even though Jackson was from Tennessee, a southern state, many southern leaders were uncomfortable with his calls for greater democracy. Conservatism in the North attempted to "conserve" the financial order and to model American society on traditional European structures. Conservatives in the South wanted to "conserve" the southern order, including a plantation economy, the institution of slavery, and a strong opposition to concentration of power in the national government. As president, Jackson was seriously challenged by southern leaders who believed that the federal government was becoming too powerful. Jackson's own vice president, John Calhoun of South Carolina, endorsed a proclamation of nullification from the South Carolina legislature that stated that any federal law could be ignored by the states if it damaged state interests. This protest by South Carolina involved a tariff that had been imposed by the federal government. Jackson was able to work through that controversy, but a line of southern conservatism had been set. If the federal government attempted to regulate the southern economy or challenge the institution of slavery, southern leaders would rise up and demand relief from federal law.

Scholar Patrick Allitt argues that the Civil War was a "conflict between two types of conservatives."[4] Southern conservatives were trying to maintain their traditions and their way of life, and Lincoln and his allies were trying to "conserve" the Union. While abolitionists in the North were calling for an end to slavery and full citizenship for all black males, many northern Republicans including Lincoln were not looking for dramatic change at the beginning of the war. A year before he was elected, in 1859, Lincoln argued that he, not the pro-slavery forces in both the North and the South, was the real conservative. "What is conservatism? Is it not adherence to the old and tried against the new and untried?"[5] Lincoln argued that he was trying to conserve the founders' view of slavery in the United States: that it be restricted to the southern states but not abolished. As the war progressed, the views of abolitionists became more accepted, and Lincoln would adopt most of their positions.[6] Above all, Lincoln was looking to preserve the Constitution and government. Yet even many northerners would remain wary of granting too many civil liberties to blacks. These two groups of conservatives would be separated by region and political party for many years following the Civil War. Conservatives would not begin joining together in a political party in the United States until the 1960s.

Jeb Bush represented the Republican Party that finally brought conservatives into the same party in the United States by the 1990s. As governor, he strongly believed in states' rights. However, with his brother as the sitting president, he called for federal action in education to give power to his ideas concerning education reform, and he also accepted hundreds of millions to restore the Everglades and sought increased military spending in the state.

Capitalist Conservatives

The post–Civil War period saw dominance at the presidential level by the Republican Party. This war spurred industrialization in the North and wrought fundamental changes in the northern economy. The ascendant industrial capitalists constituted a new conservative faction within the country. As the techniques of mass production were implemented in American industry, they created opportunities for vast wealth. The new business class in America did not want government regulation of their business practices. These practices included child labor and low wages for manufacturing employees. The conservatives in the North who once advocated for strong national authority as Federalists were now wary of too much federal power. For completely different reasons, they shared this view of federal power with southern conservatives. While southern state legislatures did not reinstitute slavery across the region, Jim Crow laws were passed that mandated racial segregation in education, business, and society as a whole. After the humiliation of losing the Civil War and the military occupation that followed, the last thing that southern leaders would tolerate was a heavy federal involvement in the lives of southerners.

After the Republican domination of the presidency for most of the post–Civil War period, the election of Democrat Woodrow Wilson in 1912 provoked new debates in the nation's political system. Even though he was elected with the help of southern conservatives, Wilson was a "progressive" Democrat. Republican Teddy Roosevelt had begun these important debates inside the Republican Party in the first decade of the 1900s. Wilson advocated for laws that favored employee unions, and he challenged monopolies with an antitrust law. Most important, he supported a constitutional amendment that made the taxing of individual income legal in the United States. The passage of the Sixteenth Amendment would become a matter of the greatest regret to many economic conservatives. Allowing the federal government to tax income would in turn allow it to expand greatly.[7] The granting of this power has been lamented by conservatives as the largest mistake in the history of the republic.

The expansion of government power was not confined to domestic politics. When the United States reluctantly entered World War I, the power of the federal government grew exponentially. During his two terms, Woodrow Wilson managed to concentrate more power in the federal government than at any time since the Civil War. This concentration of power set the stage for the two vastly different approaches to governing in the United States. The Republicans in the 1920s would be unabashedly pro-business and wary of international involvement.

The 1930s would bring in Democrats with a strongly activist view of government in response to the worst economic crisis in the nation's history. An understanding of the differences between these two approaches is central to understanding the rise of conservatism after World War II. Many of the arguments advanced by conservatives in the late twentieth century were born around reaction to the New Deal policies of the 1930s. How much money the government acquired and spent would determine the scope and reach of the federal government. Jeb Bush in 1995 wrote that "money is the key to growth in any government, and the more government has, the more control it can intentionally or unintentionally wrest from families and communities."[8] The New Deal was central in giving the federal government much more power in the economic affairs of the United States and would accelerate the need to generate more revenue from American citizens.

Yet even the Depression did not bring a unified voice for more activist government. When Democratic governor Franklin Roosevelt of New York ran against embattled incumbent president Herbert Hoover in 1932, he criticized the Hoover administration as the "greatest spending Administration in peace times in all our history."[9] In fact Roosevelt on occasion claimed that he would *cut* government spending 25 percent if he were elected. At other campaign venues, he promised more vigorous government action. As the economy worsened, there was little doubt that Roosevelt and the Democratic Party would win easily.

In June 1932, President Hoover ordered General Douglas MacArthur to disperse an encampment of jobless World War I veterans in Washington after the District of Columbia police failed to oust them and two veterans were killed. The veterans were seeking immediate payment of deferred service bonuses to ease their dire economic circumstances. With tanks and cavalry, the U.S. Army attacked the encampment. Veterans and their wives and children were forced to run from Washington to safety. The so-called Bonus Army incident showed the depth of the Depression's ravages on many Americans, and Hoover's inability to respond humanely. Instead of protecting Americans in need, the federal government was using the military against them.

After Roosevelt's landslide victory, he would not take office until March 1933. The four months between his election and inauguration were the worst four months of the Depression. No matter what Roosevelt had said in the campaign, he needed to take drastic action. The major producer of steel in the nation, U.S. Steel, would reduce its full-time workforce from 225,000 in 1929 to zero in April 1933. By inauguration day, thirty-eight states had closed all of their banks. Most financial exchanges including the stock market were closed. In short, the American economy was collapsing. By some estimates, the unemployment rate in 1933 was near 25 percent of the adult population. Moreover, the public and political leaders were looking for someone to blame. Herbert Hoover, who was seen a business-friendly president, had initiated an investigation of Wall Street financial institutions in a desperate move to win reelection. This investigation revealed a system of insider trading and the manipulation of bond pricing. For their part, the businessmen who ran America's largest corporations believed that business owners suffered much more than average workers during the beginning of the Depression. The desperate economic situation brought serious debates about the future of American capitalism.

Roosevelt answered with an aggressive program that attempted to stabilize the national economy by intertwining it with the federal government. In the first hundred days of the Roosevelt administration, Congress passed a sweeping agenda. Legislation creating the National Recovery Administration allowed the federal government to set prices in certain industries and institute regulations such as limiting the hours worked by individuals to ensure that more adults could be employed. For the first time in its history, the federal government guaranteed bank deposits up to a certain amount. The federal government also offered assistance to millions of homeowners who were falling short on their mortgages. By the end of Roosevelt's first term, Congress passed even more far-reaching legislation. A massive federal works program, the WPA, put millions of Americans to work in everything from public art to the maintenance of national parks. The National Labor Relations Act of 1935 put the federal government squarely behind the idea of collective bargaining for employees and also allowed for increased unionization of industries. Finally, the landmark Social Security Act of 1935 offered cash benefits to citizens sixty-five and over, funded by taxes on working Americans.[10]

This increase in government involvement would not be confined to domestic affairs. With the attack on Pearl Harbor in 1941, the isolationism and so-called neutrality that marked United States foreign policy during the previous two decades was gone. The United States moved to a war footing and moved quickly. Mobilization required a large expansion of the federal government. In 1939 the United States Army had about 200,000 men in uniform. By 1945, 12 million Americans were engaged in some type of military service, and 162 government agencies had been created to help maintain America's war effort. The War Production Board, which exercised federal oversight over all industries that were supplying the war effort, had power over ordering materials and setting prices. To finance the huge buildup that the war entailed, taxes had to be raised and money borrowed. In 1940 approximately 4 million Americans paid individual income taxes; by the end of the war 42 million Americans filed individual income tax returns. Meanwhile government debt increased fivefold.[11]

By the end of the war the United States was the largest economic and military power in the world, and it had a federal government to match. The expansion of government power during the Depression and the war sparked a countermovement in American politics. Most scholars and observers date the beginnings of the true modern conservative movement to postwar America. The federal government had amassed tremendous power to fight the Depression and World War II; after the victory in 1945, the question became what would the government and its leaders do with all of these new powers and resources. Even though they would not come on the political scene until after the Roosevelt/Truman years, modern conservatives like Jeb Bush would base their political ideology partially on the idea that Roosevelt and the New Dealers had gone too far and the nation needed to turn back from liberalism. Especially in regard to business regulation, Bush and other conservatives believed that government regulations had multiplied so much since the New Deal years that business development was being hindered across the country. If there had been no New Deal, there might have been no modern conservative movement.

The Intellectual Conservatives

Among conservative intellectuals in the United States after World War II, a lively debate ensued on how to translate conservative philosophy to a political and governing strategy. In domestic affairs, the conservative movement in the United States during the last half of the twentieth century focused on four major issue areas: 1) the effort to reduce government spending (with the exception of defense and law enforcement), especially in regard to the social safety net; 2) the limitation of government regulations on the private business sector; 3) reduction of both personal income taxes and taxes on businesses; and 4) reformation of the current American culture, including increased emphasis on religious/moral issues and values.

The conservative philosophy as a framework for government was in disarray during the 1930s and early 1940s. The best-known conservatives had been wrong on the two transforming issues of the time. Most conservatives in the country strongly opposed Roosevelt's New Deal. This massive expansion of government in the economy was not always successful, but it did give Americans the sense that the government was trying to help them in their time of need. Moreover, many prominent conservatives were isolationist in their views concerning foreign policy. Before Pearl Harbor, they accused Franklin Roosevelt of having a secret plan to get the United States involved in World War II. With the attack on Pearl Harbor, the isolationists were discredited. After twenty years of progressive leadership under Franklin Roosevelt and Harry Truman, the United States had come through the Depression, won a world war, and become the most powerful nation in the world.

Yet in the immediate aftermath of World War II, Republicans won both the House and Senate in 1946. Conservative Republicans became important again with two basic arguments. Learning from their isolationist past, they were now strongly anticommunist—seeking to challenge the Soviet Union's expansionism directly, even though the

Soviets had been U.S. allies in the war. The second plank of their resurgence was to advocate for less government regulation of the economy. The Wagner Act passed in 1935 had given unions and labor groups significant power in relation to management with a collective bargaining structure. Conservatives in the Republican Party along with southern Democrats sought to restore management's authority in labor relations, since there was significant labor unrest in postwar America.

Senator Robert Taft of Ohio, the Senate majority leader and de facto leader of the Republican Party, led the efforts to pass the Taft-Hartley Act of 1948. Seeking to redefine labor-management relations in the nation, Taft-Hartley was a powerful rejoinder to the Wagner Act of 1935 that established collective bargaining and protected the rights of unions to organize and strike. The Republican answer outlawed mandated union shops and placed conditions on the right of employees to strike.[12] From a business perspective, this legislation was the most important assistance to management that came out of Washington in the twentieth century.

Taft became a hero to conservatives for his leadership. With Harry Truman vulnerable in the 1948 election, conservatives wanted Taft to run. However, the liberal northeastern wing of the Republican Party wanted Governor Thomas E. Dewey of New York. Dewey got the Republican nomination and lost the general election in a famous election-night surprise.

The disappointment over Dewey was the first in a long line of problems conservatives would have with Republican nominees. They again sought to nominate Robert Taft in 1952, but war hero Dwight Eisenhower came and basically ripped the nomination away from Taft. Eisenhower was almost a sure winner, and Republican Party officials wanted a winner after losing five consecutive presidential elections. Yet conservatives paid a heavy price for Eisenhower's ascendance in the Republican Party. Many conservatives saw Eisenhower's philosophy as a continuation of greater reliance on government. Patrick Allitt submits that Eisenhower had a serious disconnect with conservatives because he adopted most of Roosevelt's New Deal programs.

Interestingly, the beginnings of the modern conservative movement that would come to dominate politics in the latter half of the twentieth century began with a group of intellectual writers and academics. These intellectuals would inspire future candidates, party leaders, and talk show hosts. Foremost among these influential conservatives was William F. Buckley Jr. (1925–2008), who wrote a strong challenge to the academic and secular establishment in 1951 called *God and Man at Yale*. Buckley argued that Yale and other academic institutions had turned against both religion and the free enterprise system.[13] He also believed that conservative politicians had no support or intellectual backup. The New Deal and its increase in the role of government had changed the paradigm under which the United States government operated. Buckley wanted both conservative intellectuals and elected officials to offer a clear alternative. He also learned an important lesson coming from the isolationism of the 1930s. Conservatives could not ignore American influence abroad. Even with the disaster of the Joseph McCarthy investigations, conservatives should be the leading voices in opposing Communism around the world. Buckley also argued that individual liberties were endangered by an encroaching federal government. He forcefully made these arguments in a new conservative publication called the *National Review*. Unlike many media outlets in the twenty-first century, Buckley clearly articulated the basic principles that would guide his magazine, most importantly that centrist political ideology was a danger to American democracy. He wrote: "Middle-of-the-Road . . . is politically, intellectually, and morally repugnant. We shall recommend policies for the simple reason that we consider them right (rather than 'non-controversial'); and we consider them right because they are based on principles we deem right (rather than on popularity polls)."[14] Buckley then went on to frame the outlines of conservative government.

While Buckley gave the conservative movement its intellectual core, Russell Kirk (1918–1994) gave the movement its history. Kirk was an intellectual who taught at Michigan State University and ran a bookstore in Lansing, Michigan. When his 1953 book *The Conservative Mind* came out, the positive reviews changed his life. The modern conservative movement of the twentieth century can be traced back to a harsh reaction to the government activism that was unchecked through the Great Depression and World War II. In Kirk's work, conservatism was not born in the 1940s but had a long history all the way back to the eighteenth century and Edmund Burke. The first coherent conservative political action took place in Britain and United States after the French Revolution began in 1789. The horror that American merchants and British elites felt when many elites of French society faced the guillotine created a conservative backlash. Kirk believed in a literal meaning of conservatism—change was neither desirable nor necessary—and called for a return to traditions and a class-based society. He lived these words throughout his life, led a minimalist existence, and refused to do any of his writing on anything but a manual typewriter.[15]

The voice of free-market conservatism in the 1950s and 1960s was Milton Friedman (1912–2006). Friedman was the mainstay of the University of Chicago economics department, well known for its emphasis on free-market economics. Friedman's urging of minimalist involvement by the government in the national economy put him in direct contrast with the philosophy of targeted government intervention in the economy developed by British economist John Maynard Keynes, who had helped industrialized countries make the transition from war economies to economies based upon trade and commerce.

Friedman, in rejecting this Keynesian espousal of enhanced government involvement to combat cyclical changes in the overall economy, placed himself squarely in opposition to the idea that federal and/or state governments can truly help the economy in substantive ways. In an interview in 1973 that summarized his lifelong contribution to the field of economics, he talked about his clear philosophy. "I think the government's solution to a problem is usually as bad as the problem and very often makes the problem worse."[16] His consistent economic prescription for almost every sector of American life was simple: freedom takes care of most problems.

The number of policy areas to which Friedman applied this philosophy was truly amazing. He argued against the minimum wage because he felt that it priced poor workers out of the market. He believed the New Deal relief programs that most of the nation embraced actually did very little to improve economic circumstances of the average American. He criticized higher-education aid programs because they ended up providing assistance to middle- and upper-class families and did not target students from poor families. He believed that government regulation of the food supply was unnecessary and ineffective. When asked what the public should do if they were harmed by tainted food or other faulty products, he replied, "You sue."[17] He also argued that government should not be attempting to limit pollution, and he again wanted the free market to take care of any externalities coming from the operation of the business. School choice would become the hallmark of Jeb Bush's time as governor, and of his post-gubernatorial career. Friedman's consistent view of the power of markets provided the framework for Bush's involvement in this policy area, and Jeb Bush has cited Friedman as an inspiration to his governing philosophy.[18]

Buckley, Kirk, Friedman, and other intellectuals like them would provide the principles and intellectual momentum for the conservative movement to grow and prosper. Buckley inspired young conservatives by making it acceptable to remain outside the political center. He also talked about the importance of religion and moral growth that conservatives should embrace along with a hawkish foreign-policy based on strident anticommunism. Kirk provided the historical framework to highlight the fact that conservatism was not a passing fad—it was a historical movement. Friedman provided an economic blueprint that offered market solutions to almost any conceivable public policy issue. When conservatives in the 1930s and 1940s objected to the government involvement in many areas of American life, they had no real policy framework to fall back upon. Friedman's consistent and comprehensive championing of free-market solutions gave conservatives strong arguments to contradict greater government involvement in the second half of the twentieth century. As governor fifty years later, Jeb Bush would embrace many of the basic principles that these three writers and intellectuals provided.

Goldwater Shows the Way

Yet before any governor could even dream of attempting a strong conservative agenda, conservatives had to move from an intellectual framework to electoral politics. The movement needed leadership and political savvy. They found this leader in Republican senator Barry

Goldwater of Arizona, who was an important predecessor to many of the conservative leaders of the late twentieth century.

Barry Goldwater's family ran a series of successful department stores in Arizona. Goldwater was a veteran and in the 1950s became a leading voice against the moderation of the Eisenhower administration. Goldwater did not like Eisenhower's acceptance of the New Deal legacy of Franklin Roosevelt. Moreover, as conservatives became even more assertive in foreign policy, Goldwater rejected the containment policy advocated by leaders in Congress from both parties.[19] Goldwater made his views clear with the publication of the 1964 book *Conscience of a Conservative*. Ghost written by another conservative intellectual, Brent Bozell, the book was an important tonic to conservatives who had watched Democratic liberals take over the nation's political structure in the 1930s and 1940s. The Dewey nomination in 1948 and the Eisenhower nomination and victory in 1952 had frustrated the conservatives even more. For example, Eisenhower said, "I am conservative when it comes to economic problems but liberal when it comes to human problems." Goldwater's book made the argument that human beings must be viewed as individuals and not as part of groups. This strong emphasis on individuality minimizes the role of government action to achieve public policy goals and emphasizes the responsibility of each individual human. Goldwater stated that "the Conservative looks upon politics as the art of achieving the maximum amount of freedom for individuals that is consistent with the maintenance of social order."[20]

Even with the publication of his book, Goldwater had to move from the attractive outsider to the nominee of the Republican Party. This effort would reflect one of the first real grassroots movements to collect delegates state by state in order to win a party's presidential nomination. The political conventions would usually decide the nominees of the respective parties until the reforms of the 1970s. County and state political leaders would meet and decide which candidate the state would back for the nomination. The Goldwater forces were not going to wait for the 1964 convention. The last four Republican conventions had produced moderates Thomas E. Dewey, Dwight Eisenhower, and the unpredictable Richard Nixon. If the conservative movement wanted to nominate a true conservative as the candidate of the Republican Party, they would have to run a nomination campaign that was very different.

However, moderates in the Republican Party were not just going to hand Goldwater and the conservatives the nomination. Republican governor Nelson Rockefeller of New York was seen as a likely nominee for 1964. Rockefeller forces understood the real threat that Goldwater's young conservatives posed. Rockefeller called the conservative faction led by Goldwater "extremists." This label would stick with Goldwater throughout the 1964 campaign. In early 1963 the Goldwater forces had to face the difficult reality that they were going up against two of the richest men in America, Republican Nelson Rockefeller and Democrat John Kennedy.[21]

After Goldwater's surprising loss in the New Hampshire primary in 1964, other Republican establishment members turned against Goldwater. The media in general and former president Dwight Eisenhower and Governor Rockefeller continued to paint Goldwater as an extremist. Yet Goldwater had the heart of most of the party's new activists. When Governor Rockefeller was condemned by religious leaders in the country for divorcing and remarrying during the election year, Goldwater had his opening again. He won the state of California, and after that win he was the presumptive nominee. It was an unlikely victory for the senator from Arizona. At the Republican convention in San Francisco in 1964, Goldwater gave his infamous speech that appeared to defend "extremism." He had been labeled extreme by so many establishment figures in the Republican Party that he felt he had to answer.[22]

Incumbent president Lyndon Johnson with his tough political instincts was ready for Goldwater after the convention. In a nation still recovering from the violent death of President Kennedy, removing his successor would be almost a political impossibility. Goldwater fought the good fight, but he was never really close in the general election.

What Goldwater did accomplish was launching the modern conservative revolution. Lyndon Johnson had begun to lay out his vision of a Great Society in the campaign of 1964. The stated goal of the Great Society was to end poverty. In a capitalistic system this would be no easy feat. Goldwater derided the antipoverty programs as a "hodgepodge of handouts."[23] At an agricultural field day in North Dakota in front of a large crowd of farmers and agricultural workers, Goldwater bravely denounced price supports for agricultural products.[24] Goldwater was not adopting a winning strategy for November 1964, he was offering the conservative vision for the future. Johnson continued to play upon the theme of extremism, and his campaign ran an ad of a little girl being blown up by an atomic bomb while counting the petals of a daisy. The ad did not run often, but this infamous "Daisy" ad added to the narrative that Goldwater did not have the temperament for the White House.

Lyndon Johnson's massive victory over Goldwater swept more Democrats into the House and Senate and offered Johnson the opportunity to pass a large amount of legislation. Yet even though Goldwater's campaign turned out to be an electoral disaster, his conservative movement within the Republican Party would change American politics for the next fifty years—and, along the way, help the Bush family become national political players. Goldwater's losing campaign set the conservative movement on a winning course in several important ways:

- Conservatives began to take over the leadership of the Republican Party.
- Goldwater began the pushback against the Great Society programs. Such "handouts" would be cited by most modern conservatives as the ultimate example of government overreach. This theme, initiated by Goldwater's campaign, was a staple of Jeb Bush's political philosophy.
- Goldwater's campaign began the real conversion of white southerners to the Republican Party. No longer would the base be in the Northeast; the new Republican Party would be based in the South and the West. After Goldwater's campaign in 1964, Democrats would win a majority of southern states in a presidential race only one more time—when southerner Jimmy Carter ran in 1976. This major trend carried over into Florida politics. From 1964 to 1996, the only Democratic

presidential candidate to win the state was Jimmy Carter in 1976. Carter would lose by a large margin in 1980 in Florida and in the nation.

- Goldwater's campaign helped launch the political career of Ronald Reagan. Without Reagan's famous speech in the 1964 campaign, his rise to become the standard-bearer of the conservative movement in the 1970s and 1980s would have been less certain.

The Bushes and Conservatism

Jeb Bush's grandfather Prescott Bush started his political career in 1950 with a run for the United States Senate in Connecticut. He ran as a strong fiscal conservative and as an anticommunist. However, his Democratic opponent wanted to talk about different issues. During the week before the election, his opponent painted Prescott Bush as a supporter of birth control because he had offered some support to Planned Parenthood.[25] In 1950 Connecticut politics, this was a volatile issue because the state was overwhelmingly Catholic. Prescott Bush lost the election by fewer than 1,200 votes. The Bush family had to learn the difficult lesson that in some elections controversial social issues become more important than all other issues. Prescott Bush would go on to win a U.S. Senate seat two years later.

Prescott Bush was a typical northeastern Republican, strongly conservative on fiscal issues and moderate to liberal on social issues. He advocated for increased government payments for poor Americans and was an early supporter of the civil rights movement. This balancing of fiscal conservatism and social moderation was not the future of the Republican Party in America.

George H. W. Bush could have followed in his father's footsteps. After a stellar career in the military during World War II and upon his graduation from Yale, he could have gone straight to Wall Street. But he wanted to strike out on his own, so he chose instead to move his wife, Barbara, and young son, George W., to Texas in 1948. Politically, Texas was an extremely conservative Democratic state in the Solid

South, a world away from the Wall Street Republicanism of the Northeast.[26] After nearly a decade in the oil business, George H. W. Bush started his political career as chairman of the local Republican Party in Houston's Harris County. A year and a half later he ran for the United States Senate, challenging a Democratic incumbent, Ralph Yarborough. Yarborough had supported the civil rights movement, which was very unpopular in the state of Texas in 1963. Unlike his father, George H. W. Bush made it clear that he opposed civil rights legislation. After the Kennedy assassination and with Texan Lyndon Johnson at the top of the Democratic ticket in 1964, Bush was soundly defeated. However, he began to make a shift to southern conservatism and away from the moderation of his father. George H. W. Bush constantly had to battle the perception in Texas that he was a Connecticut liberal and a visitor to the state. After two brief terms in the House of Representatives, he ran again for the United States Senate and lost again, to conservative Democrat Lloyd Bentsen, who also framed Bush as an outsider. Bush would gain political revenge against Bentsen when he defeated the Dukakis-Bentsen ticket for the presidency in 1988.

George H. W. Bush's difficulty navigating the terrain of southern politics in the 1960s was not an exception. After the initial acceptance of the Civil Rights Act of 1964 and the Voting Rights Act of 1965, many white southerners turned against the national Democratic Party. The cultural upheaval of the time, with its volatile mix of race relations, war protests, and real changes to traditional social customs, was too much for most white southerners to take. Their frustration with politics and culture manifested itself in the 1968 presidential candidacy of Alabama governor George Wallace. Wallace's campaign centered on his message of the decline of American culture and how the two political parties were contributing to its downfall. Wallace relished the social upheavals involving race and the Vietnam War because he could use student protesters as a convenient foil. For white southerners and other working-class whites around the nation, Wallace represented their frustration with the real changes in American society. Running as an independent, he went on to win five southern states and collect millions of other votes across the nation. On the presidential level, the

Democratic Party was being replaced in the South. Republican candidate Richard Nixon picked up on this frustration and also made an appeal to white southerners who mostly were Democrats, particularly by announcing his opposition to forced busing (the policy of addressing segregation by busing schoolchildren away from their neighborhoods). Wallace's cultural appeal was not lost on other candidates in the region. From the 1960s onward, strong cultural conservatism would become a major part of most political campaigns in the South. Without the Watergate scandal in the early 1970s, the Republican Party would have carried the South in every presidential election since 1968. While Wallace had been too extreme and outlandish during his public appearances in 1968, the core appeal of his message was heard and repeated by most candidates in the region in the latter part of the twentieth century.

Earl and Merle Black in *Politics and Society in the South* summarized the attitudes of white southerners this way: "Economic development shifted most whites out of poverty and into stable working-class or middle-class jobs," which meant that white southerners were being asked to pay higher taxes and "being forced to contribute, against their convictions and desires, to programs for which blacks were highly visible beneficiaries."[27] By the end of the 1960s, Black and Black write, it was the perception of many in the region that the "federal government was becoming an enemy to the average white person in the South."[28] Because of Lyndon Johnson's support for the civil rights movement and the programs of the Great Society, the Democratic Party was seen as the strong advocate for an expansive federal government. After the scandal of Watergate had subsided, this dynamic presented huge political opportunities for Republicans, and after 1976 they took advantage of it.

If the vast changes begun by Barry Goldwater in 1964 within the Republican Party were not clear, the election of 1980 became a fulfillment of the Goldwater legacy. After challenging an incumbent president in 1976 and almost winning the nomination, Ronald Reagan, the former governor of California, seemed to be the obvious choice as the Republican nominee in 1980. However, George H. W. Bush had been toiling in national politics for sixteen years and relished the opportunity to run for president. The Bush-Reagan fight in 1980 for the Republican presidential nomination reconstituted a familiar battle within the party. Bush called Reagan's economic plan that relied upon huge tax cuts "voodoo economics."[29] Bush shocked campaign observers by winning the Iowa caucuses in 1980. After the Iowa victory, the conservative movement that had waited so long for Reagan to win struck back. Bush was criticized for his moderate positions on social issues. Reagan's campaign had also worked hard to win over southern evangelical voters who had tired of the presidency of Jimmy Carter. Before the Florida primary, George H. W. Bush was called a "liberal" by a prominent political activist.[30] These attacks damaged Bush's campaign immensely. He even lost his adopted home state of Texas. When he withdrew from the race, his national political career looked like it was over. However, Reagan saved George H. W. Bush's political career by offering him the vice-presidential nomination. This selection would also allow a political dynasty to evolve.

Reagan's presidency showed the promise and limitations of conservative governance in America. However, his presidency made one point very clear to Republicans who were seeking office. The Republican Party was no longer the home of the eastern establishment. The Republican Party of the future was conservative, and only committed conservatives would be elected in Republican primaries. Reagan's own vice president understood the message. To become Reagan's running mate, George H. W. Bush changed his position on abortion, and he tried to appear more conservative when he ran for president in the 1988 general election. At every opportunity in that campaign, Bush would call his opponent, Michael Dukakis, a liberal. Two of George H. W. Bush's sons, George W. and Jeb, also learned the lesson of Reagan's success. They did not grow up in their grandfather's Republican Party as Connecticut liberals; they were movement conservatives from Texas who sought not only to continue Reagan's legacy but to enhance it by using the power of government to implement conservative domestic initiatives. These conservatives did not want just to stop the growth of government. They wanted to actively *reverse* it except in the areas of law enforcement and the military. Their movement saw the 1960s Great Society programs as not just failing to address social problems but actually causing social problems. They would use the executive power of government to experiment with a conservative approach to social issues.

The Bush brothers would provide an opportunity to test many of these conservative proposals at the state level. George W. Bush stayed in Texas and tried to start a career in the oil industry. Jeb Bush moved to Florida in 1980 to get out from under his father's shadow and find a more hospitable place for his Hispanic spouse, Columba, who came from Mexico. His move to Florida also coincided with the strong growth of the Republican Party in the state. Because of Reagan's success on the presidential level, more state and local politicians in Florida were running as Republicans. Jeb Bush became active in investment real estate in Miami, where he created a strong political base among the city's Cuban community. The Cuban community was generally more receptive than other Hispanic groups to Republicans because of the party's strong stance against communism. Jeb Bush served as secretary of commerce for the state of Florida for a brief period from 1987 to 1988. He worked on his father's presidential campaign in 1988. When his father lost his reelection bid in 1992, Jeb Bush decided it was now time for his opportunity. He announced his run for governor of Florida shortly thereafter. Surprisingly, his older brother George W. would also run for governor in 1994, in the state of Texas.

While his father had been accused throughout his political life of not being conservative enough, Jeb Bush made sure in his first political campaign that he would be known as the true conservative. Southern conservatives were leaving the Democratic Party in droves, and the Republican Party became their home. In Jeb Bush's first campaign, he was so conservative that he risked being called an extremist. Thirty years before, Goldwater had run a strong conservative campaign that aided the conservative movement immeasurably, but he also lost in a landslide. Jeb Bush's approach in his first campaign alienated Florida's center-right voters in a diverse state. As in other southern states, Democrats had won the vast majority of gubernatorial elections since the Civil War. Bush believed the Florida electorate was ready for real conservative change. In this campaign, he

- threatened to end the Florida State Department of Education— the department with the largest budget in state government,
- said he would send back to the federal government any welfare payments to the state,
- described himself as a "headbanging conservative,"[31] and
- when asked what he would do to help African Americans in the state, said "probably nothing."[32]

Even with these provocative statements, Bush was ahead of the incumbent governor and onetime Democratic U.S. senator Lawton Chiles until mid-October of 1994. Bush had made the issue of crime the most important issue in the campaign. However, he overreached when he complained that the Chiles administration was holding up the execution of a murderer of a ten-year-old child. The case was working its way through the courts on appeal, and there was nothing that Governor Chiles could have done to speed up the process. In a debate Chiles, a Florida political legend, chastised Jeb Bush for exploiting the death of a child for political gain. The issue backfired, and Bush lost the closest gubernatorial election in Florida history (until 2010). The defeat was particularly difficult because his brother George W. won an upset victory in Texas. This surprise turn would allow George W. to become a national figure and eventually a presidential candidate before Jeb.

Bush was determined to change his image and his rhetoric. He saw education policy as the perfect vehicle to do both. He sought out T. Willard Fair, the African American head of the Urban League of Miami. They found that they agreed on education policy, and they put together a joint proposal for opening Miami's first charter school. Along with Bush's working group, the Foundation for Florida's Future, Fair and Bush convinced the state to allow them to open a charter school in 1996.[33] The school had a profound impact on Bush and his views about urban poverty.

While Bush realized the manner in which he campaigned in 1994 had turned off too many independent voters, he was not about to change his basic belief that state government needed conservative changes. A year after his loss, Bush wrote about the state: "Now is the time for the rebirth of character and virtue in Florida. We need to recapture the spirit of self-government."[34] Bush started his second run for governor a full year before the November 1998 election. Since he had run so closely last time, he was the overwhelming Republican favorite and faced no primary opposition. Term limits had left the governor's seat open, and he ran against the sitting lieutenant governor, Buddy MacKay. With a huge fund-raising advantage and no incumbent to run against, Bush won the race easily. In a famous commercial, the Bush campaign used a word feared in southern politics. The tagline for the commercial said, "Hey Buddy, You're Liberal."[35] Bush had softened his campaign appearances in the 1998 race, but he made clear to everyone that he wanted to attempt a complete conservative reinvention of Florida state government. His victory was a statewide sweep. He carried the conservative northern Panhandle, most of the central part of the state, and, most impressively, Miami-Dade County, his adopted home in the middle of the strongest part of the state for Democrats.

Bush as the Activist Conservative

After Jeb Bush won the governor's office—a goal he had been working on for six years—he had a real opportunity to put into practice fundamental conservative ideas. His policy proposals and executive actions would show the different streams of historical conservatism. To implement his agenda and bring about an administrative revolution on the state government level, he would combine various strains of the conservative movement: executive, intellectual, states' rights, and southern conservatism.

Two major factors accompanied Jeb Bush when he came to power in 1999. The voters changed the Florida state constitution so that the governor would share executive power with fewer cabinet officers. The new constitution would leave only the attorney general, the agriculture commissioner, and the chief financial officer in the cabinet along with the governor to run the state. By 2003 the elected education commissioner would be gone and the governor gained the right to appoint the leader of K–12 education in the state. Even before 2003, Bush let it be known that he was in charge of education policy. Bush also came into office with a friendly legislature. For the first time since Reconstruction, the governor's office and both houses of the state legislature were in Republican hands. Bush thus had a new governing structure that favored executive power and a legislature that owed him because they had run on a ticket with his name at the top in 1998. Then in the year 2000, state legislative term limits passed in 1992 took effect, bringing in a wave of new Republicans who aligned themselves with Governor Bush.

Even though Bush talked repeatedly about limiting the power of government, he did not believe in limiting the power of the executive. Just as the Federalists in the early days of the nation believed that strong executive power was needed to maintain the nation's conservative values, Bush also believed that executive power was needed to implement conservative policy changes throughout state government. Bush made it clear throughout Florida state government that he was in charge. Mid-level bureaucrats in many different departments would get e-mails and phone calls from the sitting governor demanding certain actions. In Bush's view, state bureaucracy was out of control and only a strong executive could rein it in.

Bush's views on a strong executive also guided his relationship with the other two branches of government. For the state judiciary, Governor Bush had a thinly concealed contempt. The Republicans in the legislature pushed through a law that gave the governor sole authority to appoint members of state judicial nominating commissions. Bush clearly stated he was looking for more judges who would be "ideologically compatible" with him.[36] The Florida Supreme Court had almost cost his brother George W. Bush the presidential election in the year 2000. In the infamous Terri Schiavo case in 2003, Bush lobbied the Florida state legislature to pass a law that would overturn judicial decisions concerning Schiavo's medical care. Schiavo's husband, Michael, and her parents had been involved in a long court battle because her husband wanted her feeding tube removed. Not only did the Florida legislature respond to Jeb Bush's call for action, the U.S. Congress passed a law that applied only to Terri Schiavo, asking the federal court to review her medical care. Because Governor Bush had disagreed with

Florida state courts, he had mobilized the entire United States government to try to negate the state's judicial branch. After the federal courts agreed with the state court's decisions in the case, the feeding tube was eventually removed and Terri Schiavo died. This case will be reviewed in detail in the next chapter, but it illustrates Bush's view of an all-powerful executive and also shows his distrust of the judiciary.[37]

Bush's views on limited government and strong executive action seem to be contradictory. However, he was a strong believer in states' rights versus the power of the federal government. The appropriate power and authority for the states versus the federal government had been a fundamental issue since the founding of the country. "States' rights" was the rallying cry of conservatives in the South who wanted to expand slavery before the Civil War. The states' rights movement became potent again in the South with the issue of desegregation after the *Brown v. Board of Education* decision. Reagan and other Republican conservatives in the late twentieth century made the argument for states' rights as well. Jeb Bush picked up on this theme in a variety of ways. He sought to completely remake the Medicaid program in Florida. This federal-state partnership funding medical care for the poor was taking a larger and larger share of the Florida budget. Instead of following federal government regulations, Bush wanted to revamp the program through the use of HMOs (health maintenance organizations). In the end Bush received permission to pilot the program in a few counties in Florida, but he made it known that he had limited use for most federal programs. Much of his Medicaid experiment would become law in the 2013 in the Florida legislature. Ironically, his own brother as president would ask Congress to pass a large education bill called No Child Left Behind. This legislation mandated that the states achieve certain average scores in standardized testing in their public schools. In many ways this legislation was copying what both Bush brothers had done at the state level. Governor Jeb Bush would have to request a waiver from the federal government of President George W. Bush to release Florida from some of the more onerous requirements of the bill.

In his first inaugural address in Tallahassee in 1999, Bush made it clear what he thought the state government's priorities should be.

"Government will be unencumbered to make a true difference where it is most needed and where it can be most effective: education, public safety, public works, and the protection of the frailest and weakest among us."[38] Education was listed as his first priority, and he acted upon that priority.

Jeb Bush rejected the proposition that economic status is determinative of student performance. Seizing the opportunity to remake Florida education from kindergarten through high school, Bush initiated several fundamental conservative reforms. The changes, all tied to the concepts of accountability and consequences, clearly shifted the burden of performance from policymakers and parents to the schools, teachers, and students themselves. The measures of accountability and the consequences coming from the measurements would reshape the entire focus of school districts throughout the state of Florida. Governor Bush announced his education reform policies immediately on taking office in January 1999. These changes are examined in detail in chapter 5.

Governor Bush also showed that he was strong believer in the ideas of the capitalist conservatives. During his first legislative session he slashed the intangibles tax—a tax on financial instruments that hit many wealthy investors. He moved to cut other revenue streams as well, because the Florida economy was still expanding. And he privatized government services including personnel services, foster care, and management of state parks. For business leaders in the state, Bush would be the strongest advocate.

Finally, Bush had a deep understanding of the cultural conservatism that was and is a huge presence among southern Republicans. He openly expressed the view that government had become way too hostile to religious beliefs. Besides the Terri Schiavo case, Bush's legislative agenda attempted to limit abortions, use faith-based rehabilitation programs in Florida prisons, and ask Florida public schools to adopt religious materials.[39] Unlike other Republicans in the region, Bush had excellent relations with Hispanic groups throughout his state. The Hispanic population in Florida is much different than in other states. Hispanic Americans in Florida come from a variety of places, including Cuba, Venezuela, Puerto Rico, and Nicaragua. Hispanic voters in

Florida are generally culturally conservative, and Bush reflected these cultural ideas. As of this writing, Governor Bush is also a leading voice for immigration reform in 2014. Yet like most southern Republican leaders, he has had strained relations with African Americans. His father had opposed the Civil Rights Act in his run for the U.S. Senate in 1964 and had received little African American support in his presidential campaigns. Jeb Bush had his own problems with African American leaders with his One Florida initiative. This executive order sought to end all preferential admissions and hiring programs in the state. They would be replaced by taking the top 20 percent of students from all high schools and guaranteeing them university admissions. With state high schools reflecting the segregated living patterns of its citizens, this plan should have ensured that minorities would be represented in Florida universities. Yet because Governor Bush did not reach out to African American leaders across the state before he announced his initiative, it met stiff resistance. This resistance culminated in a large march on Tallahassee to protest the end of affirmative action programs. Governor Bush held his ground, but his relations with the African American community were never the same.[40]

Again, with a real examination of Governor Bush's record in Florida, a direct conclusion is that he was a solid conservative leader. With the passage of time since his gubernatorial tenure ended in 2006, some national commentators have labeled Bush a moderate. His time as Florida governor is a direct refutation of that description. The reason for the view of Jeb Bush as a moderate has to do with the emergence of the Tea Party movement in 2008 and 2009. Tea Party conservatives argue they want a severe reduction in government expenditures and power. This philosophy would be in conflict with some of Jeb Bush's initiatives that relied upon strong executive power.

However, in some ways Jeb Bush's conservatism allowed the Tea Party to find a space in Florida politics. His turn away from the moderation of Florida Democrats such as Reubin Askew, Bob Graham, and Lawton Chiles made the Republican Party the dominant party in Florida on the state level. When the Tea Party backlash occurred in 2010, Republicans had been in the governor's office in Florida since

1999. Although Bush's preferred gubernatorial candidate did not win the Republican nomination in 2010, it is difficult to see how the Tea Party candidate Rick Scott could have won the governor's race in Florida in 2010 if the Republican Party had not been the dominant party in state elections since the 1990s. Governor Bush's relationship with the Tea Party movement has been mixed. The Bush name also carries the impression of American political nobility, while most Tea Party activists want to completely clean out the political "establishment." Bush's relationship with the new Tea Party wing of the Republican Party will be examined in the last chapter in detail, but while Governor Bush is certainly not a typical Tea Party Republican, his successes in Florida made it more likely that Tea Party candidates would be competitive in state races.

Moreover, there is little doubt that his policies as governor of Florida produced important achievements in conservative governance on the state level. States have been called the laboratories of democracy; Bush made Florida into a laboratory of conservative governance, and the effects are still being felt today in the state and around the nation. If Jeb Bush decides to run for president in 2016, a crucial test in the Republican primaries may be whether these policies are conservative enough for the new vocal Tea Party base of the Republican Party.

4

. . . .

Jeb Bush, Culture Warrior

Jeb Bush is known as a policy wonk. He would much rather discuss public policy at a think tank than attend a campaign event with music and cheering. This affinity is somewhat of a contradiction for a man who argues for limited government. Jeb Bush's time as governor of Florida showed that he could use government to advance conservative principles. Bush did not want to be separated from government; he wanted to lead state government to a new way of operation. However, the core of Bush's approach to government was not based on levels of expenditure or figuring out how grants from the federal government could be used more efficiently. Bush's core approach to government was much more fundamental: he believed a citizen's relationship with his government depends upon character and virtue. In order to take the emphasis from government action and dependence, Bush believed that state government and Florida society must focus on changing individual moral behavior.

This is a tall order for any politician, government, or even individual family, but Bush wrote extensively on the subject in the mid-1990s. He shared the view of the Reagan revolution that, more often than not, government was the problem and not the solution. Bush even offered a more damning indictment—not only was state government not helping Florida citizens, it was eroding their character and virtue. In short, government was helping to put more people into poverty, was destroying traditional families, and was crowding traditional faith and religion out of the public square.[1] However, the most famous episode regarding Jeb Bush and issues of morality was the Terri Schiavo case, where Bush fought the state and federal government to try to keep a woman in a chronic vegetative state alive. This chapter will first examine Bush's ideas about the connection of virtue, faith, and government and why approaching these moral issues through government is tremendously difficult. Then five policy areas will be examined to assess the impact of Bush's efforts, including the Schiavo case. Against historical precedent where many politicians talked about moral issues but did little, Jeb Bush actually made serious efforts to change public policy involving several contentious social issues, among them abortion, gun control, prison rehabilitation, affirmative action, and end-of-life issues. As with his brother George W. Bush, these social and cultural concerns were not casual campaign slogans for Jeb Bush; they represented the core of what he believed about governance and society.

Bush's Philosophy

Jeb Bush believed that government had attempted to take over ensuring "goodness" in American society and had failed miserably. He wrote that individuals, families, and societal institutions had for too long attempted to "delegate our goodness" to government.[2] Bush argued that because President Lyndon Johnson's Great Society initiative in the 1960s attempted to use the federal government to solve race relations, poverty, and urban decay, individuals at the community level had been crowded out of making society better. Bush cited the legendary political scientist James Q. Wilson, who believed that societal success was dependent upon the self-control of individuals. Bush argued that too many individuals had lost their self-control.

In Bush's view the largest obstacle to promoting a more moral society in Florida and in the United States was the fact that "character-forming" institutions such as families, schools, and community groups were too often prevented from engaging in character-building work. Before he took office, he viewed public schools as "receptacles of social experimentation." In other words, schools were devoting too much time and effort to trying to ensure the individual rights of students and parents instead of focusing on the basics of educational achievement. This belief drove Governor Bush to push for fundamental changes to the Florida school system, examined in chapter 5.

Too often, Bush felt, schools and other societal institutions were "justifying a wide variety of deviant behaviors." In his view, "children need direction, not choices"—thus schools and community groups should be less concerned about what children can say and wear and more about building fundamental character traits. He argued that public policy too often emphasizes our differences and not our similarities. He believed that most Floridians have different political values but not different human virtues—which he defines as "agreed-upon standards of right and wrong." For example, Floridians believe the vast majority of criminal acts defined by Florida statute are indeed wrongful acts that harm society. Bush suggests using these unifying principles for "renewal of virtue and character."

In the mid-1990s, Bush examined social indicators in Florida such as the crime rate, the poverty rate, the number of abortions performed in the state, and the percentage of out-of-wedlock births and concluded that the trends in the state were heading in the wrong direction. He argued that Florida's families were at a crossroads. Comparing the plight of the Florida family to the surrounded platoon at the Battle of Gettysburg in the Civil War, he said that Florida families were being attacked on all sides by an uncivil society and an ineffective government. It would take a monumental change in state government to combat all of the negative trends, and Jeb Bush was ready to start this movement.

Bush's attempt to use government to restore character in Florida society was ambitious and strangely difficult. Religion, values, and morality all require living under specific standards of conduct. Some patterns of conduct, such as committing murder or stealing property, are universally condemned.[3] Yet other issues that involve moral judgments do not have societal consensus. Even if a values issue is a concern to the majority of a society, that does not necessarily mean that most citizens should be involved in that issue.

Politicians and many social scientists agree that single-parent families are at the core of many modern-day problems. Yet it is not clear that action or lack of action by government can do anything to stop the trend of single-parent families. Many conservative critics of public assistance to the poor have argued that the levels of assistance were too high and were encouraging single-parent families. Yet after the welfare reform efforts of the Clinton administration and the reduction of public assistance benefits during Governor Bush's administration in Florida, Florida still has one of the highest percentages of single-parent families in the nation.[4] This is a stark example of the limits that government action or inaction can have on societal indicators. For example, in a free society it is difficult if not impossible for the court system or legislation to regulate the consensual sexual conduct of adults. What is a society and a government supposed to do when a child is born into a single-parent household that may be doomed to poverty? Even though the child's parents may have not acted responsibly, is it the responsibility of government to help? These are not simple questions, and while many politicians talk about religion and morality in their campaigns, they end up doing very little to advance the causes when elected. Jeb Bush was different: he believed that state government should play a large role in honoring religion and restoring moral character. Yet how far should government go? Should it attempt to regulate the content of movies that might be objectionable? Should it attempt to regulate the use of alcohol and drugs in the home? Jeb Bush would later have to confront these questions in his own family when his daughter, Noelle, was referred to a drug treatment facility after being arrested for trying to obtain the antianxiety drug Xanax without a prescription.[5] After another relapse, she successfully completed a drug rehabilitation program in 2003.

Different institutions in American society tried to answer these questions in the late twentieth and early twenty-first century through the court system, legislation, and political campaigns. Yet more times than not, the answers from these institutions were incomplete and unsatisfying. As I wrote in another book,

> Those who seek to resolve moral dilemmas through the political process may strongly believe that no compromise is possible on their core beliefs. Conflict between moral certainty and political reality is inevitable. Yet this conflict has not stopped moral and religious factors from becoming central to American politics.[6]

Jeb Bush sought to advance conservative positions on religious and moral issues and did so in ways that many governors had not attempted until the 1990s. He also made these efforts in an unyielding fashion despite the fact that politics often requires some type of compromise.

This attitude would bring him to the front and center of several political firestorms, but it also allowed him to advance a more conservative social agenda farther than many other governors at that time. It also helped to set the stage for an even stronger advancement of conservative social policies in Florida and throughout the nation. Republican governors have been much more active on social issues since the 1990s. Bush believed that religion was being pushed out of the public square, and during his time as governor he did more to integrate religion and religious organizations into Florida politics and administration than any governor in Florida history.

The melding of politics and religion was actually not as commonplace in the American South as some might believe. For most of southern history since the Civil War, religion was not a main political force either in elections or in administration. Since southern states including Florida were for so many years part of the conservative Democratic Solid South, no partisan divisions and few other political divisions were evident regarding religion. There are exceptions to this trend, including the Florida governorship of Sidney Catts, who in 1916 ran on a virulent anti-Catholic platform. The Scopes "monkey trial" of 1925 in Tennessee brought the issue of evolution to the forefront, but after national condemnation, it quickly faded from the public arena. Prohibition was an important issue in the 1920s, but its repeal in 1933 showed the limits of combining moral beliefs with public policy. Moreover, societal mores were generally conservative for most of the first half of the twentieth century. Since there was more agreement then on moral and political issues, there was no reason to inject religion into most political debates.

This dynamic changed dramatically in the 1950s and 1960s during the civil rights movement in the South. African American churches were the political base for those courageous organizers who sought to change the status quo of racial segregation. Rev. Martin Luther King Jr. as leader of the civil rights movement appealed to the morality of American citizens in religious terms. In 1965 the civil rights march from Selma, Alabama, to Montgomery helped to spur the passage of the Voting Rights Act, and the march was populated with religious figures from around the nation.

White Protestant churches and Catholic churches basically tried to stay out of politics in the 1950s and 1960s. This attitude changed dramatically with the *Roe v. Wade* abortion decision in 1973. The American Catholic Church reacted strongly and began to organize to reverse the decision. This political activity took place at the same time that many conservative religious leaders around the nation were asking for a return to traditional values. The cultural and political upheaval of the late 1960s, including widespread use of drugs and more permissive sexual behavior, had shocked some religious and political leaders. They believed that political participation by religious leaders and religious voters could stem the fundamental changes occurring in American society.

In 1976 many white conservative religious leaders supported Jimmy Carter for president because he described himself as a born-again Christian. Yet these leaders became dissatisfied and angry at the Carter administration for its lack of action on social issues including abortion. Republican Ronald Reagan's presidential campaign of 1980 moved quickly to take advantage of this division. At a meeting of evangelical leaders in 1980, Reagan stated that he was not asking for their endorsement but said, "I endorse you and what you are doing." Later in that same session a minister addressed the crowd and said, "I'm sick and tired of hearing about . . . all of the perverts and the liberals and leftists . . . coming out of the closet, it's time for God's people to come out of the closet."[7] Religious conservatives were an important part of Reagan's landslide presidential victory in 1980.

Since the 1980 election, these religious conservatives have played a central role in the Republican Party in the United States. This important role can be seen in the Bush family itself. Jeb Bush's grandfather Prescott was a northeastern Republican who was a traditional Protestant. Jeb's father was an Episcopalian and was viewed warily by some Christian conservatives during his political life. The political sons of George Herbert Walker Bush made their religious leanings as clear as they could: George W. became an evangelical Christian and Jeb became a Roman Catholic. Jeb Bush's Catholicism, to which he came later in life, seems to have had a major impact on his decision making. Without hesitation the Bush brothers both combined their strong religious beliefs with their public policy decisions. White conservative Christians became a major voting bloc within the national Republican Party from the 1980s onward. Both George W. Bush and Jeb Bush could appeal to this bloc with their rhetoric and their political actions. In many ways Jeb Bush was even more vocal than his brother George about using his religious beliefs to impact public policy.

Abortion

Jeb Bush made it clear that he was going to try to impact the issue of abortion in Florida immediately upon becoming governor. Since Republicans had gained control of the state legislature in 1996, two years before Bush became governor, a number of antiabortion bills had reached the desk of Bush's predecessor Governor Lawton Chiles. These bills were quickly vetoed, as the efforts of Christian conservative advocacy groups were blunted in the state capital. In the first two months Governor Bush was in office, he met with the Christian Coalition of Florida and promised quick public action on moral issues. The director of the Christian Coalition of Florida said, "For years we could not get a phone call back from the governor's office, much less a meeting." A

Republican state senator from Leesburg confirmed the idea that Governor Bush was going to bring in a new era of moral accountability; she sponsored a limit on late-term abortions and said, "We have to draw the line somewhere on what's right or wrong."[8]

Accordingly, in Bush's first session as governor, the legislature would again consider abortion legislation that had been vetoed by Governor Chiles. This social agenda would set Jeb Bush up against the one Florida political institution that did not back away from challenging his conservative agenda: the Florida courts. The Florida state court system would time and time again balk what Governor Bush wanted to do regarding social issues. This conflict would lead to a constitutional showdown over the Terri Schiavo matter. However, the courts intervened in Governor Bush's attempts to implement bold conservative public policy long before the Schiavo issue.

From the beginning of his first session in 1999, almost every social or cultural issue that Jeb Bush and the Republican legislature attempted to address ended up in the courts. Unlike the federal court system, which had become more populated with Republican conservatives during the presidencies of Ronald Reagan and George Herbert Walker Bush, the Florida judicial branch had mostly been nominated by moderate Democratic governors. These judges would serve as the only effective check on Governor Bush's conservative social agenda. Under Bush's direction, the Florida legislature gave him much more power to control the nomination process for future state judges. Yet he could do nothing about the judges currently on the bench. The conflict between the two branches of government during Bush's tenure brought into question the basic premise of the separation of powers and the ability of a governor to implement his agenda. The fact that the courts became the only real barrier to Jeb Bush's political power in the state is a testament to how he increased the power and effectiveness of the office of governor.

Bush's first challenge in the court system over a social controversy involved the seemingly innocuous issue of what phrase it was permissible to put on a Florida license tag. In the mid-1990s, antiabortion advocates had pushed the Republican legislature to let Floridians purchase a license tag that included the phrase "Choose Life" with an outline of two children with their hands raised. Democrats and pro-choice groups like the National Organization for Women believed the state was endorsing a political message with the license tag. They saw this as the first shot in a battle to severely limit access to abortions in the state of Florida. The sponsor of the legislation rejected the argument that it endorsed an antiabortion message. Representative Bev Kilmer from the Panhandle region of Florida said in February 1999 that "it's the kind of issue that the people of my district feel strongly about. My district is pretty much considered the Bible Belt. . . . [The bill,] it's not antiabortion anything . . . it's an adopt a child tag."[9] A version of the bill that changed the language from "Choose Life" to "Adopt a Child" failed to pass a Senate committee. It took most of Bush's first legislative session to get the "Choose Life" license tag approved by both houses of the legislature. The proceeds of the license plate would go to organizations that supported financially needy pregnant women who chose not to have abortions.[10] After Bush signed the legislation in May 1999, it was immediately challenged in the Florida state court system. The opponents of the tag argued that it was an unconstitutional approval of religion by a state entity. Florida circuit court judge Nikki Clark ruled that the sale of license plates could continue because adoption was a secular issue, not a religious issue.[11]

Another major issue regarding abortion during Bush's first legislative session involved legislation that would require minor women to notify their parents if they wanted to get an abortion. Notification is different from a consent provision, which is more difficult to implement where parents are either negligent or abusive. The notification legislation passed with strong Republican support and mostly united Democratic opposition. Governor Bush signed the bill and showed that with his election he could advance an agenda promoting socially conservative issues. Yet two months later a Florida circuit judge ruled that the law violated Florida's constitution. Florida has a broad privacy provision in its constitution that states: "Every natural person has the right to be let alone and free from governmental intrusion into the person's private life except as otherwise provided herein." The judge ruled that since children can receive other services such as mental health counseling and treatment for sexually transmitted diseases without notification, notification for abortions would be an exception.[12] This decision was seen as a major blow to Florida's Christian Coalition and to Governor Bush's attempts to push forward conservative social issues. But supporters of this bill and the governor countered with a smart tactic to get around the court system. If the Florida constitution would not allow a parental notification bill, then the Florida constitution would need to be changed. In 2004 the Florida legislature voted to put on the ballot in November an amendment that would carve out an exception to the privacy provision in the Florida constitution. Any woman seventeen or under would have to notify her parents within forty-eight hours of seeking an abortion. There was a waiver provision in the amendment that would exempt a woman whose parents were abusive from notifying them, if a judge ruled the exemption was warranted. Opponents argued that this was insufficient protection. Yet voters overwhelmingly approved the amendment, and it was signed into law after the following legislative session.[13] This episode showed that the Florida constitution would become a main battleground between Governor Bush and the Florida court system.

In the second legislative session for Governor Bush, in 2000, the legislature passed a ban on late-term abortions. The medical procedure known as extraction is called partial-birth abortion by antiabortion advocates. These advocates argued that late-term abortions could result in a viable fetus being killed. When Bush signed the legislation, a lobbyist for the Florida Women's Political Caucus said that it showed "a total disregard for the Florida Constitution and the U.S. Constitution." However, Bush's spokesperson said that the governor could not wait to end "this gruesome procedure," and added, "The Legislature felt it was important to address this issue this year and Governor Bush agreed."[14] Bush and his administration likely knew the legislation would be ruled unconstitutional. Yet this did not deter them from pushing the issue. Less than two months later, the United States Supreme Court ruled that a similar law in Nebraska was unconstitutional. After that ruling, a federal judge in Miami declared the Florida law unconstitutional.

Such a legal setback would have deterred many governors from taking on the abortion issue again, but not Governor Jeb Bush. He would ensure that the state of Florida went to unprecedented lengths to make changes to the state's abortion policies in a post–*Roe v. Wade* America. In 2003, Governor Bush asked the state courts to appoint a legal representative for the fetus of a mentally handicapped woman who had been raped in a state group home. The state courts rejected this effort as invading the privacy of the pregnant woman. She eventually gave birth, and the baby was later adopted.

Another case involved a thirteen-year-old girl, a longtime responsibility of the state, who was living in a state shelter under the care of the Department of Children and Families. In 2005 the girl, then more than two months pregnant, asked a caseworker to help her get an abortion. The caseworker scheduled an abortion on a specific date and agreed to drive the girl to the appointment. Florida's Department of Children and Families moved for an injunction to stop the caseworker from assisting the girl in obtaining the abortion.

The American Civil Liberties Union took up the girl's case and argued that the state did not have a right to intervene. ACLU attorney James Crane argued that the state should be more concerned about how the girl became pregnant than about preventing the abortion. The ACLU director in Florida at the time, Howard Simon, said that "forcing a thirteen-year-old to carry an unwanted pregnancy to term . . . is just plain cruel. This is what you get when ideology dictates child welfare decisions." A spokeswoman for the state's Department of Children and Families countered that the DCF was "acting in the best interest of the child." Bush and DCF won an early victory in this case: the judge issued an injunction blocking the abortion procedure until the teenager could have a psychological evaluation. However, the girl told the judge that she was too young to have a baby and had no way to support a child. The girl apparently became pregnant when she ran away from the state shelter. The judge finally sided with the girl's position, and she was allowed to have the abortion. Governor Bush commented, "It's a tragedy that a thirteen-year-old girl would be in a vulnerable position where she could be made pregnant, and it's a tragedy that her baby will be lost."[15]

Again, not many governors would be so absolute in their beliefs as to use the entire state government to intervene in two difficult and emotionally wrenching pregnancies. Jeb Bush would use the same template for action with a different set of facts in the case of Terri Schiavo. Simply put, when it came to the difficult and emotional cases involving abortion or other right-to-life issues, Bush believed in strong government intervention to support pro-life causes, and if that meant intervening in someone's private life, he would do it. He called himself "probably the most pro-life governor of modern times."[16]

In the same month in 2005, Governor Bush also signed legislation that would greatly increase the oversight of clinics that performed second-trimester abortions. Abortion rights groups argued that the legislation was intended to shut clinics down. Bush said that it was needed to enhance their safety. This stance was a departure for Bush in the matter of government regulation. From his first inaugural speech, he argued strongly for fewer restrictions on businesses that offered services to Floridians. Yet right-to-life issues brought Governor Bush to another conclusion: government needed to be involved in these life issues, even if it meant becoming involved in an individual's private decision making. When speaking to the Georgia Republican Convention after the Florida legislative session of 2005, Bush received the most applause when he talked about the stance he took on abortion in Florida. He said Republicans cannot back away from these issues "in a time of moral ambivalence." He went on to say, "There is such a thing as right and wrong. Republicans cannot continue to win unless we talk with compassion and passion about absolute truth."[17] In the view of political theorists and observers, politics is supposed to be the art of compromise, but Governor Bush talked about "absolute truths." The question remains, how does a concept like "absolute truths" work in a democratic system that demands majority rule? Moreover, the governor attempted these changes with a legislature in which less than 25 percent of the members were women.

The Open Gun State

The idea that elected officials talk often about social and cultural issues but do very little when they get a chance to legislate is refuted by Jeb Bush's record on gun issues during his time as governor. In the 1990s the protection of gun rights had become a central tenet of Republican politics in most states. Some southerners viewed access to guns as part of their cultural heritage. Governor Bush and the Republican legislature methodically and completely changed gun regulation in the state of Florida during his two terms. Ironically in the same election in which Governor Bush came to office, the voters of Florida approved a constitutional amendment that would allow local counties to implement tighter restrictions on gun shows in their localities. At that time in Florida anyone could go to a gun show and buy and sell guns without any criminal background check or any waiting period. The amendment allowed counties to have their own say on the matter.

Yet this unusual setback for the gun lobby in Florida did not deter the governor or the National Rifle Association from pursuing an aggressive course. While gun issues have not received as much publicity as social issues addressed by Governor Bush, his support of broadening gun rights marks the most conservative part of the agenda. His policy initiatives on gun issues arguably left a broader legacy than in many other areas.

The depth and consistency of the changes that Governor Bush sought regarding gun rights is truly remarkable. The National Rifle Association, led by its lobbyist Marion Hammer, had more influence and sway over Florida politics during Jeb Bush's time as governor than any other interest group. Hammer is a state legend and a national figure in the gun rights movement. During Bush's two terms, she was a feared presence in Tallahassee. Bush's gun agenda and Hammer's priorities became almost identical and would transform Florida into one of the most pro-gun states in the Union.

Before he started to advocate for a broadening of protections for gun owners, Governor Bush followed through on a campaign promise when he signed the 10–20–Life law. Under this law, a person convicted of committing a crime while carrying a gun gets a mandated 10 years in prison. The term becomes 20 years if the gun is fired, and 25 years to life if a person is injured or killed by gunfire during the commission of a crime. Judges and defense attorneys publicly argued against the law because it took away all discretion in handing out sentences. The mere possession of a gun during the commission of a crime would mean 10 years in prison, even if the gun had nothing to do with the criminal violation. The legislation smartly focused on guns used in the commission of a crime. When Bush and the state legislature passed this legislation that targeted criminal activity with guns, it gave them political cover to go to extraordinary lengths to protect the rights of legal gun owners.[18]

The first major piece of legislation the governor approved that aided the gun rights cause allowed non-Floridians with a concealed weapons permit from their own state to cross state lines into Florida and still lawfully conceal their weapons. Democrats in the Florida legislature complained that this would allow thousands of people into the state with firearms without proper background checks. Regulations on carrying concealed firearms varied tremendously from state to state in the late 1990s, and this new legislation would allow unknown citizens from other states to carry guns in public. Yet the Republican state senator who sponsored the bill, Charles Bronson, called this criticism misguided and said, "The people you should be afraid of are not the people that went to their state and got weapons permits, you should be afraid of the people who are carrying their weapons illegally."[19] The respected Florida author and commentator Martin Dyckman was not convinced; he criticized the governor and the state legislature for ignoring the will of state voters who had voted in November 1998 for more regulation, not less.[20]

Highlighting the power of the gun lobby over the Florida legislature and Governor Jeb Bush in 1999 was the refusal to pass legislation that would require gun locks for weapons "on premises where children can reasonably be expected." The Democratic sponsor of the legislation, Senator Betty Holzendorf from Jacksonville, said the Senate Criminal Justice Committee would not consider the legislation because they were "scared of Marion Hammer"[21]—the NRA lobbyist. The fact that legislation that attempted to protect children in their own homes from accidental shootings was not even considered by the full Florida legislature showed the amount of resistance to even minimal regulation.

It was in Bush's second term that he solidified his legacy as a champion of gun rights. In 2004 Bush signed legislation that protected gun ranges from being sued for contamination of nearby land and water. The Southwest Florida Water Management District, a regulatory agency that monitors the water supply, was suing a gun range in Pinellas County because of the damage the range had done to a nearby pond. The new law made it impossible for gun ranges to be sued for environmental contamination, with certain restrictions. The 2004 session also produced legislation that restricted police departments in the state from keeping an electronic list of gun owners if they committed no crime.[22] Bush signed that legislation after he made changes that satisfied some in law enforcement.

The most comprehensive and controversial gun legislation during Bush's tenure, the law known as Stand Your Ground, came in 2005 when the legislature with the support of the governor vastly expanded the so-called Castle Doctrine. Florida had already passed a detailed law that allowed homeowners to use firearms to defend themselves in their own homes and cars. The basic premise of this protective legislation was that a home or a car was a person's "castle." Accordingly, a homeowner or car owner did not have a "duty to retreat" under duress. The 2005 version of this law extended the right to public areas such as streets and highways. Proponents of this Stand Your Ground law contended that people who were attacked in the streets should not have to retreat before defending themselves. Representative Dennis Baxley, a Republican from Ocala, argued that "if I'm attacked I shouldn't have a duty to retreat. . . . Some violent rape will not occur because somebody will feel empowered by this bill. Somebody's child will not be abducted . . . you're going to prevent a murder."[23] Sarah Brady, chair of the Brady Campaign to Prevent Gun Violence, was strongly opposed to the bill. She said at the time of passage, "This is just a license to kill." Brady and others were concerned that any small personal conflict in any location could give a Floridian the right to fire. The controversy underlines Governor Jeb Bush's importance in advancing conservative legislation like this. Six years after he had been inaugurated, Jeb Bush was still the most important force in Florida politics. He had won reelection and was the brother of the sitting president of the United States. If Jeb Bush wanted changes to the legislation or threatened to veto it entirely, it would have happened.

Yet Bush strongly supported the legislation, saying it's "common sense to allow people to defend themselves."[24] Moreover, the

Democratic Party that was in the minority offered little resistance to this gun legislation. By 2005, a year after Jeb Bush's brother won the state in convincing fashion by Florida standards, some Democrats were trying to establish themselves as more conservative on social issues. Democratic representative Will Kendrick was a sponsor of the House legislation that dealt with the Stand Your Ground Issue. He said about the state Democrats that "a majority of Democrats have gotten away from basic principles. They realized they were way out in left field, and I think some of them voted for this one in an attempt to get back up to balance."[25] Thus Democrats put up weak opposition to the most conservative change to the self-defense doctrine in the nation. From 2005 to 2012, 199 Floridians invoked the Stand Your Ground doctrine when they had killed someone. A third of them had been accused of violent crimes in the past. Many others who claimed the defense had a history of drug offenses on their records.[26]

Two recent controversial cases also brought the Stand Your Ground legislation into question. From a legal standpoint, they did not involve the Stand Your Ground doctrine, yet opponents argued that Stand Your Ground principles are part of most jury instructions in self-defense cases in Florida. The famous Trayvon Martin case generated a national discussion on Stand Your Ground laws. The defendant, George Zimmerman, claimed that he was attacked, even though the victim, Trayvon Martin, was walking to his father's girlfriend's house in the neighborhood. This case and Bush's law highlighted inconsistencies in how self-defense laws were interpreted by juries and the public at large. The case also highlighted for the nation the fact that gun restrictions in Florida were almost nonexistent. In another case in 2013 a jury in Jacksonville acquitted Michael Dunn of first-degree murder in the shooting of an African American teen, Jordan Davis, who had been sitting in a van with his friends listening to loud music at a convenience store. After an exchange of words, Dunn fired into the vehicle ten times. Dunn was found guilty on lesser charges, but the jury did not convict him on the first-degree charge because Dunn claimed self-defense. No other weapon was ever found at the scene. Because of laws such as Stand Your Ground, Floridians could expand the concept of self-defense to almost any situation.

Even after this seminal change in gun regulation in Florida with the 2005 legislation, gun rights advocates in the state pushed for even more during Governor Bush's last year. Their efforts paid off beyond expectations when Bush signed six separate pieces of legislation that vastly expanded the rights of gun owners and protected gun manufacturers. This last blitzkrieg of gun rights legislation included:

- exempting concealed weapon permit holders from the state's public records law—which meant the names of people who applied for concealed weapons permits would not be made public even if requested by the media;
- requiring stores that sell hunting and fishing licenses to offer voter registration applications—a clear attempt to connect political power and support for expanded gun rights;
- removing the power of the sitting governor to order the collection of firearms during a hurricane or other natural disaster—this in response to the terrible looting in the aftermath of Hurricane Katrina in 2005 when, to stem the violence, New Orleans police confiscated weapons; Governor Bush and the Florida legislature wanted to make sure that that would not occur in Florida, where such a situation is likely to arise because of the state's vulnerability to hurricanes; and
- allowing firearms into state parks and national forests in Florida.

In his last legislative session, Governor Bush had thus changed the state's open records laws to accommodate gun owners, mandated that hunting and fishing retail outlets become voter registration centers, allowed gun owners to keep their weapons in the event of a natural disaster, and for the first time allowed weapons into Florida's national forests and state parks, where thousands of families vacation every year. It was a stunning array of policy changes and legislative achievements for the gun lobby.[27]

The NRA failed in one attempt to get a priority passed. The NRA wanted to penalize businesses that did not allow their employees to have guns at work even if the guns were locked in their personal cars. Yet this bill faced a counterattack from the business lobby in Florida, which did not want the liability of employees having guns at work. The legislation never made it out of committee to both houses of the state legislature. This rare defeat could not overshadow the complete dismantling of any regulation on gun owners or gun manufacturers in the state.

Ending Affirmative Action

Governor Bush did not limit himself or his agenda to such controversial social issues as abortion and gun rights; early in his administration he took on a policy that had been ingrained in most state and local governments since the civil rights movement of the 1960s. In the late 1990s a conservative activist from California named Ward Connerly had started a nationwide movement to put affirmative action policies on state ballots for voter approval or disapproval. While affirmative action legislation and policies had been challenged in the courts since their inception in the 1960s, most state legislatures and governors worked to implement them. Connerly wanted to put the policies on the ballot, because whenever limits to affirmation action were put up for a vote, the public tended to favor these limits. Governor Bush wanted to avoid this type of divisive vote, especially in the 2000 election where his brother George would be on the ballot for president. Instead of waiting on Connerly to get enough signatures to place his anti-affirmative-action initiative on the ballot, Jeb Bush moved swiftly in his first term to drastically alter and essentially end affirmative action in the state of Florida.

By executive order in late 1999, Bush released his One Florida initiative. Under the provisions of One Florida, state public universities and colleges could no longer consider race or gender in their admissions policies. Moreover, businesses could not be awarded state contracts on the basis of minority participation in those businesses. In exchange for these fundamental changes, Bush ordered state universities to accept all students who were in the top 20 percent of their class. Bush believed that this would actually allow greater minority participation. Even thirty years after the civil rights movement, many Florida high schools were still heavily racially segregated. His proposal would allow the top 20 percent from suburban high schools that were predominantly white and the top 20 percent from urban high schools that were predominantly African American or Hispanic to be admitted to public universities.

Bush believed that he had struck the right balance, blocking off Ward Connerly's divisive efforts but still enabling qualified minority students to make it to Florida universities. Bush said he was trying to "transcend the entire debate about affirmative action" by changing rules "that discriminate or pit one racial group against another." He understood the historical context for affirmative action policies, he said, but their time had come to an end. "These policies were intended to deal with the real and tragic legacy of more than a century of segregation in our state." Bush went on to say that the affirmative action regulations were now increasingly controversial and divisive. "What is viewed as an opportunity by one Floridian is too often correctly viewed as an unfair damage by another Floridian."[28]

Initially Bush's arguments won the day even with some minority lawmakers. Democratic state senator Daryl Jones, an African American from Miami, agreed to chair a panel that would help implement the new initiative. Yet even with this support, Bush's policy shortly ignited a political firestorm that created the divisiveness that he was hoping to avoid. Just a week after Bush announced the new initiative, Senator Jones withdrew his support. Other African American lawmakers came out strongly against the One Florida idea. Democratic congresswoman Corrine Brown from Jacksonville declared her opposition to Bush's plan, saying, "Unfortunately, Florida is not a colorblind or gender-neutral place . . . discrimination is widespread and persistent."[29] The interim president of the University of Florida said the plan might harm minority enrollment. He also complained that the policy was approved by the state Board of Regents without any consultation with universities and students.[30] Most dramatically, two prominent African American state lawmakers held a vigil at the office of the governor for twenty-five hours to protest the policy and the way policy was being approved. Democratic state senator Kendrick Meek and Democratic representative Tony Hill launched the protest before the Board of Regents gave final approval to the policy. More than a hundred people came to the Capitol to support the protest by Meek and Hill. Bush reacted strongly, calling the protest "childish, sophomoric and unbecoming an elected official." Earlier in the day Bush had said into an open microphone, "Kick their asses out."[31] Bush claimed to be talking about reporters and not the state legislators. In the end Bush did agree to postpone the decision on One Florida after considering some suggestions from African American lawmakers. However, the core of the One Florida plan remained intact and was implemented beginning in the year 2001. Although his policy created a strong backlash and heavy media coverage, Governor Bush did not back away from these fundamental changes. He continued the pattern of strong conservative leadership on social and cultural issues even when they led to controversy and divisiveness.

Faith-Based Prisons

With his views on gun rights and Affirmative Action, Governor Bush showcased his cultural conservatism. Yet these issues did not highlight a more important aspect of this belief system in regards to social issues—his religious beliefs. Governor Bush converted to Catholicism in 1995 after losing his first bid to become Florida's governor. He made no secret that his policy proposals would be influenced by his religious beliefs. Even more important, he wanted those who were using state services to also be able to interweave their religious beliefs with state action.

Florida became a laboratory of sorts for one of President George W. Bush's major initiatives: faith-based public policy programs. President Bush had established a national office for faith-based programs, and Governor Jeb Bush led the way among governors to implement this idea throughout state government. The best example of this faith-based initiative was creating two faith-based prisons—one for men and one for women. Beginning in 2003, the Lawtey correctional institution became a faith-based prison. Using volunteers, religious programming was made available to prisoners who were close to completing their sentences and who had served their time with good behavior. This combined a state function, the punishment and rehabilitation of criminals, with an overtly religious approach. The American Civil Liberties Union in Florida protested and said the prison was a "church prison at taxpayer expense." Bush rejected the criticism and said that this religious approach to rehabilitation could "make a tremendous difference . . . by creating a pathway out of the criminal justice system."[32] Interestingly, the religious initiative was focused not on the most hardened of criminals but on those inmates who would soon be released. This was not the sole mixing of religion and government policy in Florida; by 2005 the legislature had established a faith-based advisory board that would distribute funds for public purposes carried out by faith-based institutions.

Moreover, the state legislature worked to protect prayers at Florida public school events and also established a drug treatment program that allowed recovering addicts to take a state voucher to the rehabilitation center of their choice, including those that were religiously affiliated. Republican legislator Steven Wise from Jacksonville sponsored a number of bills with Governor Bush's support that included faith-based provisions. Wise talked about the nation returning to its values: "I think America feels like it needs to come back toward its roots."[33] Governor Bush worked the legislature with leaders like Wise to implement the most wide-ranging religious initiative in the history of Florida state government.

The Schiavo Case

Nowhere in the two terms that Governor Jeb Bush served in Florida was the connection between religion and politics so prominently displayed as in the case of Terri Schiavo. This personal family tragedy involving the Schiavo and Schindler families became a national test of what government should or should not do when individuals confront end-of-life issues. The controversy also showcased Bush's stubbornness, his belief in executive branch supremacy, and his wariness of the judicial system.

For more than a decade, the case of Terri Schiavo had been an intense family battle between her husband, Michael Schiavo, and her parents, Bob and Mary Schindler. The tragic case began in 1990 when the twenty-five-year-old woman collapsed at her bedside at her home in St. Petersburg. Because of an unknown condition, she did not receive oxygen to her brain for at least five minutes as she was transported to the hospital. This lack of oxygen caused Terri Schiavo to enter a comatose state from which she never recovered. Her doctors and the hospital were able to prevent her death, but she was diagnosed as being in a "chronic vegetative state,"[34] kept alive with nutrition provided through a feeding tube. In 1993 the Schindlers and Michael Schiavo had a severe falling-out about the course of treatment for Terri Schiavo. The dispute centered around a monetary settlement that Michael Schiavo received to help take care of his wife. From that point, the Schindlers and Michael Schiavo engaged in a twelve-year legal marathon to determine the fate of Terri Schiavo. The conflict grew greater when Michael Schiavo decided to ask the medical authorities in 1998 to remove her feeding tube and allow her to die.

Three major issues emerged in this case that focused on end-of-life issues. The Schindlers challenged Terri's husband, Michael, on all three.

1. The Schindlers believed that Terri Schiavo was not in a chronic vegetative state, and they believed she consciously reacted to their presence during their many visits with her.
2. Contrary to what Michael Schiavo believed, the Schindlers said their daughter, because of her religious faith, would never consent to the withdrawal of medical attention. Michael Schiavo and his sister-in-law and brother testified in court that Terri told them she would never want to live in the way she was living.
3. The Schindlers also challenged Michael Schiavo as being a fit guardian for his wife, Terri. They believed he was not providing the proper care for her, and they also criticized him for having a long-term romantic relationship with another woman that began several years after Terri Schiavo's incapacity.

Two important court cases would act as the controlling legal precedent in the Schiavo case. On the federal level, *Cruzan et Ux. v. Director, Missouri Department of Health* in 1986 involved a thirty-two-year-old woman, Nancy Cruzan, who had been in vegetative state for several years after a car accident in Missouri; as part of her medical treatment, she received nutrition through a feeding tube. This court decision defines a persistent vegetative state as a "condition in which a person exhibits motor reflexes but evinces no indications of significant cognitive function." This situation is difficult for relatives and friends to understand, because the patient is still moving even though brain function is essentially over. Like Terri Schiavo's, Nancy Cruzan's brain was denied oxygen for a sustained period. From medical testimony, the trial court in the *Cruzan* case found that permanent brain damage results after a denial of oxygen for six minutes.[35] Cruzan was in a sustained unconscious state and had difficulty taking oral nutrition. Without the outside nutrition, Nancy Cruzan would have died shortly after the automobile accident. Nancy's parents and sister believed that she was in a medical condition from which she would never recover and thus requested that her feeding tube be removed and that she be allowed to die.

The state of Missouri moved to block the implementation of this request. In a precursor to the politics that would surround the Terri Schiavo case, the Republican governor of Missouri at the time, John Ashcroft, pushed the state's Department of Health to challenge the Cruzan family's decision. (Ironically, twelve years later former Missouri governor John Ashcroft would become attorney general of the United States under President George W. Bush, although Ashcroft was no longer the attorney general at the time of the Schiavo case.)

The *Cruzan* case worked its way up to the United States Supreme Court after the Missouri state supreme court ruled in favor of the state of Missouri to block the extraction of the feeding tube. In a 5–4 decision, Chief Justice Rehnquist wrote the opinion, joined by Justices White, O'Connor, Scalia, and Kennedy; the Court found that the families of patients who are incapacitated do have the right to refuse treatment if the supporting family had a real understanding of the patient's wishes in such circumstances. The Court returned the case to Missouri and directed the Missouri courts to allow evidence into the record that showed that Nancy Cruzan would not want to continue to live under these medical circumstances. The parents were able to find friends of Nancy Cruzan to validate her wishes. After years of court battles, the Cruzan family finally could direct their daughter's nursing home to remove the nutrition and hydration. As Nancy Cruzan lay dying, protesters camped out in front of her nursing home and threatened to storm the door to restart her nutrition and hydration. These protests shocked the Cruzan family and underscored the controversial and emotional nature of these end-of-life cases. But the Cruzan case established as the law of the land that patients and families could refuse life-sustaining treatment as long as there was "clear and convincing" evidence of the patient's wishes.

When the Schiavo case emerged, Florida state law followed the basic principles articulated in *Cruzan*. In the state case *In Re: Guardianship of Browning,* the Florida Supreme Court makes it clear that a patient's decision making should be the controlling legal factor. This decision also echoed an earlier Florida decision that externally delivered nutrition or hydration was a treatment and not part of basic care. A medical treatment could be denied to a patient upon request, but basic care could not. This distinction is important because Florida courts have ruled that Florida's constitution with its explicit "privacy" clause puts such medical decisions in the hands of the patient or the patient's legal guardian. Florida law also goes a further step to outline who controls decision making when the patient is incapacitated. In the statute FS 765, the Life Prolonging Procedure Act, the state of Florida clearly writes that in case of incapacitation, the person first in line to make decisions on medical care is a legal guardian. Yet most people do not have a court-appointed legal guardian, so this provision does not apply to the vast majority of citizens. The next person who has decision-making authority is the patient's spouse. Since this provision of the law would apply to most patients, including Terri Schiavo, the spouse as decision maker is given an elevated status in Florida law. The act does go on to say that the status of the patient's spouse as proxy can be challenged if the spouse/guardian is not acting in the best interests of the patient. However, if negligence by the spouse/proxy is alleged, the burden of proof is on the challenger.

Thus Florida law in the early 1990s was relatively settled in regard to decisions about end-of-life issues when the patient is incapacitated. The courts had ruled that artificially supplied nutrition when the patient was in a vegetative state was not part of basic care and could be refused by the patient or the patient's proxy. Florida case law also clearly stated that patients or their proxies had a right of privacy to refuse medical treatment. Finally, going beyond what most states had done on the issue, Florida law stated that unless the patient had a court-appointed guardian, the spouse was the rightful decision maker about medical care if the patient was incapacitated. Thus the Schiavo case seemingly should have been settled as soon as Michael Schiavo decided in 1998 to end nutrition and hydration for his wife, Terri.

The reason the Schiavo case went on for over a decade can be found in a missing topic in Florida law. Florida law and the law in most other states presumed that when dealing with end-of-life issues, family members would agree on what was in the best interests of their incapacitated relative.[36] The relationship of the Schindlers and Michael Schiavo obviously tore apart this assumption. The Schindlers challenged Michael Schiavo's handling of his wife's medical care with a three-pronged religious, legal, and media strategy. They challenged the basic premise that Terri Schiavo was in a chronic vegetative state, because she could move and show reflexes when they visited her. They also challenged the idea that Terri Schiavo would agree that her feeding tube should be removed. They claimed that Terri as a practicing Catholic would never consent to ending her life. Most important, they challenged the fitness of Michael Schiavo to be the decision maker for their daughter. They claimed that after 1993 he did not have the best interests of their daughter in mind when he was making these medical decisions.

Again, the Schindlers had most of the stated public law on this topic against them, but they would find tremendous support for their position in religious circles, and their political arguments would find a number of strong advocates and eventually include the governor of Florida, Jeb Bush, the United States Congress, and the president of the United States, George W. Bush.

Michael Schiavo's decision to ask for the removal of his wife's feeding tube resulted in a 2000 case before a circuit court (trial court in Florida) that focused on what would be the last wishes of Terri Schiavo and the fitness of Michael Schiavo as her guardian. Florida circuit court judge George Greer would ultimately decide whether Terri Schiavo could be taken off life support. The trial heard from fourteen witnesses, including one doctor who testified that Terri Schiavo was in a "persistent vegetative state" and that "nothing known to science will help this woman." The parents testified that their daughter reacted to them when they visited with movements and eye gestures.

Since Terri Schiavo did not leave a will making her wishes clear, Michael Schiavo was her legal medical decision maker. Michael Schiavo's sister testified in court that "Terri [told her] didn't want to live like that." The Schindler family said that Terri would never consent to removal of life support. Schiavo's attorney Michael Felos said in court, "Should she be kept alive to keep her parents happy? . . . This is about letting go."[37] Judge Greer acknowledged what a difficult case he had before him. With the medical evidence and the testimony from the Schiavos, Judge Greer granted permission for Michael Schiavo to have the feeding tube removed from his wife. This decision in a circuit court in Florida would be vigorously challenged until it reached the United States Congress, the president of the United States, and the United States Supreme Court. The political figure who would lead this fight was Governor Jeb Bush.

For three years the case moved through the Florida state court system and the federal court system with no real change in its outcome. However, the Schindlers were successful in delaying the removal of the feeding tube while they appealed and appealed. In 2001 the feeding tube was removed, but the Schindlers quickly started another court case by accusing Michael Schiavo of perjuring himself in the 2000 case. Florida circuit court judge Frank Quesada ordered the feeding tube reinserted while the facts of the case were being considered. The Schindlers spent the next two years trying to prevent their daughter's feeding tube from being removed again. Finally in August 2003 the Schindler family had run out of appeals before the Florida Second District Court of Appeals and the Florida Supreme Court.[38] The case was put back in the circuit court of Judge George Greer. Judge Greer began to consider how to implement his original decision from three years ago to remove the tube.

It was at this point, after five years in which the Florida state courts had wrestled with the issue and then federal courts including the United States Supreme Court had declared that no federal question existed to examine, that Florida governor Jeb Bush decided to intervene. Governor Bush requested in August 2003 that Judge Greer assign another guardian ad litem (court representative for minors and incapacitated adults) for Terri Schiavo before the feeding tube was removed again. Bush seemed to realize that he was stepping into uncharted territory. Having a sitting governor take sides in a family battle presently in the court system was unusual. Bush wrote: "I normally would not address a letter to the judge in a pending legal proceeding. However, my office has received over 27,000 e-mails reflecting understandable concern for the well-being of Terri Schiavo." Judge Greer responded in a clear way to tell the governor that he was moving beyond the powers of his office. Greer said, "I respect the governor's position. Beyond that, the letter is going into the court file." Greer went on to say that he was not involved in a popularity contest. "I don't go out on the street and survey how I'm supposed to rule."[39]

Michael Schiavo reacted strongly to Bush's intervention: "This case has been in litigation for five years and all of a sudden Governor Bush wants to be involved? This isn't his concern; he should stay out of it."[40] Although Greer allowed Terri Schiavo to continue receiving medical treatment, he eventually ordered that her feeding tube be removed on October 15, 2003. These actions by Judge Greer did not dissuade Governor Bush. In early October 2003, Bush filed a friend of the court brief asking a federal district court to prevent the feeding tube from being removed. Bush's actions came after Florida's Republican attorney general Charlie Crist refused to become involved. (Interestingly, Crist, who did not want to touch this case, would succeed Bush in the governor's office in 2007. Later Crist would leave the Republican Party and become an independent in 2010 and a Democrat in 2013.) Even with Governor Bush's appeal to a federal district court, the scheduled removal of the feeding tube in the middle of October 2003 would stand, because the federal court ruled it had no jurisdiction.

The day before the feeding tube was to be removed, the Schindlers made one last appeal to Florida's Second District Court of Appeal. The appellate court refused to block the removal of the feeding tube. On

October 15, 2003, the feeding tube was removed from Terri Schiavo, and most medical authorities gave her about two weeks to live. The Schindlers and their allies lobbied Governor Bush to intervene more forcefully. On the day the feeding tube was removed, Bush met with Bob and Mary Schindler to figure out a way to circumvent the court's ruling. After the meeting, Bush's spokesman said that the governor's legal advisors were trying to figure out a way to challenge the constitutionality of Judge Greer's decision to allow the removal of the feeding tube. The spokesman said, "I could just also add that the Governor respects the separation of powers here. . . . He does not have the authority to overrule a court order, and he has a dual responsibility here to uphold the laws of the state and give a choice to the citizens of the state as well."[41] Thus the governor's office knew that they were headed into a constitutional crisis if they tried to avoid the court ruling. The political pressure on the governor was increasing. Some 40,000 people went to a website to sign an online petition requesting that Governor Bush intervene. On the website, supporters of the Schindlers could see pictures of Terri Schiavo moving and groaning. Groups representing the disabled also added to the debate, because they were concerned that anyone who might be seen as mentally incompetent could be threatened by the actions in the Schiavo case.

On October 21, 2003, six days after the feeding tube was removed, Governor Bush made his move. Fortunately for the Schindlers and for the governor, the Florida legislature was holding a special session at the time. Usually there is no legislative session during the fall, but the legislature was at the Capitol in Tallahassee to consider measures for economic development. The governor requested that the Schiavo issue be added to the agenda. Although legislation usually takes months of working its way through committees to reach a vote in both legislative chambers, the Schiavo legislation was introduced and voted on in one day in both houses. The bill, which would grant the governor power to issue a "stay" to stop the denial of nutrition and/or hydration to patients that had no clear written guidelines or directives, did not go through any committee and had no legal analysis attached to it. Republican representative Sandy Murman from Tampa said, "No one should take God's power in their own hands. We need to step in here."[42] With a vote of 68 to 23, the Florida House of Representatives passed what became known as Terri's Law. Members of the Florida Senate seemed to be more conflicted about the legislation. The Senate voted quickly 23 to 15 to give the governor the unprecedented power of ordering the feeding tube to be reinserted. The Senate majority leader, Republican Jim King, said, "I hope, I really do hope we've done the right thing. I keep thinking, 'What if Terri Schiavo really didn't want this at all?' May God have mercy on us all."[43] The legislation did not even take up more than one page, and it was specific to the Schiavo case. House Bill 35-E read

1) The Governor shall have the authority to issue a one-time stay to prevent the withholding of nutrition and hydration from a patient if as of October 15, 2003
A) the patient had no written advance directive
B) the court has found the patient to be in a persistent vegetative state
C) the patient has had nutrition and hydration withheld and
D) a member of that patient's families challenges the withholding of nutrition and hydration.

The legislation set off a flurry of activity at the hospice facility where Terri Schiavo was staying. The next day an attorney for the Schindlers pushed through a crowd of protesters and police officers guarding the entrance to the hospice. The attorney showed the police the governor's order, and the crowd let out a cheer and began to sing "Amazing Grace."[44] Terri Schiavo would have to be moved to a hospital to safely replace her feeding tube. As an ambulance arrived at the hospice, the crowd cheered again. Terri Schiavo was put in the ambulance and rushed to the hospital, escorted by two police cruisers. At the hospital, her feeding tube was eventually reinserted—the second time within two years that she was taken off a feeding tube and then had it reinserted after legal and political action.

Put simply, Terri's Law challenged the legitimacy of the Florida state court system to make judgments about Terri Schiavo. It was a direct repudiation of the judicial process in Florida and set up a constitutional conflict between the governor and the court system. It also demonstrated again that even though Governor Bush proclaimed the importance of smaller and less intrusive government, he believed in a powerful governor's office—as seen earlier in his administration, when he was given almost total control of state judicial nominations. However, the Florida judiciary was still primarily made up of judges appointed or elected before Bush became governor. The fact that he could not persuade the judiciary as he could the legislature was a major source of irritation to the Bush administration. This frustration led to direct challenges to judicial power, such as this legislation. When introducing one of his appointments to the Florida Supreme Court in 2002, Bush railed against the power of the courts. He said, "The increasing power of courts . . . should not come at the expense of institutions that have a more legitimate claim to govern our lives." He decried the personal influence of judges, saying that "our courts . . . have substituted their own personal views for the laws enacted by the people and their representatives." Finally, he said, "Increasingly, courts have seized control over policy decisions that are not theirs to make."[45]

Essentially, if the governor could overrule the Florida courts on the Schiavo issue, what would prevent Governor Bush or any future governor from doing the same on another issue? Michael Schiavo's attorney George Felos said, "The citizens of Florida should be alarmed by what is happening. What is happening here is a gross and illegal intrusion into the private liberty of citizens. . . . This is not the former Soviet Bloc."[46] This action would set in motion another seven-month battle between the governor's office and the Florida courts. Michael Schiavo immediately challenged the constitutionality of Terri's Law in state court. Schiavo's attorney believed that Terri's Law was a clear violation of the separation of powers under the Florida state constitution. The state circuit judge who heard Michael Schiavo's challenge did not immediately ask the governor to lift the stay. The constitutionality of the law would be tested in the Florida district court and then move directly up to the Florida Supreme Court because of the public importance of the case. Of more importance to the Schindlers, all of the legal and political maneuvering gave more time for Terri Schiavo.

In September 2004, two months before the presidential election, the Florida Supreme Court decided the case of *Jeb Bush, Governor of*

Florida, et al., v. Michael Schiavo, Guardian of Theresa Schiavo. The title of the case showed the odd position where the governor of Florida was suing one of his own citizens about the health care of the citizen's wife. The Supreme Court made it clear that they were not deciding the facts of the case surrounding Terri Schiavo, including whether Michael Schiavo was an appropriate guardian. What the Supreme Court focused on was whether Governor Bush had the legal authority to order the reinsertion of the feeding tube in direct challenge to the opinion of a Florida judge. Bush's attorney Ken Connor argued that the courts do not have the "exclusive domain" to protect the rights of the disabled. Michael Schiavo's attorney told the Supreme Court justices, "It is absolutely extraordinary for the governor to argue that the Legislature in 18 hours . . . somehow possess some inherent wisdom . . . that could not be ascertained by justices of this state over a six-year period."[47] The Florida Supreme Court made it clear that they believe the governor had overstepped his bounds. In its unanimous decision in *Bush v. Schiavo*, SC 04-925, the court found:

We recognize that the tragic circumstances underlying this case make it difficult to put emotions aside and focus solely on the legal issue presented. We are not insensitive to the struggle that all members of Theresa's family have endured since she fell unconscious in 1990. However, we are a nation of laws and we must govern our decisions by the rule of law and not by our own emotions. Our hearts can fully comprehend the grief so fully demonstrated by Theresa's family members on this record. But our hearts are not the law. What is in the Constitution always must prevail over emotion. Our oaths as judges require that this principle is our polestar, and it alone. . . .

The continuing vitality of our system of separation of powers precludes the other two branches from nullifying the judicial branch's final orders. If the Legislature with the assent of the Governor can do what was attempted here, the judicial branch would be subordinated to the final directive of the other branches. Also subordinated would be the rights of individuals, including the well established privacy right to self determination. . . . No court judgment could ever be considered truly final and no constitutional right truly secure, because the precedent of this case would hold to the contrary. Vested rights could be stripped away based on popular clamor. The essential core of what the Founding Fathers sought to change from their experience with English rule would be lost, especially their belief that our courts exist precisely to preserve the rights of individuals, even when doing so is contrary to popular will.

The unanimous decision was a massive repudiation of what the governor and the legislature attempted to do in this case. Jurisdiction in the case was returned to the Florida circuit court judge for implementation. The Florida Supreme Court had upheld the circuit court's decision to remove the feeding tube.

In a combination of stubbornness, lack of regard for the Florida court system, belief in executive power, and genuine concern for the Schindler family and Terri Schiavo, Governor Bush would not give up. During his first six years as governor of Florida, he had not been told no very often by the legislature. He had made sweeping policy changes that previous Florida governors could never have imagined. Accordingly, after the Florida Supreme Court issued its ruling, Governor Bush would not back down. Three months after the Florida Supreme Court decision, the state of Florida appealed to the United States Supreme Court. With the Schindlers and the governor still fighting the case, the ultimate status of Terri Schiavo would remain in limbo for several more months.

Even after the clear rejection by the Florida Supreme Court, Governor Bush's involvement in the case was just beginning. The state of Florida appealed the Florida Supreme Court decision directly to the United States Supreme Court. In late January 2005, the U.S. Supreme Court declined to hear Bush's appeal without comment. Nearly five years after Florida circuit court judge George Greer had ruled in favor of Michael Schiavo, the United States Supreme Court had essentially upheld what the Florida courts had done in the Schiavo case. The long series of appeals and motions, review by three levels of the Florida courts, a specific piece of legislation passed by the Florida legislature and signed by the governor, and finally a rejection by the United States Supreme Court would have ended most cases. Yet even after the highest court in Florida and the highest court in the United States had ruled against Terri's Law, Governor Bush did not back away. He warned that he would engage in "other options" to help Terri Schiavo. He went on to say, "I will do whatever I can within the powers that be granted to me by law and by statute, . . . I will do whatever I can."[48]

The month of February 2005 showed that Governor Bush had no intention of giving up the fight. Judge Greer again ordered that Terri Schiavo's feeding tube be removed, but he did not set a date for removal while waiting on other appeals. In the meantime Randall Terry, a controversial pro-life activist, brought his organization called Operation Rescue into the controversy. The Catholic bishops in Florida issued a clear statement of support for the Schindlers.[49] Undaunted by the rejection of the appeal regarding Terri's Law, the Florida state legislature began the process of passing a new law to protect Terri Schiavo. In the midst of all this activity, Governor Bush's executive branch made its move. The Department of Children and Families—the Florida agency in charge of protecting disabled adults—made a motion to Judge Greer to stop any removal of the feeding tube while the agency investigated possible charges of abuse toward Terri Schiavo. In this emotional case, many accusations of abuse had been leveled at Michael Schiavo and at Terri Schiavo's caregivers by the Schindler family and their supporters. The Department of Children and Families had not investigated these allegations before, but with the governor of the state of Florida losing in the courts, the DCF asked for time to do so. A representative of the DCF said that the law made it the department's responsibility to investigate when someone had "direct credible information" regarding abuse. The Schindler family rejoiced at the state intervention. Their attorney said, "We are deeply grateful. . . . I believe they are looking at the entire treatment of Terri Schiavo." Michael Schiavo's attorney said that the case had now become a serious constitutional issue. He said the investigation by DCF was an attempt by the governor and the legislature to do an "end run around the court system." The same day the investigation was announced, the Schindler family was petitioning to have Michael Schiavo removed as guardian of Terri Schiavo. The Schindler family appeared in court that day with Randall Terry and two Franciscan monks.[50]

Even with all of this activity and appeals and motions, at the end of February 2005 Judge George Greer set a date of March 18 for the removal of Terri Schiavo's feeding tube. The countdown was on, and the only two major institutions of government in the United States that had previously stayed out of the case—the United States Congress and the president of the United States—now became heavily involved.

On the very day that Terri Schiavo's feeding tube was to be removed, a committee of the United States House of Representatives issued five legal subpoenas in the case. The subpoenas included the unusual demand that Terri Schiavo—a woman who had been in a persistent vegetative state for fifteen years—appear before the committee. They also requested that Michael Schiavo appear along with his wife and the nutrition equipment that could keep Terri Schiavo alive.[51] The idea was that the subpoena would force Michael Schiavo to allow the feeding tube to remain connected to his wife until the appearance before Congress. When Michael Schiavo refused this weird suggestion, the U.S. House Committee on Governmental Reform asked the Florida courts to intervene to stop the removal of the tube until the United States Congress could investigate. When the Florida courts rejected the congressional request, the committee appealed to the United States Supreme Court. The Supreme Court declined to hear the case. On the afternoon of March 18, 2005, Terri Schiavo's feeding tube was removed for the third time, abiding by Judge Greer's order of February 2005.

At a time when most bills introduced before the U.S. Congress are never passed into law, and those bills that do become law may take years before final passage, the Terri Schiavo case became a startling exception. The very next day Congress postponed its Easter recess to pass a bill that gave the Schindlers new legal standing to press their daughter's case in federal court. In the middle of two wars in Iraq and Afghanistan, the president of the United States then flew back from his Easter vacation at his ranch in Texas in the middle of the night to support his brother. In the White House at 1 a.m. President George W. Bush signed the bill that would grant the Schindlers some relief. Essentially Congress was telling the federal courts that they must hear the

Schiavo case. The courts understandably did not react positively to this mandate. After passage of the law, the Schindlers again petitioned the federal court system seeking an order to reinsert Terri Schiavo's feeding tube. Within four days a federal district court, an appellate court, and the United States Supreme Court denied the Schindlers' request.

Yet even with this series of losses, Governor Bush was not finished. He publicly disclosed that a doctor whom the state of Florida had asked for an opinion on the status of Terri Schiavo concluded that she was not in a persistent vegetative state. In his written affidavit to the state, Dr. William Cheshire from the Mayo Clinic in Jacksonville wrote, "I asked myself whether if I were her attending physician, I could in good conscience withdraw her feeding and hydration. No, I could not. I could not withdraw life support if I were asked. Withhold life-sustaining nutrition and hydration from this beautiful lady whose face brightens in the presence of others."[52]

Even though Dr. Chesire's analysis ran counter to the reports from most of the other medical doctors who had examined Terri Schiavo, he was a well-known physician, and Governor Bush again challenged the Florida state courts and the Federal courts. The day that the United States 11th Circuit Court denied the Schindlers' request to have the feeding tube replaced, Bush requested that his Department of Children and Families take custody of Terri Schiavo in order to protect her after alleged abuse by her husband and caregivers.[53] Again after five years in the court system where Governor Bush's position had continually lost, he still could not give up. If the Department of Children and Families came to take custody of Terri Schiavo in late March 2005, the governor and the state police would be contravening a court order and the state of Florida and the federal courts would be locked in a constitutional crisis over the separation of powers. Judge Greer moved quickly to grant a restraining order against the governor, and to block the Department of Children and Families from taking custody of Terri Schiavo in order to reinsert her feeding tube.

After this latest rejection, Governor Bush realized that he could go no further without risking a constitutional showdown. On March 27, 2005, he told CNN, "I cannot violate a court order. I don't have the power from the U.S. Constitution, and the Florida Constitution for that matter, that would allow me to intervene after a decision has been made."[54] The governor who had remade Florida government and had found success in pushing cultural issues on several different fronts had met the limits of his power. On March 31, 2005, Terri Schiavo finally died.

The governor who for the last six months had worked to fight the Florida court system in the Schiavo controversy was now being criticized by Terri Schiavo's father for not doing enough. Amazingly, these comments came after the governor had almost taken the Schiavo case to a constitutional conflict. His next step could only have been to literally capture Terri Schiavo and take her away from her hospice. Noted Florida political scientist Susan MacManus commented that Bush's actions might hurt him politically, but that was not his concern: "Those of us who watch him think this is Jeb and how he truly believes and what he truly believes."[55]

Bush's dedication to the case was evident. Yet his lack of judgment was on display when he could not let the case go, even after Terri Schiavo's death. More than two months later, the results of the official autopsy on Terri Schiavo were released. Dr. Jon Thogmartin, the medical examiner in Pinellas County where Terri Schiavo died, found that her brain had shrunk to half of its normal size and that no medical treatment would have improved her medical condition. The examiner said about her brain damage: "No amounts of therapy or treatment would have regenerated the massive loss of neurons."[56] However, the autopsy could not address why Terri Schiavo collapsed in 1990. This medical fact gave Governor Bush one last opening to pursue the Schiavo case. Even after an autopsy showed that Terri Schiavo had no chance of recovery, Governor Bush wanted more information on what Michael Schiavo might have done fifteen years earlier. The day after the autopsy results were released, Governor Bush requested that a state prosecutor look into the circumstances of Terri Schiavo's 1990 heart attack and the actions of Michael Schiavo regarding his wife's health during her medical crisis.

This reckless accusation regarding Michael Schiavo showed how Governor Bush could not give up the fight. Little evidence existed to support the charge that Michael Schiavo did anything wrong. The

Pinellas County prosecutor took only ten days to conclude: "If the available facts are analyzed without preconceptions, it is clear that there is no basis for further investigation. While some questions may remain following the autopsy, the likelihood of finding evidence that criminal acts were responsible for her collapse is not one of them."[57] Finally in early July 2005 Governor Bush announced that he would not ask for any further investigation into the Schiavo case. Yet this did not mean that he thought his actions were wrong. He wrote in a letter to the *Tampa Tribune* on July 12, 2005:

> On Thursday, I closed the state inquiry into the Terri Schiavo case. This puts to rest a sad chapter in Florida State history. Although I'm saddened and Terri had years cut from her life, and I do not agree with the Court's decisions, I respect those decisions.

It took five years for Governor Jeb Bush to accept what the courts had done in the Schiavo case. His doggedness almost led him to a political and legal place where he would have been in violation of a court order. Public opinion polls published during and after the controversy showed that a majority of Floridians believed the governor should have stayed out of it. However, unlike most political dialogue and positioning in the early twenty-first century, Bush's stance on Terri Schiavo was not based upon political polls and media pressure. He believed in her cause and worked tirelessly to advance his point of view. No other episode in Governor Bush's tenure showed so clearly the strength of his political beliefs and at the same time the worst of his judgment and political leadership.

The Impact of Bush's Cultural Agenda

Governor Bush's agenda met his campaign promises about social and cultural issues. He provided a template for other governors to not simply talk about cultural issues during election season but also act upon them in legislative sessions. Since Jeb Bush believed the core problem facing the state and the nation was a lack of moral character among politicians and citizens, his cultural activism should not be a surprise. However, making a real impact in the policy arena involving controversial issues is difficult. His record here is mixed, but the mere fact that he confronted these issues says a great deal about his version of conservatism and his belief that changes in government policy can strengthen society and the culture of a state.

Attempting to definitively connect government policy with certain social outcomes is complicated by a plethora of variables, and assigning too much credit or blame to a government policy is a mistake. However, it is instructive to look at what occurred before Governor Bush took office and what happened after he left office. For example, regarding the issue of abortion, his policies had somewhat more success in limiting providers than in reducing the number of abortions. In 1998, the year before he took office, the abortion rate (number of abortions per 1,000 women in the state) was 31.2. The year after he left office in 2007, the abortion rate in the state was 27, a drop of 13.5 percent. By 2008, more than 95,000 abortions were still being performed in the state—a slight decrease from the time Governor Bush took office—but the population in the state had increased substantially. During Bush's tenure, the number of providers of abortion decreased by 15.7 percent, from 108 to 91, and 70 percent of the counties in Florida did not have an abortion provider in residence.[58] Thus the serious abortion restrictions that Governor Bush and the Republican legislature passed during his term apparently did in fact reduce the number of providers. These restrictions may also have contributed to the decrease in the number of abortions performed annually in the state. While that number remained near 100,000, Governor Bush did provide a template for other Republican governors and state legislators to engage on the issue of abortion. Florida's restrictions were adopted by many other states. For example in 2011, forty-seven states considered legislation to reduce access to abortions and eighty laws were passed. Mississippi had only one abortion provider in the entire state and needed a decision by a federal court to keep its doors open.[59]

Examining the impact of the numerous changes to gun regulations in the state of Florida during Jeb Bush's two terms also yields a mixed result. According to the Florida Department of Law Enforcement, firearm-related crimes decreased slightly from 1998 to 2007. The index of gun-related crimes per 100,000 people dropped noticeably in the early years of the new century but began to rise again by the time Governor Bush left office.[60]

Firearm-related murder over the same time span doubled in raw numbers. Yet it needs to be noted that the overall crime rate generally went down. This trend caused concern in many quarters that lessening gun regulations and passing a Stand Your Ground law would combine to make Florida into a shooting gallery. Indeed, after the Stand Your Ground legislation passed in 2005, the number of justifiable homicide cases more than doubled in the two years after the law's passage—indicating more use of deadly force in confrontations.[61]

As Governor Bush accomplished his goal of making Florida one of the most pro-gun states in the nation, the effects of his policies are mixed and their future impact is a bit unclear. After the pro-gun legislation passed, there was no dramatic increase in gun crimes during or immediately after Governor Bush's tenure. The results of the Stand Your Ground legislation passed late in his administration may be more ominous. Stand Your Ground seeks to protect citizens forced into self-defense. The claims of justifiable homicide have increased dramatically since the law's passage in 2005, with the 2012 Trayvon Martin case highlighting the controversy that accompanies the law. The law put Florida again on the front line in the cultural conflicts over the regulation or nonregulation of guns in America.

Another area where Governor Bush dramatically changed social policy in the state was his attempt to end affirmative action in college admissions and hiring. From 1998 to 2010, diversity at Florida's universities increased. However, this increase was due mainly to the larger number of Hispanic citizens who attended universities in the first decade of the 2000s. The African American percentage of admissions to universities slightly declined over the same period. Two state universities actually had fewer African American freshmen in 2008 than in 1999—even with a large population increase among all ethnic groups in Florida. In particular, African American men have been more difficult to recruit to the larger state universities after Bush's policies went into effect. In sum, diversity at Florida's universities has increased since Bush's policies were put in place, but African American enrollment remains a concern.[62]

On the issue of gay rights, Bush as governor took a more moderate line than others in the Republican Party. He argued that same-sex marriages should not be "sanctioned" in Florida but that civil arrangements for same-sex couples should be possible. With the Defense of Marriage Act as federal law at the time, Bush did not see the need for a state initiative to ban gay marriage. Ironically, such an amendment was approved by Florida voters in the 2008 election two years after Jeb Bush left office.

The difficulties in impacting social policy are exemplified by the Terri Schiavo case. After the case captured the nation's attention in 2005 and almost provoked a constitutional showdown, the subject of providing legal guidance to relatives in case of an incapacitating injury was prominent in the nation's consciousness. Yet even with this publicity and public angst, the number of Americans having so-called living wills—documents that state clearly the person's wishes in the case of incapacity—has not increased dramatically since Terri Schiavo's death in 2005.[63]

5

. . . .

Jeb Bush's Education Revolution

After a heartbreaking defeat in Florida's 1994 gubernatorial race, Jeb Bush found his political footing once again when he turned to the issue of education in the mid-1990s. He founded the Foundation for Florida's Future as a think tank that became focused on conservative educational reforms including charter schools, vouchers, and other forms of school choice. This focus on education was an unusual place for the self-described "head-banging" conservative.[1]

Traditionally, K–12 education is one of largest expenditures in the state budget.[2] Jeb Bush was not only attempting to reform educational policies, he was trying to transform the entire educational system of the state. The match pitting a conservative who talked about smaller government against the largest government bureaucracy in the state was unusual and volatile. However, Jeb Bush had lofty expectations for

K–12 education—expectations that would be difficult to meet under any circumstances. The governor viewed K–12 education as the key to three major policy outcomes: 1) increasing economic opportunity for high school graduates, 2) providing the state with a more educated workforce, and 3) helping students become high-character individuals. No matter the background of the students who came through the schoolhouse door, Bush thought that schools could overcome a difficult upbringing, provide businesses with better employees, and give society citizens who understood the importance of morality and practiced that morality. Bush's involvement with education became the core of his public life and his private business dealings as well. Bush and his foundation would develop strong ties with educational companies like Pearson and a company called K12 that would benefit from the policy changes he was advocating by selling products and services.[3]

A high expectation for the redemptive quality of education is not new in the United States. Political figures, civic leaders, and some academics have stated that education could transform students into model citizens. Ironically, these leaders believe(d) that children and their schools could successfully meet these broad expectations even though many adults could not. Before examining the reforms offered by Jeb Bush, the historical context of public education in Florida needs to be considered.

How Schools Became Public

A central question when discussing K–12 education: Is education a public good that should be provided by Florida state government or any state government? After the Revolutionary War, families, churches, and apprenticeships provided most of the educational guidance for preteens. Not all of these arrangements were poor in quality. By some estimates, white citizens in the United States had one of the highest literacy rates in the world in the early 1800s. Yet education was available to only a small number of children in the nation, and the curriculum varied widely.

As more citizens came to live in cities and communication improved, the focus on quality education for all children increased. Apprenticeships in skilled trades had been the launching pad for millions of young men in Europe and America. With the Industrial Revolution, the need for skilled artisans decreased, and the number of genuine apprenticeships plummeted. A new form of education for the young was needed to replace the apprentice system. For many reformers, secular public education was the answer. One newly naturalized citizen wrote about providing public education in the 1830s to everyone in the United States, "Give to education . . . a clear field and fair play, and your poor houses . . . and hospitals will stand empty, your prisons and penitentiaries will lack inmates, and the whole country will be filled with wise, industrious, and happy inhabitants. Immorality, vice and crime, disease, misery and poverty, will vanish from our regions."[4] Any form of education would have a difficult time meeting these expectations.

The expansion of free public education was advocated most heavily in the northern United States. The North was dealing with a population that was becoming more and more urban. Public schools for white children were seen as the magic solution to all of society's ills. In the mid-twentieth century, Supreme Court decisions regarding the separation of church and state have drastically reduced religious influence in modern American K–12 public education; no such separation existed in America's schools as they were coming into existence. In fact, a main reason cited for the establishment of public schools was centered on Christian morality. In many ways, free public schools were seen as a necessary institution to create a civic identity and morality in the nation. Horace Mann, a public school advocate and intellectual, wrote in 1841 that in order to prevent authoritarianism in the nation, "schoolhouses are the republican line of fortifications, and if they are dismantled and dilapidated, ignorance and vice will pour in their legions through every breach."[5]

Since public education was equated with moral training, moral arguments added political momentum to the free public school movement in antebellum America. These public schools were referred to as common schools. With the emphasis on increasing access to education for all white students, standardization of curriculum became more of a reality. However, the governance and funding of common schools remained a local endeavor—a critical characteristic of American public schools that has been a dominant factor in the governance and funding of public education. With the governance of public schools being decentralized, standardized changes and reforms would always be difficult. This factor became especially important when the federal and state governments mandated so many reforms in the late twentieth and early twenty-first century. Such top-down efforts would always meet with resistance, because public schools were created at the local level. As Jeb Bush believed in strong direction to local districts, it is unsurprising that relations between the governor's office and school districts were uneven and controversial during his tenure and have been a continued source of tension in the state after his governorship.

In the early 1800s, the fact that education was increasingly seen as a public good was a major impetus for the expansion of government. While prejudice against African Americans and other minorities kept the expansion of education from being too widespread, providing a free public education to all white children was still a massive undertaking for local and state governments in the nineteenth century. It would establish a tradition of government involvement in one of the most important endeavors a society encounters: the raising and development of its children.

The local nature of public school governance remains an administrative and political obstacle to widespread reform throughout the nation. Yet by the 1830s and 1840s, a common curriculum was emerging in northern schools. Arithmetic, reading, and writing were common subject areas in most public schools by the time of the Civil War. There was one other important subject that was constantly infused into the public school curriculum: religion and morality. Protestants viewed public schools as vehicles for students to learn about religion and moral values. The "Our Father" was the morning prayer in most schools. As waves of Catholic immigrants came into the nation during the three decades before the Civil War, Protestants also viewed public schools as a religious bulwark against the encroaching influence of Catholic immigrants in large cities. School texts reflected the influence of Protestant beliefs; these texts praised the Reformation and condemned the Catholic religion. Intolerance of Catholics and other minorities would be the notable exception to the idea that schools would truly be "common." To their credit, some education reformers in the North believed that common schools could unite children from diverse backgrounds. Horace Mann believed that schools would become "great leveling institutions." He recognized the challenge of bringing together children who would be starting with different skill levels. He said that schools needed to be "good enough for the richest, open to the poorest."[6] Mann's challenge of the 1830s and 1840s remains a challenge for education in the twenty-first century. How do you have a common school system that promotes excellence for all while at the same time not excluding students who have educational challenges? In many ways Jeb Bush concentrated his reform efforts on the lowest-performing students during his time as governor.

This emphasis on a common public school education in the North was difficult to find in the antebellum southern United States. While northern education reformers sought to use public education to assimilate varying parts of American society, southerners were much more hesitant to establish common schools. Any hint of reform might be targeted at bringing together white southerners and black slaves. Moreover, the South was still dependent on agriculture as its main economic driver. Southern children were an important part of the labor force. The ability to read and write were not essential skills for doing chores on the farm. Accordingly, education in the South was a patchwork of church instruction and homeschooling with some common schools. While attempts to bring about common public education were present in Virginia and North Carolina, the possibility that a common education would be shared by poor whites and slaves was blasphemy to most southerners of the planter class. The aftereffects of the Civil War would cause some southerners to reassess the need for public education.

Education in the South after the Civil War

Part of the Reconstruction effort after the Civil War included expanded rights for former black slaves and creation of the Freedman's Bureau. This bureau helped to establish a network of public schools specifically for former slaves. Protestant missionary groups assisted in the staffing of new schools. As southern states were gradually removed from military control, these states had to write new state constitutions. Many of these Reconstruction constitutions included a provision to educate former slaves and all southern children.

Florida's educational system reflected all of these challenges. When the territory of Florida was transferred to the United States in 1821, public lands were set aside for public education. This promising start did not lead to development of a coherent and funded system of public education before the Civil War. Florida's educational system was similar to the disjointed and underfunded school systems across the southern region. In 1885, Florida's white conservatives passed their version of a Redemption (post-Reconstruction) constitution for the state. A positive feature of this constitution was its attention to public education. As we have seen, Reconstruction had led to a strong fear of centralized government, whether directed from Washington or from Tallahassee. However, a notable exception was made for state education. The 1885 Constitution contained a provision for a state superintendent of education. This office would help to bring some standards to curriculum throughout the state. With leadership from the state superintendent's office, a conference on public education was held in Gainesville at the University of Florida in 1918. Even in a state with a frontier mentality, a commitment to low taxes, and a fear of centralized government, public education for all was seen as critical for the development of the state.[7]

Yet the strident racial politics of the time led the writers of the new Redemption constitution to create a dual school system based upon race. After the constitution passed in 1885, it would be unconstitutional for black students and white students to attend the same school. A decade later the Florida legislature passed a law that made it illegal for white and black students to be taught by the same teacher or even to be taught in the same building. White students could not be taught by black teachers and vice versa. In a particular low point in 1916, Florida's governor ordered the arrest of three white Catholic nuns because they taught black children in a school in St. Augustine.

This separation would exacerbate one of the main problems with Florida's schools: how to pay for them. Southern states and localities could barely pay for one school system, much less dual school systems. In many rural counties and towns, there was not enough money to build two public schools, so black schools were often held in church houses, barns, and sheds with limited supplies and no bathrooms. Since many black families were still dependent upon agricultural work for a living, black students went to school only three months out of the year, compared to nine months for white students. Expenditures per pupil were also extremely unbalanced. Generally white students received four times as much financial support as black students. These financial disparities would lead to legal challenges and would help to bring about reforms after World War II.[8]

Florida Education after World War II

The victory by the United States and its allies in World War II brought new urgency to the cause of public education in America. America's new position as the world's economic and defense superpower high-lighted the importance and the deficiencies of America's education system. In Florida, Democratic governor Millard Caldwell believed that the industrial boom in the postwar economy showed the need for more state involvement in local public schools. The funding of most public schools in Florida was overwhelmingly dependent upon local property taxes. Accordingly, a poor county with little in the way of property tax revenue would automatically have underfunded schools. After forming a commission, Governor Caldwell convinced the state legislature in 1947 to pass the Minimum Foundation Program, intended to equalize funding across counties. This program set funding levels by teaching unit and set the funded class-size level at 27 students—no matter if counties had more or fewer students per class. The legislation also set a minimum statewide property tax, so no counties could go below a certain rate. Finally, the legislation mandated a 180-day school year and set a salary scale for teachers.[9]

This legislation by no means was the cure for Florida public education, but it was an important moment in the governance of public education. The state was now more heavily involved in local education than at any point in Florida history. While variations in funding across counties would still exist, this legislation made the clear statement that involvement in education by the governor and the state legislature would never go back to the days when local counties were on their own. This would be a blessing and a curse to local counties; they needed the resources from Tallahassee, but the calls for accountability for the money delivered were immediate. Fifty years later Jeb Bush took accountability measures to a new level, and he was not the first governor or legislature to ask for results in exchange for state money. Bush's critics who have lamented his efforts to tie accountability to state resources for education often overlook the fact that this type of trade-off has been present in Florida for more than seventy years.

These attempted reforms in the governance of Florida public education did not include efforts to end the dual school systems in most counties based upon race. As legal challenges to segregation increased in the late 1940s, Florida officials were some of the staunchest defenders of segregation. As the famous *Brown v. Board of Education* case worked its way through the courts, Florida chose to partner with six other states to advocate for the maintenance of segregation in public schools. Moreover, the Florida attorney general wrote the most extensive and detailed argument for segregation in public schools among the six states in that partnership.

A change in this approach came with Governor LeRoy Collins in 1955. Collins originally advocated continuance of segregation in education, but his position evolved, and he became a legend in Florida history for his leadership on the issue of desegregation in the state. Still, with segregation and the civil rights movement and other cultural issues dominating Florida politics in the late 1950s and most of the 1960s, the political environment made it extremely difficult to propose and implement educational reforms. The rural legislators were fighting attempts to reapportion state legislative districts. As long as the Pork Chop Gang remained in power in the legislature, they could block efforts to make representation and funding across the counties of Florida more equitable. When both state and federal courts forced the legislature to redraw legislative districts, new reforms were possible.

As Florida slowly came into compliance with the *Brown v. Board of Education* decision during the 1960s and 1970s, a huge population boom was occurring. The state population grew nearly 40 percent in the 1960s. Not only had Florida state government always prided itself on low taxation, but the state constitution forbade a state income tax. Property taxes at the county level were very low compared to midwestern and northern states. Accordingly, Florida's education system had to deal with the legacy of segregation, a strong increase in demand, and a low tax base to provide funding.

Financial reforms in the 1970s under Governor Reubin Askew helped to add state aid to the property tax revenues at the county level. The heavy reliance on property taxes made for large resource differences between counties in Florida. At Askew's behest the legislature passed the Florida Education Funding Program, which changed the allocation of state funding to counties for schools from a teaching-based unit to a student-based unit. This full-time equivalent measure or FTE would help take into account the vast differences across the state. The FEFP produced a complicated formula that attempted to be fair in the distribution of funds based upon the cost of living, the number of special-needs students, and the differing population density of the Florida counties. The creation of this formula began a long battle over funding formulas for education that would persist in Florida government to this day.

Some of the more rural Florida counties were not happy with this approach, but distribution of state funds by this formula did achieve more equity. With property values in Florida so unpredictable, no system of financing that had a significant element of revenue coming from property taxes would ever truly be equal across the state. Yet the FEFP made an important difference for many counties and also increased state involvement in public education. Along with the additional funds came new calls for accountability. Askew made student assessment a major part of his program. All high school seniors would have to pass a state student assessment test in order to graduate. This requirement came under heavy legal scrutiny when representatives of African American students and other groups called the test culturally biased. The courts delayed implementation of the tests, and by the time the court case was resolved, the testing was no more.

When state senator Bob Graham became governor in 1979, he likewise focused on education issues. Graham instituted a program called RAISE, intended to toughen requirements for high school graduation. Yet even this modest goal came under legal scrutiny. If the state was going to have a graduation requirement in the form of a test, the counties had to make sure the material tested had been covered in some way during the students' school year. With the courts monitoring how the students were being tested, it was difficult for state and local officials to be innovative and demanding. The courts were blocking the use of tests for measuring student achievement.[10]

In 1991, when former U.S. senator Lawton Chiles took the governor's office, he too had an education program. Called Blueprint 2000, it listed the skills and abilities that students should have when they graduated from Florida public schools. It also set up student advisory committees across the state that would help schools develop standards. The goals of Blueprint 2000 were so general that it would be difficult to see immediate progress. Yet this program created the testing process that would become instrumental in Florida's educational future. To see how students were measuring up to Blueprint 2000, the Florida Department of Education had students in grades 3 and 11 take a Florida Comprehensive Assessment Test or FCAT. This test would become the platform on which Jeb Bush started his education revolution. First used in the Chiles administration as a reporting tool, the FCAT was based upon the Sunshine State Standards passed by the legislature in 1996. These guidelines emphasized analytical thinking, communication skills, and mathematical computation. Converting such broad goals into meaningful evaluations would be a continuous challenge for the Florida education system. Even with all these attempted reforms under different governors, Florida's education system fell behind in national and international comparisons. Simply put, Florida state government was always playing catch-up with the education demand. From 1980 to 2000, a million additional children were born or moved to the state.[11]

In 1995 the Florida Department of Education identified 158 low-performing schools. The vast majority were in urban areas, especially Dade (Miami), Duval (Jacksonville), and Orange (Orlando) Counties.[12] Many policy analysts and political leaders pointed to the socioeconomic background of the students in the lowest-performing schools. Not surprisingly, many students in these schools came from poor families.[13] It was concluded that socioeconomic background might determine student performance. The changes that Jeb Bush would make to the K–12 system rejected this argument.

Jeb Bush and Education

After losing his first run at the Florida governorship in 1994 as an unyielding conservative, Jeb Bush positioned his 1998 bid for the office as a conservative policymaker, not a conservative ideologue. He saw the issue of education as a way of testing new conservative ideas while focusing on an issue that had widespread bipartisan appeal. His focus on education actually began long before his second gubernatorial campaign. In 1996 the Florida legislature passed and Governor Chiles signed a law that would allow public charter schools in the state. The Florida education commissioner at the time, Frank Brogan, said that the only people against this legislation were the "education establishment," which was code for the teachers' union.[14] Florida teachers and administrators were concerned that charter schools—schools run by nongovernment groups with taxpayer money—would drain money from other public schools. The charter schools would be allowed to bypass many regulations that governed public schools in Florida. This charter school initiative was an effort to try something new in response to poor graduation rates in the state, especially in the urban areas. Bush took the distressing data on public schools and tried to make both political and policy overtures to African Americans. After his infamous comment in his first campaign for governor in 1994, when he was asked what he would do for African Americans and replied, "Probably nothing,"[15] Bush was determined to change his image and his rhetoric. He saw education policy as the perfect vehicle to do both. Along with Bush's think tank, the Foundation for Florida's Future, Miami Urban League head T. Willard Fair and Bush convinced the state to allow them to operate a charter school in 1996.[16]

The relationship between Fair and Bush highlights how important the education issue had become to Jeb Bush after his election defeat.

Fair said he was skeptical at first but came to believe Bush really had an interest in urban education issues. Moreover, decades of Democratic dominance in Florida politics had not brought serious change to Florida's public education system. Even with the reforms of the Askew and Graham administrations, Florida's policymakers never could catch up to the huge population growth the state was experiencing in the 1980s and 1990s, and the large ethnic and socioeconomic diversity of its students that this influx created. While the state boasted some high-achieving public schools, the urban school districts were continually struggling for resources and advancement. Low graduation rates reported by the state Department of Education brought new urgency to the problem.

Fair had seen enough of the problems of educating students in Liberty City, one of the poorest areas in Miami. When asked why he was partnering with the Republican Jeb Bush, Fair said, "Blacks always voted Democratic because we were caught between Tweedledum and Tweedledee. . . . We have an obligation to look beyond party, to look to the future." Fair said that, through his experiences with the charter school, "Jeb Bush has proven himself to be decent, caring, compassionate and committed to the things that are important. . . . I've grown to know and love him." When Fair was asked if his relationship with Bush was political, Fair said, "My relationship with Jeb is quid pro quo, and it survives on mutuality of admiration and respect." Fair then talked honestly about how they needed each other: "Yes, Jeb wants the black vote. And I, T. Willard Fair, wanted and got his charter school."[17]

The voters of Florida not only elected Bush governor in 1998, they also passed Amendment 8, the constitutional amendment that downsized the cabinet form of government that had been in effect since the end of Reconstruction. In particular, the amendment changed the commissioner of education from an elected official to an office appointed by the state Board of Education. And by 2003 the state Board of Education, now consisting of seven members appointed by the governor, would administer education in the state at all levels, kindergarten through university. Even before the formal handover of power in 2003, Bush was in charge of education policy in Florida. Bush made clear to his appointees on the new Board of Education that he would have a strong influence in selecting the education commissioner. The Florida constitution, which had long been a restraint on gubernatorial power, had now in effect made the governor the "czar" of Florida education.

However, with this new power the voters also gave Florida government a clear mandate. Amendment 6 declared that education was a "paramount duty of the state" and that the state must provide "free public schools" of "high quality." Thus the new constitutional changes invigorated the office of governor by delegating new powers to the office while making public education the main priority of state government. This scenario provided an unprecedented opportunity for Jeb Bush to shape public education policy in the state—an opportunity he met with force and vigor.

Bush's proposed reforms rested on these elements:

1) **A+ Plan:** The A+ Plan mandated that students in Florida public schools in grades 3–10 take a yearly assessment test. The results of these tests would be translated into an overall letter grade for schools, from A to F. Schools that posted the highest learning gains would be given additional financial resources.

2) **Public school choice:** If a public school received an F grade for two consecutive years, students in that school would be allowed to transfer to another school in the county with a grade of C or better.

3) **Vouchers for private schools:** If a school in a Florida public school district received an F grade in two out of four years of assessment, students would be able to transfer to private schools that accepted the state vouchers. This program was found to be unconstitutional in 2002 and 2004 by the Florida state courts. In order to bypass the hurdles presented by the use of taxpayer money, a Corporate Tax Credit Scholarship program was established by the Florida legislature to replace the vouchers program. This granted Florida businesses a deduction from the state corporate income tax if they contributed to a fund that public school students could use to transfer to private schools. Moreover, to access these funds, students did

not have to come from F-rated schools—they could transfer from any public school. Changes made in the 2010 legislature may expand this program dramatically over the next decade.

4) **Merit pay for teachers:** The A+ Plan provided for student learning gains to be evaluated. School districts were given four years to develop a system to reward teachers whose students posted the most significant learning gains. In effect, part of teacher raises would be based upon student performance.[18]

5) **Removing the universities' Board of Regents:** In 2000 Bush continued his assault on the Florida education system by moving his attention to higher education. Over the objections of his chancellor, Bush and House Speaker John Thrasher proposed and passed legislation to end a separate governing board for the university system. As of 2003 the entire educational system of Florida would be under one Board of Education, with the universities having separate local boards of trustees. Dr. Adam Herbert, chancellor of the university system, warned that this proposal would create "turf wars," with each university seeking to get the most out the legislature.[19] To restore system-wide control of the university system, U.S. senator Bob Graham led a drive to put an amendment on the ballot that would create a Board of Governors to oversee the system. The drive and the vote were successful. Thus Florida ended up with a Board of Governors and local boards of trustees to oversee the universities with duplicative bureaucracies.

The core of Bush's accountability policies rested upon grading individual schools. The huge transformation that this concept entailed made teachers and administrators concerned. Even before Bush took office in 1999, some school districts positioned themselves against the reforms. In December 1998 the Broward school district lobbyist Georgia Slack released the statement "We are against grading schools." Some of the administrators who were against the idea said that school grades "are simplistic and unfairly stigmatized individual students."[20]

However, Bush had momentum and events on his side. In a Florida cabinet meeting in February 1999, the graduation rate for Florida's students was discussed. The new education commissioner, Tom Gallagher, said the true graduation rate for the state of Florida was much lower than the 70 percent that had been reported previously. Gallagher argued that the number was near 49 percent. The methodology for arriving at the 70 percent figure relied upon looking at the number of graduates and then dividing by the number of ninth-graders in the state four years earlier.[21] This approach could be contested on numerous grounds. Bush said whatever the figures, they were "lousy."[22]

This debate in the Florida cabinet highlights a central part of the controversy surrounding measurement of educational progress. The exact measurements used are open to different interpretations and levels of importance. A constant theme of Jeb Bush's attempt to reform education in Florida was disagreement regarding educational outputs. The issue would dominate the implementation phase of Bush's reform proposals. Yet even with the uncertainty regarding educational measurement, the consensus among elected officials was that the education system was in trouble. Bush received help from an unlikely ally, the sitting president of the United States, Democrat Bill Clinton. During the same month that Jeb Bush introduced his reforms in Florida, President Clinton met with the nation's governors in Washington to discuss education reform. Clinton remarked, "Let's not kid ourselves. We are not doing our children any favors by continuing to subsidize practices that don't work and failing to invest in practices that do." At that meeting, Clinton praised Governor Jeb Bush for what Bush was doing on children's issues in the state of Florida.[23]

With political momentum and the huge Republican advantage in the Florida legislature, Bush introduced his first budget, with educational reform front and center. The 2000 budget reflected a different economic time than the severe fiscal constraints of the post-2008 recession economy. Governor Bush was able to introduce a budget that cut taxes by more than $1 billion, increased education spending, and set aside money for the purchase of environmentally sensitive lands. This budget proposal, with its increases in revenue and spending, would be the envy of any governor in the second decade of the twenty-first century. At the beginning of his administration Jeb Bush enjoyed the benefits of a strong economy, a fully funded state pension fund, and a huge multibillion-dollar settlement from the tobacco industry. As Bush said, the budget represented more than just revenues and expenses; to Bush, budgets were a "compilation of priorities. It is policy. It is ideas."[24] However, increases in K–12 education spending came with important restrictions and consequences. Some of this increased money would go for merit pay for teachers, school voucher alternatives for students, and rewards to schools that saw substantial increases in overall test scores.

Bush would face a serious fight to get his educational plan passed in the legislature. He was taking on the teachers' union and local school boards. Yet because Bush enjoyed strong influence over Republicans in the Florida state legislature, his priorities were well received. The Florida House, which served as Bush's "champion" for most of his initiatives, passed his A+ Plan by a comfortable margin of 70 to 48 after only two hours of debate. In the Senate, moderate Republican Jim King of Jacksonville challenged the vast scope of the plan. King wanted a slower approach to test the ideas before applying them to every school in the state. He wanted to restrict the use of vouchers to only those students who scored near the bottom on state tests. In the end, this amendment was taken out of the bill; King decided to support the measure anyway. He said that "it was very, very, difficult with the first major issue of a Republican governor to vote no." He did warn, however, that the voucher issue would be tied up in the courts for years to come.[25]

Bush worked up until the final moments to ensure that the A+ Plan would pass in the Florida Senate. He asked supporters in both the House and the Senate to meet with undecided legislators at his office in an attempt to convince them. He was able to get seven of eight Republican senators to switch from opposing parts of his plan to total support. With the passage of the plan by a 25-to-15 margin, Bush accomplished his number one legislative priority in his first session. By any account it was an impressive legislative achievement. Bush had put Florida at the vanguard of the movement to reform public education using conservative policies. What happened in Florida in May

1999 would have a major impact on the educational debate in the nation. Yet the most difficult time for the A+ legislation was about to begin: the implementation phase.

Early Conceptual Doubts

Because of the substantial changes to the K–12 educational system that Bush proposed, many teachers and administrators expressed real doubt about the basic idea of school accountability based upon student test scores. The consequences of Bush's program would mean an end to promoting students who were not up to grade level and would provide extra money for schools that increased their grade scores and graduation rates. Many educators believed this framework was doomed to failure. A guidance counselor at a school in Hillsborough County (Tampa area), Sue Powell, said that the idea of getting most public school students up to standards was unrealistic: "A lot of kids are just not motivated." A difficult student population to reach was those students who were struggling but not labeled for special or exceptional education. Hillsborough County had auctioned off bicycles and given away CD players in 1999 to encourage students to read. A principal in the district said, "I know of no way to make a child learn if he doesn't want to. We are not going to catch them all up." In one Hillsborough high school, more than a hundred ninth-graders were seventeen or older when school began for the year.[26]

The comments were typical of many administrators and teachers. The Bush legislation fundamentally challenged the K–12 education system like no other government change in Florida history. The idea that test grades for individual schools would have so many real consequences dramatically altered the educational landscape in Florida. As the A+ legislation moved from passage to implementation, the focus moved from the conceptual to the practical.

Implementation

The A+ Plan was based upon the results of the Florida Comprehensive Assessment Test. While this test actually began in the Lawton Chiles administration in the mid-1990s, the Bush administration made a major contribution to the debate on school accountability with its focus on attaching consequences to the test scores. Testing for school results was not a new concept in educational policymaking. However, basing punitive actions upon the outcome of these tests was new. Adding consequences to test results had been tried with almost no success in North Carolina and Kentucky. These states found it difficult to enforce the consequences of bad test scores.[27]

Under Bush's reforms, these consequences centered on resources. Financing has always been at the center of the debate on how to improve public education. When Jeb Bush promoted a program that rewarded schools that showed progress with more money and took away resources from schools that were struggling, the standardized test that triggered these rewards and sanctions took center stage.

The FCAT test now brought to Florida's public schools a mixture of focus, fear, and organizational change. The impact of the FCAT process is difficult to exaggerate. In many schools, the entire school calendar had to be reordered to allow for preparation for the FCAT. Principals and teachers lived with the reality of the FCAT hanging over them. As the new system was being put in place, resistance and apprehension were inevitable. In February 2000, as the testing process was beginning in many schools, an official for Miami-Dade schools said, "I don't think you will find an educator who will say that the FCAT is a bad test. . . . [If it] shows teachers how to better prepare students, then the test is the best thing that has happened, but the purpose is the bitter part of the pill."[28]

The superintendent of Broward County Schools remarked in the same year, "The system [now] focuses almost exclusively on teaching to the test. I have examples of schools that have dropped arts and physical education so they won't risk losing their A rating. I know schools where they stopped teaching geometry so they could drill their students on the basics to prepare."[29]

However, some educators would not deny the positive impacts of the A+ Plan. An assistant superintendent in Hillsborough County said, "While we have some serious concerns about the A+ Plan, the one positive that you can't ignore is that it is helping us to refocus our attention."[30] The attention that the superintendent was referring to was a concentration on poorly performing schools. The A+ Plan's pressure caused some school districts to add more resources to struggling schools so that D schools would not become F schools. These additional resources included Spanish-speaking teachers, more guidance counselors, and quicker bus routes to school.[31] Not all struggling schools in the state received additional aid, but many districts responded to the threat of a scarlet letter F on their schools by paying greater attention to these schools.

Those who were hoping that the A+ Plan would go away were fighting a losing battle. The Republican legislature gave Jeb Bush the political support he sought. Bush also used the changes to the Florida constitution to wield the authority to make changes in educational policy. With one large exception, the A+ Plan and its consequences would dominate educational policymaking in the state and in some ways the nation for the first decade of the twenty-first century. Bush would use standardized testing as a political club to pound the educational establishment, especially the teachers' union, into implementing his ideas.

The FCAT Process

The FCAT was seen as an improvement over previous standardized tests because it attempted to emphasize critical thinking. Bush's predecessor, Lawton Chiles, had initiated a program called BluePrint 2000. Out of this effort the Florida Department of Education began to develop testing methods to measure student progress. The Florida Comprehensive Assessment Test was a major part of this assessment. When Bush came to office, he used the FCAT that was already in place to implement his broad system of educational accountability.[32] For the first time, individual student results were aggregated to give schools grades from A to F. To the frustration of local school districts, the standards of measurement to achieve these grades often changed, but the simple A-to-F grade scale made the results easily understandable to the public and media. In 2000, fourth-graders were tested in reading and writing, fifth-graders in math, and eighth- and tenth-graders in all three subjects. Individual student test results were then translated into a score from 1 to 6, with 6 the highest score possible. A passing score was 3/6. By the year 2001, all grades from 3 to 10 engaged in yearly testing. The most important academic activity for the vast majority of students in Florida's public schools was taking the FCAT.

The individual student scores were then translated into an overall school grade based upon the percentage of students who passed the different portions of the test.[33] In the early iterations of the overall school grade, other factors such as graduation rates and percentage of students taking advanced courses were considered. The calculation of the school grade included a number of factors, but the final product was an easy-to-understand single grade for a school. The simplistic approach of labeling a school based solely on the number of students who passed a particular test would come under enhanced scrutiny as the A+ Plan became a permanent part of Florida's educational system.

School Choice

While Jeb Bush could rightfully claim that he transformed Florida's educational system with the A+ Plan, he suffered a rare policy defeat regarding the issue of vouchers or opportunity scholarships. As part of the original A+ Plan, if a student attended a public school that received a grade of F for two consecutive years, the student's family would be eligible for an educational voucher worth $3,400 to be used at a private school. This proposal would allow more than a thousand private elementary, middle, and high schools in the state of Florida to receive substantial amounts of public money. Governor Bush and his allies argued that it also allowed for real competition in the K–12 educational system, which would force local public school boards and schools to try to improve their schools' academic profile so that they would not lose students to private schools. If this new project to help student achievement in K–12 took hold, it would mark the largest combination of public money and private schools in American history.

Many different types of school choice emerged in the latter part of the twentieth century to answer the call for substantive school reforms. Yet most of these forms of school choice occurred within the public school system itself. Perhaps the most important type of school choice is one that is often overlooked: the choice of where families live. Since most school districts in the country are based upon geographic districts, the place of residence determines for many students where they go to school. Many realtors and other relocation specialists emphasize the quality of the school districts when they are selling homes. This dynamic is important, because national data suggest that moving rates among families with young children are higher than other types of families. Some of these families are searching for a quality school system before their children are in kindergarten. Hard data on these residential choices are difficult to find, but the National Center for Education Statistics has estimated that about half of families with children in public school are influenced by the quality of the public schools when making residential location decisions. Since Florida has a much more mobile population than other states, this residential school choice decision may be even more important for Florida parents. The ability to choose a residential school district is dependent on income. Even when lower-income families are mobile, the move may be forced upon them by economic circumstances. Accordingly, moving to a new school district may not be an act of choice for lower-income parents.[34]

Another type of public school choice is choice *within* districts. Some districts allow families to choose any school within the district. In Florida even before the A+ Plan came into existence, the Broward school system was a leader in public school choice, with students able to attend schools anywhere in the Broward district.

Magnet schools also afford choice within districts. Magnet schools—schools that specialize in a particular subject or professional area like medicine or engineering—began in the 1970s and 1980s to help districts racially desegregate their school systems. Many of the most attractive magnet programs were placed in inner-city schools so that white students would come to these minority-dominated schools. The schools have a mixed record in solving segregation issues, but they have become firmly entrenched in many urban school districts across the country.[35] For example, in Jacksonville two magnet high schools located in the urban core have become nationally ranked as centers of educational excellence. Unfortunately, some of the other high schools in the city have continued to struggle. Supporters of these other urban schools claim that the magnet schools drain quality students and families away from traditional residential-area high schools.[36]

Charter schools, where approved by local school boards, are another attempt to expand choice in the public school system. Separate from the general administration of the school district in which they are located, charter schools are run by management teams that may be made up of policy entrepreneurs, community leaders, or former teachers and administrators. While these schools are given funding per student similar to normal public schools, they are freed from many of the regulations and mandates under which public schools have to operate. Charter schools have become the main vehicle for public-school choice across the nation. Since Jeb Bush started the first charter school in Florida, more than three hundred have opened across the state. The level of student achievement at these schools is a source of controversy in educational circles. Depending on the research study examined, charter schools have a mixed record. Some have made important gains in student achievement when compared with similar public schools, while others, with weaker management teams, have not produced these gains.[37] In fact, the Liberty City Charter School that Jeb Bush founded earned a D on its first evaluation because students struggled with the reading and writing portions of the FCAT.[38] The Liberty City school also had serious financial problems and was recommended to be closed in 2008.[39] The success of a charter school is most likely dependent upon the quality of the management team and the economic resources the school can acquire. Whatever their impact on student achievement, these charter schools have remained popular with parents as an alternative to the traditional public school setting. More than 100,000 Florida students were attending charter schools by the time Jeb Bush left office.[40]

Private School Vouchers

Private school vouchers or opportunity scholarships were the perfect marriage between conservative free market ideology and the largest state government policy area, K–12 education. For conservatives, private school choice was the best way to introduce meaningful competition into the education sector. As noted in chapter 3, this idea was promoted by the paragon of conservative economics, Milton Friedman. Friedman began writing on this subject in the mid-1950s, but it was rejected as too radical at the time. Yet the changes in public schools during the tumultuous 1960s would give private school vouchers another chance in the marketplace of American educational reforms.

When busing and other forms of school integration came into practice in the late 1960s and early 1970s, interest in private schooling among some white parents increased tremendously. The idea that government would pay for private education was of course appealing to parents. A federal agency, the Office of Economic Opportunity, sponsored a private school voucher plan in the state of California. Yet the proposal met immediate fierce opposition from the teachers' unions and district administrators.

In 1983 the report A *Nation at Risk* detailed substantive problems with the United States educational system. This report by a federal commission sparked widespread debate and discussion around the nation. One response was a renewed emphasis on choice, but generally focused on public school choice. The state of Minnesota in particular was a leader in implementing school choice through the use of charter schools. Yet again the performance of charter schools was decidedly mixed, with some successes and some failures. As a consequence, in the 1990s momentum returned to the private school choice movement.

The private choice movement was supported by an unusual mix of economic conservatives and African American leaders—particularly where urban school systems were on the verge of collapse. For example, a school choice program began in Milwaukee in 1990. However, it was not launched by a conservative public policy think tank; it was begun by a Democrat, an African American state representative from the city. She had soured on efforts to desegregate urban public schools because she felt the brunt of the desegregation efforts fell upon black students and parents.[41] Many African American parents in the city, unhappy with the state of public schools, looked for other alternatives. An unusual coalition of African American parents, the Catholic Church

in Milwaukee, and several conservative think tanks supported legislation to give vouchers financed by tax dollars to parents who could then
use them to pay for private education. In 1995 the state legislature
expanded the program by allowing religious private schools to participate. By the end of the decade, more than 6,000 Milwaukee children
participated in the voucher program.[42] Cleveland had a similar program in which more than 2,000 students participated.

Even with these examples, voucher systems still faced large hurdles
to become a major part of K–12 educational reforms nationwide. The
use of public money for private schooling faced an array of opposition from the teachers' union, parents, and many in the legal community. In particular the issue of using public money at private religious
schools could be a constitutional issue if this intermingling of public
money and private schooling violated the Establishment Clause of the
U.S. Constitution. The U.S. Supreme Court had taken up the issue of
restricting the use of public money for private schools in the *Lemon
v. Kurtzman* case in 1971. In the *Lemon* decision, the Court found that
the use of public money in private schools did not violate the Establishment Clause if the money was used for a secular purpose, and that
the money did not advance religion and produce "excessive entangle-
ment" between the state and a private religious school.[43] This decision proved problematic in its implementation. The Supreme Court
decision made federal courts the referee in questions involving public money and private schools. How public money could be used in
a religious school became the fodder for many court challenges over
the last forty years. Would vouchers mean that the government was
promoting a particular religion? Would private religious schools that
received public money have to limit their religious practices? These
are important questions, because any widespread voucher program
would have to include religious schools, which make up more than 80
percent of all private schools in the country.[44] In *Zelman v. Harris* in
2002, in a 5-to-4 decision, the Court ruled that the Cleveland voucher
program did not violate the Establishment Clause. After this decision,
supporters hoped that voucher programs would expand dramatically
across the country. This did not occur, and what happened in the state

of Florida is a good illustration of why the publicly funded voucher system did not take hold nationwide.

The private voucher program was a major part of Governor Bush's A+ education initiative. The proposal allowed families to get a voucher if their child's school was deemed failing for two years in a row. By the time a circuit court (trial court) judge in Florida ruled in 2000 that the voucher program was unconstitutional, only a few dozen children from the city of Pensacola were using vouchers and private schools. The circuit court ruled that the voucher program diverted funds from public schools to private schools, and the Florida constitution made it clear that public schools were to be the first priority of state government.[45] This decision barred new students from attempting to join the voucher program but allowed those students already in the program to continue in the program pending appeal.

The appeal finally reached the Florida Supreme Court in 2006. In a 5-to-2 ruling, the court found that the voucher program was unconstitutional because it violated the "paramount clause" of the Florida state constitution, which made public education "a paramount duty of the state." The clause, added to the state constitution as Article 9 Section 1 by a ballot initiative in 1998, read:

> The education of children is a fundamental value of the people of the State of Florida. It is, therefore, a paramount duty of the state to make adequate provision for the education of all children residing within its borders. Adequate provision shall be made by law for a uniform, efficient, safe, secure, and high quality system of free public schools that allows students to obtain a high quality education and for the establishment, maintenance, and operation of institutions of higher learning and other public education programs that the needs of the people may require. To assure that children attending public schools obtain a high quality education . . .

Again, the constitutional changes of 1998 afforded Governor Bush more authority over education than any previous governor. Yet this amendment made sure that "a uniform, efficient, safe, secure, and high quality system of free *public* schools" would be "a paramount duty of the state." The justices believed the use of vouchers in private schools would take away resources from public schools and thus violate the constitution. This amendment, approved by Florida voters the same year as Bush's election, put more pressure and expectation upon state government to improve education. The 2006 decision was a major loss for the Bush agenda and increased Florida conservatives' mistrust of the state court system in general. Governor Bush heavily criticized the decision:

> I think it is a sad day for accountability for our state. . . . [The voucher program] put pressure on school districts to focus on the underperforming schools. . . . I don't think any option should be taken off the table. School choice is as American as apple pie in my opinion. . . . The world is made richer and fuller and more vibrant when you have choices.[46]

It was another example of how Governor Bush distrusted the courts and believed the state court system had too much power.

When the decision came down, Bush also made it clear that he would seek other ways to implement a school voucher program in Florida. School choice became Governor Bush's Holy Grail of educational reform. Even with this setback, school choice options were abundant for many Florida families. In 1999 the McKay Scholarship program was created to allow students with disabilities the choice of public or private schools at public expense. Moreover, the Florida Tax Credit Scholarship Program, passed in 2001, allowed corporations to voluntarily contribute to nonprofit organizations to fund scholarships to private schools for economically needy students in exchange for a credit on their corporate tax bill to the state. The important legal distinction here is that no state tax money went directly to private schools. Later the U.S. Supreme Court in 2011 upheld the constitutionality of the tax credit programs on those very grounds. With these two programs, Governor Bush was able to accomplish a notable expansion of school choice options in Florida. These trends continue at the time of this writing. As table 1 shows, more than 20 percent of Florida K–12 schoolchildren used options other than the traditional neighborhood school in 2010.[47] Virtual online schooling and homeschooling

Table 1. Florida school-aged children in school choice options, 2010

Type of school/program	Percentage of Florida student population, K–12
Private Schools	10.8
Charter Schools	5.0
Virtual Schools	3.0
Florida Tax Credit Scholarships	1.0
McKay Scholarships for Disabled	0.07
Home Education (Schooled)	2.1

Source: Florida Department of Education, "School Choice," esp. http://floridaschoolchoice. org/Information/CTC/files/Fast_Facts_FTC.pdf and http://floridaschoolchoice.org/ Information/McKay/files/Fast_Facts_McKay.pdf and http://floridaschoolchoice.org/ Information/Charter_Schools/files/fast_facts_charter_schools.pdf.

have expanded substantially in the last few years and are expected to continue to increase. While the controversy about the effectiveness of some of these options remains, Governor Bush made school choice a large part of Florida's school system, and that has had a real impact on Florida education.

Other Implementation Issues

While the expansion of school choice was a success for Governor Bush, the issues attending implementation of the A+ program during his second term were substantial. Many of these issues came to the forefront in 2003–4, when the A+ program had been established for four years and the consequences for not maintaining the standards set out by the A+ program were being felt across the state. One issue was how disabled students were to be tested and evaluated. Since the A+ Plan demanded that all students be tested, students with serious disabilities also had to take the FCAT. For example, blind students could not use talking calculators for their testing; they had to use an abacus. Dyslexic students were expected to read the tests at the same pace as other students. Governor Bush did direct the education commissioner to correct these issues, but it took too long to change the senseless regulations.[48]

Also in 2003, tough provisions took hold that prevented promotion to the fourth grade for third-graders who did not get a passing grade on the FCAT. Similarly, students could not graduate from Florida public high schools without strong enough scores on their FCAT testing. Using this standard, almost one-third of Florida's third-graders were in danger of not being promoted to the fourth grade in 2003.[49] Many parents were understandably worried. To mitigate this concern, students were allowed to do extra work in the summer to meet the reading standards expected. Only a small percentage of those third-graders who did not pass the FCAT actually ended up being denied promotion, but the threat made it a difficult spring and summer for thousands of Florida parents.

The same dynamic occurred at the high school level with seniors who could not graduate if they did not perform well on the FCAT. Students who could not pass the tenth-grade FCAT reading and math tests were not promoted. The graduating seniors whose grades were good enough to graduate but who did not pass the FCAT were given "certificates of completion." Even with the disruption that the FCAT caused to thousands of Florida's families, Governor Bush's education commissioner Jim Horne made it clear that the consequences of failure would be severe. Commissioner Horne said in 2003: "This accountability system has a lot of bite to it, but the governor and I are strong on this. We're not backing up."[50]

Students and parents were not the only ones stigmatized by FCAT failures. Schools that received an overall F rating also had to deal with tough consequences. A teacher at an F-rated school in Hillsborough County talked about the problems with the F grade: "How can a single grade tell the story of the school? . . . Like how far behind the children were before the start of school, the small everyday accomplishments, the intangibles that make a school a school."

At the same school, another teacher complained about the FCAT but also saw the benefits of the testing program. After receiving an F, this Tampa school was given a higher priority in the district, which offered seventy teacher-training sessions. The school got a $40,000 computer lab and, for being a high-poverty school, $232,500 to hire enough additional teachers that every class could schedule an undivided two and one-half hours for reading. This Tampa school had not received this level of help for its struggling students before.[51]

Another part of Governor Bush's plans for encouraging higher student performance was reward money for schools with improved student performance on tests. In 2004 and 2005, about 40 percent of schools in the state received a portion of the $120 million to $137 million reward money. The staff and advisory committees at the individual schools could decide how the money was to be spent. A good percentage went to bonuses for teachers.[52] These resources undoubtedly aided some students and rewarded some teachers. Two unanswered questions from these types of monetary incentives: 1) Is the money shifted from other educational needs? 2) What happens when the money—both to help struggling schools and to reward schools that test well—runs out? The Florida state system had to answer these questions during the leaner years of 2007 to 2012.

Results of Bush's Educational Policies

The implementation of the A+ Plan was an important development in conservative policymaking at the state level. While many states had used standardized testing, no other state used the results of the testing for such extensive consequences as promoting school choice and rewarding or punishing teachers. Teachers and schools were held accountable for the performance of their students. With this framework, Governor Bush rejected the idea that home and other societal influences were to blame for low-performing students. Upon gaining the presidency in 2001, his brother would adopt many of the Florida reforms with the No Child Left Behind law that applied to all states.

In some regards, this approach is a paradigm shift in social policymaking. While the beneficiaries of government services have long had restrictions and expectations placed on their behavior, the government employees or contractors who provide these services generally have not. Drug testing for welfare recipients, limits on the use of Medicaid benefits for the poor, speeding tickets for motorists who violate laws on public highways are all examples of holding recipients or beneficiaries of government benefits accountable. This concept is much different from holding the government employees or providers of public benefits accountable. Wardens and prison guards are not held accountable for high recidivism rates. Doctors and nurses are not held accountable for long stays of Medicaid patients who are hospitalized. Employees of state highway departments are not held accountable for citizens' dissatisfaction with state roadway systems.

Governor Bush was attempting a real social and political experiment. Accordingly, the results of these reform efforts took on huge political and social importance.

Measurement

Attempting to measure anything in the public policy arena can be difficult. Measurement of policy outputs is part science, part art, and part politics. Unlike in the natural sciences such as biology and chemistry, a social scientist cannot hope to control all of the potential factors that impact the concepts to be measured. And broad concepts do not lend themselves to measurement according to some clearly understood numerical standard. Researchers and policy analysts must ask if the proposed measurement fully captures the concept that is being examined. In this instance, if assessing student progress and/or achievement is the goal of the measurement, what is the best standard for that measurement? Can student achievement be measured by simply looking at the results of a test at a particular time in, say, the fourth grade? For some that may be too static a measurement. They might prefer to measure student progress from year to year on a particular test. Indeed, can standardized tests themselves be a good measurement of student knowledge and achievement? No consensus exists that standardized tests used for either college entrance or graduate school admissions are good predictors of academic success. Undoubtedly some students have a high intellect that does not come out in particular tests.

When approaching a subject such as educational achievement, other factors influence the testing regime. Among parents, there perhaps is no other public policy issue as important as their child's academic achievement. The passion invested in issues impacting children's welfare is substantial. Political ideology is also a significant factor. Since educational spending is the largest item in many state budgets, the political stakes regarding K–12 education are exceptionally high. Perhaps most important, the sums of money dedicated to public education are so vast that the economic stakes in measuring student achievement are very real for teachers and administrators and elected officials. Thus the difficulty of measuring student achievement combined with the personal, political, and financial stakes involved in education makes objective assessment of outcomes extremely dicey.

Yet the alternative to confronting these considerable obstacles is to not measure at all. The only way that policy analysts can cushion themselves from criticism about their measurements is to simply not try to analyze policy outputs. After his gubernatorial term, Bush said, "We measured because we cared."[53] Some parents and teachers also argued that the yardsticks for success constantly kept changing for the FCAT. The best way to analyze the relative success of educational policies is to assess the impacts of those policies while fully disclosing the strengths and weaknesses of those assessments. As this book attempts to analyze the important impacts of Governor Bush's A+ Plan, different measurements will be examined.

The Results of the FCAT

The centerpiece of the A+ program with standardized testing was the FCAT. Florida was the first state to have this amount of testing with publicly disclosed results. The entire school system of Florida with more than 2 million children turned its attention toward standardized testing beginning in 1999. Eventually all students in grades 3 through 10 would be tested on an annual basis. As tables 2 and 3 show, the enormous focus the FCAT received in the Florida public school system was reflected in the results, especially at the fourth-grade level. After the A+ Plan had been fully implemented for two years, 53 percent of fourth-graders in the state tested at grade level on the reading portion of the test. By 2010 the number of fourth-grade students testing at their grade level had increased to 72 percent. These impressive numbers are most likely the result not only of the important attention placed upon the FCAT in the school system but also of the tougher

Table 2. Percentage of Florida students scoring at grade level (score 3 or above) on Reading FCAT

	2001	2007	2010
Grade 4	53	68	72
Grade 8	43	49	55
Grade 10	37	34	39

Source: Florida Department of Education, http://fcat.fldoe.org/mediapacket/2011/pdf/2011ReadingComparison.pdf.

Table 3. Percentage of Florida students scoring at grade level (score 3 or above) on Math FCAT

	2001	2007	2010
Grade 4	45	69	74
Grade 8	55	63	68
Grade 10	59	65	73

Source: Florida Department of Education, http://fcat.fldoe.org/mediapacket/2011/pdf/2011MathComparison.pdf and http://fcat.fldoe.org/mediapacket/2011/pdf/2011Gr10FCATMathComparison.pdf.

retention policy put in place in 2002. This policy mandated that third-grade students who scored a 1 on the FCAT could not be promoted to the fourth grade. The number of third graders who did not get promoted more than tripled.[54] This policy made sure that when students made it to the fourth grade and then were tested on the FCAT, they had some basic skills in reading and would do better on the test. The scores also reflect substantial improvement among African American and Hispanic students on the FCAT test.[55] From 2001 to 2007, when Bush left office, African American students in grades 3, 4, and 5 improved from a 33 percent to a 53 percent pass rate in reading. Hispanic students showed similar strong gains.

The grade 8 scores in tables 2 and 3 also show improvement, but not the level of improvement shown in the fourth-grade scores. The grade 10 math scores show improvement of all students testing at grade level, especially when the 2010 data are considered; this increase continued until the new version of the FCAT was implemented in 2011. However, the reading scores for grade 10 started low and remained low when Governor Bush was in office and when he left office. The purpose of any education reform is to prepare citizens to become responsible adults and to compete in the workforce. The difficulty in improving performance at the high school level is notable. If testing reveals that high school students are struggling to keep up with their grade level, the impact on the future workforce in Florida could be severe and the effectiveness of the A+ program would be questioned.

The National Assessment of Educational Progress (NAEP)

The NAEP testing program is also known as the nation's report card. The series of measurements are collected by the Department of Education in order for states to comply with the federal No Child Left Behind Act that was passed in 2001. Not surprisingly, Jeb Bush's brother President George W. Bush believed in the Florida A+ model and essentially copied it on the national level, just as Jeb Bush had borrowed extensively from his brother's experiences in Texas. The act tied Title I federal education money to performance on standardized tests. The goal of the act was to get 95 percent of the public schoolchildren in the United States to become "proficient" at math and reading. Proficiency would be defined differently by the different states. Yet the reality was that the assessment bar was raised to a higher level. The national testing scheme would continually run counter to what the states were doing. For example in 2004, 68 percent of Florida's public schools earned an A or B on the FCAT. The same year only 23 percent of Florida public schools met the requirements under the federal No Child Left Behind Act.[56] The NCLB data take into account many different sets of students and how they perform. If one small group in a particular school, such as learning-disabled students, does not meet the federal standards, then the entire school is penalized.

The national data in tables 4 and 5 show overall scaled scores that reflect student achievement. Much as they did on the FCAT, Florida's fourth-graders consistently improved on their reading scores and scored above the national average. The eighth-grade reading scores in Florida showed slower improvement than the fourth-grade scores, but they remained higher than the national average. Moreover, on a

Table 4. The nation's report card (NAEP) scaled scores on reading

	1998	2007	2009
Florida Grade 4	213	224	226
Nation Grade 4	206	220	220
Florida Grade 8	261	261	264
Nation Grade 8	255	260	262
Florida Grade 12	NA	NA	283
Nation Grade 12	NA	NA	287

Source: National Center for Educational Statistics, http://nces.ed.gov/nationsreportcard/pdf/stt2009/2010460FL4.pdf.
Note: Scaled scores are designed to facilitate item analysis and permit comparison across categories. These are on a scale of 0–500.

Table 5. The nation's report card (NAEP) scaled scores on math

	1996	2007	2009
Florida Grade 4	216	242	242
Nation Grade 4	222	239	239
Florida Grade 8	264	277	279
Nation Grade 8	271	280	282
Florida Grade 12	NA	NA	148
Nation Grade 12	NA	NA	152

Source: National Center for Educational Statistics, http://nces.ed.gov/nationsreportcard/pdf/stt2009/2010454FL4.pdf and http://www.mynaep.com/dms/published/myschool/setup/doc_20091014_Grade_8_snapsh.pdf and http://nces.ed.gov/nationsreportcard/pdf/stt2009/2011456mFL12.pdf.
Note: Scaled scores are designed to facilitate item analysis and permit comparison across categories. These are on a scale of 0–500.

comparative basis Florida's fourth-graders showed the most improvement in math and again had higher mean scores than the national average. The results were not as favorable for the twelfth-graders. The data show that Florida trailed the national average in reading and that Florida twelfth-graders remained behind their national counterparts on the math portion of the NAEP as well.

While the FCAT tests and the NAEP scores can give some confusing results, their general trends are consistent. Florida's fourth-graders improved their performance dramatically on both reading and math from the late 1990s to 2010. African American and Hispanic students were a major part of these testing gains. Eighth-graders showed some improvement but did not share the gains displayed by the fourth-graders. Finally, Florida high school students had lower scores on the FCAT and also on the national testing.

The accountability data in Florida provide a timeline to view the general impact of testing over the past decade. What these data have shown in Florida and elsewhere in the nation is that raising achievement levels is easier to accomplish in the lower grades than in middle school and high school. The goal of these educational reform efforts is to create a workforce that will be ready with the new job skills required in the twenty-first century. The ultimate measure of success is what students do in high school and beyond. Looking at these measurements shows the difficulties of trying to maintain student achievement through high school.

Graduation Rates

Graduation rates are one way of measuring the effectiveness of all the reform efforts in Florida public education. Unfortunately, as with other measurements, there is little agreement on how graduation rates are to be calculated. Beginning in the late 1990s, the state of Florida tried to measure cohorts—following the same group of students from ninth grade to graduation. This method takes more effort than simply dividing the number of graduates by the ninth-grade population of four years earlier.

The graduation rate from the Florida Department of Education showed real improvement from 1998, before A+ was implemented, to 2008. The Florida DOE data show the 1998 rate was 60.2 percent and the 2008 rate was 75 percent. However, different policy groups have come up with graduation rates that are much lower. In 2000 the Manhattan Institute, a conservative public policy think tank, reported that Florida had the lowest graduation rate in the nation at 55 percent.[57] *Education Week* magazine uses a different methodology for its annual report on diplomas awarded in all fifty states. The Diplomas Count statistic does not take into account those students who leave high school

Table 6. Graduation rates for Florida public school students

	1999	2003	2008
Florida DOE Rate	60.2%	69.0%	75.4%
Education Weekly Rate	52.5%	57.0%	63.9%
Federal Rate		56.5%	62.7%

Source: Diplomas Count, http://www.edweek.org/ew/toc/2010/06/10/index.html, and Florida Department of Education, http://www.fldoe.org/eias/eiaspubs/pubstudent.asp.

and then pass a general equivalency degree (GED) exam. It also does not take into account other categories of specialized graduation equivalencies such as certificates. Table 6 shows the different rates, with a discrepancy of more than 10 percent for the years examined. By agreement of the nation's governors and the U.S. Department of Education, a federal graduation rate will be used as the standard in the future. This federal rate focuses more on the four-year cohorts of students and not on general equivalencies and is similar to the *Education Week* measure.

Two important trends are common to the rates. First, the rates according to all of the measures have been increasing since 1998. This positive trend may be attributable to the increased attention placed upon high school graduation and performance. However, the good news about the direction of the graduation rates is tempered by the reality that Florida is in the bottom ten states in graduation rates, even with the improved numbers over the last decade. *Education Week* in its 2011 report put the national graduation rate at 71.7 percent, with Florida trailing at 64 percent. Florida also trailed other large states including California, Texas, and New York.[58] The improvement in graduation rates coupled with Florida's lag behind other states shows the challenges of improving performance at the high school level. At this writing, the last federal government graduation rate reported for the state was for 2012, and it was 74.5 percent.[59] The focus on improving graduation rates has resulted in clear improvement during the Bush administration and afterwards. The challenge that remains is for the state to compare more favorably with other states.

College Readiness

One of the most important tests of any educational reform in K–12 is how reforms prepare students to perform in college. While not all students should or will attend college, the focus of the A+ educational plan was to improve students' academic achievement and thereby set the stage for success in college. Under the A+ Plan, more students have been encouraged to take advanced placement classes and take the ACT and the SAT. The data from the ACT test will show how far Florida high school students still have to go. Table 7 reveals that Florida high school students who took the ACT trailed their national counterparts in the 1998 cohort, and the 2010 Florida cohort still is below the national average in composite scores. The Florida Department of Education emphasizes that more Florida students are taking college standardized tests like the ACT, and with a larger pool of students taking the test, large improvements in the overall scores are more difficult to attain. The state has particularly encouraged minority students to take the ACT as part of their college preparation efforts. Minority students now make up more than half of Florida students taking the test.[60] The ACT also has a measure of college readiness involving four subjects—science, reading, math, and English. Examining this measure, only 16 percent of Florida students who took ACT in 2010 were ready for college level courses, while the national rate was 24 percent. The ACT scores in math and science were particularly lower in Florida than their national counterparts.[61]

The challenges of increasing high school achievement are also underscored by the number of students in Florida placed in remedial courses as they enter college. A 2007–8 assessment by the Florida legislature's Office of Program Policy Analysis and Government Account-

Table 7. ACT composite scores for public high school students

	1998	2005	2007	2010
Florida	20.8	20.4	19.9	19.5
Nation	21.0	20.9	21.2	21.0

Source: ACT, "2010 ACT National and State Scores," http://act.org/newsroom/data/2010/profilereports.html.

ability found that more than half of students who entered Florida's community colleges or universities needed remediation courses in mathematics, reading, or writing. More than 90 percent of the students who need remediation were attending Florida's community colleges (now called state colleges).[62] For example, at Florida State College at Jacksonville, 70 percent of incoming students in 2010 needed remedial courses to begin their college coursework.[63] These numbers are problematic because they show that a large percentage of students who enter Florida colleges and universities are simply unprepared for college-level work.

Public Opinion

After years of reform based upon testing, the public and other stakeholders had mixed reviews about Governor Bush's A+ Plan. A year before he left office, Quinnipiac University released a survey of 1,000 randomly selected Florida voters. It found that Bush had a 52 percent approval rating, but 55 percent of the voters polled rated the quality of public education as "not so good" or "poor."[64] Those surveyed were also split on whether Bush had made progress in education; 47 percent said yes and 47 percent said no. Again, receiving public praise on education is rare because of the high expectations that parents and the public have. Governor Bush helped to raise these expectations, but he could not win over voters with the FCAT.

Political use of the FCAT emerged in the 2006 gubernatorial race to succeed Jeb Bush. The Democratic candidate Jim Davis argued to end the testing, and the Republican candidate Charlie Crist advocated keeping it. In another public opinion poll, conducted by the *St. Petersburg Times* in 2006, 59 percent of the respondents opposed how the FCAT was administered in the public schools.[65] In a 2006 survey of Florida public school principals, 80 percent disagreed with awarding money to schools on the basis of FCAT scores. However, 76 percent of principals believed that the FCAT helped schools develop "strategies" to improve student achievement. The principals also said the FCAT had decreased the time students spent on non-FCAT subjects like art and history. Finally, the principals believed that the FCAT put teachers "under pressure" to increase scores.[66] Nationwide, the validity of test scores has been challenged in Washington, D.C., and Atlanta following accusations of cheating involving administrators and teachers. How these tests are administered and graded will continue to be a matter for policymakers to observe. Since the end of the Bush administration, the Florida Department of Education has continually changed the rules for the FCAT and other accountability measures. These changes have called into the question the validity of the measurements. As of this writing, new end-of-class tests are being used as a replacement for the FCAT in the state. Also, the controversy over common academic standards across different states is increasing nationwide. Even in Jeb Bush's home state, there is conservative opposition to national testing standards. The conflict involving these tests may create even more confusion for local administrators and parents.

Conclusion

The two terms of Jeb Bush's governorship fostered the largest experiment in public school education in the nation's history. The A+ education plan that Bush authored and implemented has changed the public school educational experience for millions of Florida students and parents. This market-based approach to public-school education was both innovative and controversial. Placing responsibility for results of government action upon the deliverer instead of the recipient of government services was a new approach. For example, doctors who receive Medicaid are not held responsible when their patients become sick. The A+ Plan put the responsibility for student success not on the parents and students themselves but on schools and teachers. If students didn't show signs of academic achievement, both schools and teachers received sanctions through a grading system that highlighted their professional failures. Governor Bush attempted to provide choices to parents of students who were in schools that did not display increasing levels of student achievement according to standardized tests.

These market-based methods followed the tenets of conservative economist Milton Friedman, who long ago advocated for more choice in public education. Political scientists John Chubb and Terry Moe in their important book *Politics, Markets, and America's Schools* used nationwide testing data to conclude that typical public school systems are too bureaucratic and inflexible to help students achieve. Chubb and Moe advocated for more choice for parents in K–12 education and much more autonomy for individual schools. Governor Bush adapted some of these ideas and put together a system that placed extensive emphasis on the results of standardized testing. Bush believed that if schools and teachers could not produce students that did well on these tests, then market-based choices should be made available to them.

From the results detailed above, these market-based reforms had real impacts on Florida's public K–12 system. Even though Governor Bush's voucher plan for parents was found unconstitutional, school choice still increased dramatically during his tenure. From a combination of charter schools, McKay and opportunity scholarships, home-schooling, and distance learning, more than 20 percent of Florida's school-aged children receive their education outside the public school system (see table 1). Another important impact of the A+ Plan was a clear increase in test scores, primarily at the fourth-grade level and to some degree at the eighth-grade level. As Florida's public K–12 system became accustomed to the testing regime, students performed better on these tests. Moreover, the attention on testing did provide more focus on the academic performance of African American and Hispanic students. Because of this increased attention, schools that were deemed low-performing were sometimes able to improve their performance on the FCAT. The testing scheme also greatly increased attention on the subject of public education in general. Throughout Governor Bush's tenure, according to public opinion data, education was viewed as the most important issue in the state.[67] Governor Bush believed education was the most critical issue of his two terms, and in many ways he made the state of Florida believe it as well. This attention brought about real discussion of the issues facing low-performing students. Finally, graduation rates in the state increased during Bush's tenure.

This market-based approach had negative impacts as well. In a market system, there are winners and losers. With more choices for families that were ready to take advantage of them, many low-performing schools were drained of their best students. Especially at the high school level in urban areas in Florida, pockets of low-performing schools stubbornly remain. In 2011 two urban high schools in Jacksonville and Miami were threatened with closure because after a decade of the A+ Plan, achievement in these schools still had not risen. The neighborhood schools that would be shuttered in this process are important in their local communities.

Bush's attempted changes to the university system also did not go as planned. Since Senator Bob Graham backed a successful movement to restore system-wide governance, the universities ended up being governed by two different boards. As predicted, the universities have engaged in battles for their own interests, with little system-wide planning. Since 2000, two new public law schools, one public medical school, and a twelfth university—a polytechnic university—have been created. These schools were created through legislative action usually sponsored by one powerful legislator, not through planning or analysis done by a central body. And they were created at a time when the existing universities received sharply reduced subsidies from state government, adding to the urgency of yearly tuition increases during difficult economic years.

Market-based reforms also require rewards for schools and teachers that do well, and more resources for schools and teachers that need help. In the heyday of the Florida economy, these resources were available. Governor Bush campaigned for reelection in 2002 by boasting that he had increased school spending by $1 billion. After the Great Recession and the plummeting housing market at the end of the decade, school funding was cut in the 2011 budget. Schools across the state struggled to offer their basic courses. Rewards for successful teachers and schools were scarcer, and extra resources for schools that had problems with student achievement scores were either not available or severely reduced. How can market-based reforms work if no rewards are available?

Moreover, large market-based reforms or reforms of any kind on a large scale are going to have important unintended consequences. One of the consequences is that the implementation of the A+ Plan has entailed more state bureaucratic control over local schools, rather than less. This increase is in direct opposition to the recommendations of Chubb and Moe. Their research found that the strongest indicator of school success is autonomy in decision making at the school level. The A+ Plan, on the contrary, has morphed into a heavy hand from the state. Another important consequence is that the overwhelming academic focus on the FCAT in K–12 schools has led some schools to de-emphasize non-FCAT subjects such as art, music, and social studies. Florida students may be getting a more focused education in some core areas but an education that has less breadth. Finally, another damaging consequence of the A+ system is the "scarlet letter" problem. Once schools are deemed failing or low performing, this reputation is difficult to lose. Moreover, since the grading of schools is an aggregate measure, it conceals the successes of many individual teachers and students within those low-performing schools. Again, this grading system has important impacts on real estate values near schools, the desire of students to attend those schools, and their overall reputation in the communities. These are powerful impacts coming from one test taken in one week of the school year—and they are among the reasons that the FCAT is being ended in the state. Yet even with the end of the FCAT, Bush's efforts to reform education would not end with his governorship. Those efforts are examined in the last chapter.

6

Jeb Bush versus State Government

When Jeb Bush began his second term as governor of Florida, he made this bold statement in his inaugural address: "I look forward to the time when these buildings of government are empty. There would be no greater tribute to our maturity as a society than if we can make these buildings around us empty of workers—silent monuments to the time when government played a larger role than it deserved or could adequately fill." It was a direct message to state government: the private sector can do it better than state employees and agencies can do it. What the statement reflects is Governor Bush's belief in the private market to handle almost anything and his distrust of government in general. These two impulses helped Jeb Bush put forward an agenda during his time as governor that was more pro-business and more antigovernment than any Florida gubernatorial agenda since the early 1950s. Ironically, the way he implemented these policies was with an accumulation of power in the office of governor that was unparalleled in the state's history.

Bush's attitudes about the free marketplace and his views on the limitations of government created a three-pronged initiative to change the way government operated. The three factors were 1) a Reaganite belief in supply-side economics—especially a focus on tax cuts, 2) an effort to use government to support incentives for new businesses, and 3) an attempt to privatize and contract out many functions of government, which would take the day-to-day operation of the government out of the hands of state employees and lead to the elimination of thousands of state government jobs.

The fact that he was able to implement most of these ideas is another testament to his power in the state at the time. Again Jeb Bush was not satisfied with incremental conservative reforms; he wanted fundamental conservative changes in the way Florida government operated. Yet his style of governance was to strongly assert the power of the executive branch of government to bring about the changes that he wanted.

Going after Taxes

Using a strategy Ronald Reagan employed in Washington in the 1980s and his brother George W. would soon use in 2001, Jeb Bush set out to substantially reduce taxes in the state of Florida. He also had a serious advantage that any mayor or governor would love to have in 2014. A growing national and Florida economy created a surplus in the state of Florida's budget in 1999, Governor Bush's first year. Accordingly, he could offer the largest tax cut in Florida's history along with spending increases in needed areas including education. Since the 1950s, Florida state government has always been trying to catch up to the influx of new citizens. According to U.S. Census data, the state grew from fewer than 3 million people in 1950 to more than 15 million in the year 2000, with a diverse population of young and old, whites and African Americans and Hispanics. These new Floridians required more schools, more roads, and a much larger public safety sector, among a wide variety of other needs. Even with the demographic realities, Governor Bush believed that more money needed to be returned to individual taxpayers and small businesses, and he called for a $1.2 billion tax cut. Bush said that the state was enjoying a period of "unprecedented prosperity" and could afford the cut. He rejected calls from some Democrats to use the surplus to fund educational initiatives. Bush responded, "We're also going to fund public education. . . . This is not at the expense of priorities at the state level."[1]

The package included a mix of property tax cuts, lower unemployment taxes that businesses had to pay, and a sharp reduction in a unique tax called the intangibles tax. This tax brought revenue from financial assets such as stocks and bonds, and accounts receivable for businesses. The intangibles tax in particular was extremely unpopular among businesses and wealthier seniors in the state who had considerable stock portfolios. Yet as the history of the state has shown, it would be a challenge for any administration to raise revenue to meet all of Florida's needs. The state did not have an income tax and accordingly looked for revenue from other sources to make up the difference. These particular tax reductions would not impact individual taxpayers to a great extent but definitely aided businesses. Constituencies that already believed they were underfunded spoke out. A spokesman for Florida's teachers' union said at the time, "It seems like we are being penny wise and pound foolish. We've got plenty of money to help our schools if we would just put it to the best use."[2] Yet the governor was not persuaded. He told a group of business leaders, "We have a lot of dough. . . . It's a good time to get back to the people who play by the rules."[3]

There was little doubt that Bush was going to get what he wanted on taxes. The first unified Republican government in Florida since Reconstruction had only one true leader, and that was Jeb Bush. Unlike previous Democratic legislatures, which rarely gave Democratic governors much deference, both houses of the legislature would move Governor Bush's agenda through without much change. In his State of the State address to the legislature as it opened in March 1999, Bush acknowledged his political power. After he talked about his ideas for a large tax cut, he joked: "I was thinking about a vote count right now. . . .

I guess we can't do that."[4] Yet he almost could have taken a vote at the opening of the legislature without going through committees and deliberation. Jeb Bush had set the agenda; tax cuts would now be an important part of public policy in Florida for the next two decades. The tax cut agenda became so ingrained in the Florida Republican Party and among conservative groups that numerous state constitutional initiatives were put on the ballot by the Republican legislature to reduce property taxes after Bush took office. These initiatives placed a heavy strain on school districts and county governments throughout the state, and the reductions continued to challenge local governments in succeeding administrations.

The combination of a strong economy in the late 1990s and the added windfall of a billion-dollar settlement with the tobacco companies gave Jeb Bush the budgetary space he needed to implement his priorities. Even with this cushion in his first two years, he was still committed to reducing state government employees and reframing government agencies. At the end of the first budgetary cycle, Jeb Bush sent a message to legislators that he would watch their spending. Using the line-item veto, which allowed the governor to strike individual items from an appropriations bill without stopping the entire bill, he vetoed $300 million in approved projects.[5] To restore the spending, the legislature would have to override the line-item vetoes—an action not likely in the Republican-controlled legislature. Bush's vetoes broke with a tradition of the governor getting his priorities in exchange for district-specific projects for legislators. Bush wanted these projects to have an "overall statewide benefit." If they did not meet this criterion, they were vetoed.[6] The vetoes sent a strong signal of who was in charge in Tallahassee. The days of the weak-governor system were over in Florida during the Jeb Bush years.

The tax cuts also energized the business lobby in Tallahassee. Legislation that capped the punitive damages those businesses might have to pay in liability lawsuits finally passed, after numerous attempts in the 1990s. The tax cuts directed at businesses and the legal reforms together created a perfect legislation storm for business-friendly initiatives. The spokesman for the Associated Industries of Florida, one of the largest business lobbies in Florida, called Bush's first session "the best ever." Yet even the business lobby realized that the state still needed to address serious needs through education spending and workforce development. One lobbyist for the state Chamber of Commerce said that "the day-to-day inability of businesses to find educated workers is a huge problem now."[7]

During Governor Bush's two terms, even with the strong use of the line-item veto, overall spending did increase dramatically, from approximately $49 billion to nearly $74 billion in 2006.[8] A large portion of the increase came in his second term when the state had to deal with record hurricane damage and increasing Medicaid costs. Bush had to face what all his predecessors had faced over the last forty years—a surging population with demands on government along with a voting base that was lukewarm to any increase in taxes. Some of the stark tax cuts he was able to pass in his first two years in office put pressure on the Florida budget after the September 11 terrorist attacks and a slowing economy. The Cato Institute, a libertarian think tank, had given Governor Bush an A for fiscal discipline during his first term but a C in his second term because of the increased spending.[9] However, through privatization and reductions, the Bush administration did reduce the state government workforce by 12 percent.[10]

While some areas of his fiscal plans were hit hard by reductions, Governor Bush increased K–12 education spending throughout his two terms. After three years of his governorship, K–12 education spending had increased by more than $1 billion.[11] Critics argued that the spending "increases" were not adjusted to take into account inflation and a growing student population. Moreover, some of the governor's tax proposals reduced local property taxes, and thus the increases at the state level were offset by cuts at the local level. Another factor in state education spending was implementing the class-size amendment, an amendment the governor had opposed. This amendment dictated maximum student-teacher ratios for the various levels of K–12 education. To reach the mandated ratios would cost the state millions of dollars. However, supporters argued that these reduced ratios would aid student learning. In Bush's 2004 budget plan, K–12 education spending would rise by a healthy 7 percent. Yet more than half of that increase was budgeted to reduce class size. The rest was mostly targeted at the influx of new students during the growth years early in the decade. Finally, some of the increase was earmarked for rewards to administrators of schools that produced higher grades on their standardized exams.[12] In Bush's early budgets, funds for schools where students were struggling on the standardized tests were not allocated by the state but left up to the local school boards to address. Yet even with the criticisms of Bush's spending plans, they did represent increases—increases that many Florida school districts have not seen since the Bush administration ended in 2007.

After his first two years, when Bush was able to reduce taxes and also increase spending in education and some areas of social services, budget realities started to hit. The combination of the slowing economy and the terrorist attacks of September 11, 2001, hurt Florida's revenues. The September 11 attacks, which featured the use of airplanes as terrorist weapons, drastically reduced Florida tourism. For example, in the three months after the attacks, 10,000 workers in the Central Florida tourist industry were laid off. In Central Florida alone, 2.7 million fewer tourists came to the area during the two years after the attack.[13] These factors forced a special legislative session in the fall of 2001 and produced a budget reduced by $1 billion.[14] One result was that all educational spending from kindergarten through the university system had to be reduced by $600 million. Throughout this period, the Florida budget was trying to balance ever-increasing needs with a much slower rate of growth in revenues. By the middle of the decade, the economy was growing strongly again on the strength of the housing market. In the year 2006, added revenues increased the budget surplus to more than $3 billion, allowing Governor Bush to offer another large tax cut before he left office in 2007. This economic turnaround from the 9/11 attacks was impressive and contributed to a low unemployment rate of 3.5 percent when Bush left office. Along with the budget surplus, the state earned a AAA bond rating from rating agencies.

Incentives for Businesses

For too many years, Florida's economy depended upon a tourism industry that featured mostly lower-paid service workers such as waiters and waitresses, an agricultural industry where migrant farm laborers made up the majority of employees, and a housing industry that depended upon cheap capital and a constant increase in property values. Thus the dilemma, how to bring more businesses to Florida that would provide Floridians with higher-paid jobs in more resilient industries? Before it became a tourist magnet, the state had struggled to attract citizens to come to visit and live. The federal government even paid white Americans to migrate to Florida in the 1800s. After the state's post–World War II expansion, Florida tried to use a more lenient tax policy to lure businesses to the state. As international competition for manufacturing jobs increased and many states adopted aggressive incentive policies, Florida tried to respond. Enterprise Florida is the public-private agency that has attempted to lead economic development in the state since the 1990s. Yet by the time Bush came to office, Enterprise Florida's governing board had mushroomed to 125 members. This unworkable situation caused the governor and the legislature to restructure the agency and to rethink economic development policy.

The governor's new chief of economic development said bluntly at the beginning of Bush's first-term, "We don't have a cohesive economic development strategy in the state. . . . We find lots of programs, lots of good intentions that are scattered."[15] Governor Bush proposed to use more public money for business development and to bring more economic incentives under his direct control than any previous Florida governor. These public incentives have a very mixed record in improving the economic climate of cities and states. Florida attempted a strategy that moved away from economic development guided by a large committee to getting more power directly to the governor to hand out incentives. The purpose of more gubernatorial authority for economic development aid was to make sure that the aid moved more quickly through the process. Legislation early in his first term allowed Governor Bush to approve incentive funds with the approval of only a few legislative leaders, not a direct vote of the entire legislature. To access these funds, companies would have to promise a certain number of high-wage jobs. Job guarantees have always been a difficult part of implementing incentives. Yet again the focus of Florida's economic

development in 1999 was to give the governor more flexibility in nego-
tiating deals with major companies. A Republican state legislator who
chaired the Senate's Commerce Committee made clear the purpose of
the legislation: "This bill will help Jeb Bush in his role as the state's
chief economic development officer. . . . That's good news."[16]

Another problem with Florida's economic development strategy
was a lack of cooperation among counties. In August 1999, Sarasota
and Manatee engaged in a battle for Tropicana Industries and its orange juice and drink empire. Tropicana Products presented to officials of both counties a seventeen-item "assistance request" including
payment for many detailed items such as landscaping costs. Sarasota
County officials finally decided they could not meet all of the requested
items, and Tropicana remained in Manatee County. Sarasota officials
said that Tropicana may have been asking for too much. "Once you
open the door, you never shut it," according to the Sarasota county
manager.[17] Yet some efforts were extremely successful. In late 1999,
Pratt Rocket Engines agreed to keep its 800 engineers in Palm Beach
County, accepting more than $500,000 in incentives to do so.[18] The
company had threatened to move to California or Mississippi because
they were being offered better incentives. Senator Trent Lott of Mississippi, then the Senate majority leader, personally attempted to lure
Pratt to his home state. But along with their incentives, Florida officials made the point that moving the operations would have been
disruptive, and in the end Pratt remained in Florida.

Scripps Research Institute and the Biotech Initiative

No other business recruitment showcased Governor Bush's aggressive strategy more than the pursuit of the Scripps Research Institute.
Scripps Research was a nonprofit conglomerate that focused on the
development of pharmaceuticals that could combat serious diseases,
including cancer. They were not looking to move to Florida, but Governor Bush wanted them in his state. The nonprofit part of the enterprise basically acted as a start-up for industries that could bring in
massive profits. Once the drugs were developed, they would then be
marketed and sold by private pharmaceutical interests. Yet in the fall

of 2003, Governor Bush made it clear that the Scripps recruitment effort would not be the usual menu of tax breaks and persuasion. Bush wanted to go big, and he ended up offering Scripps money and benefits that were unprecedented in Florida history. Scripps had not been seeking incentives to move anywhere. Governor Bush flew to California to make the company a huge offer pending legislative approval. He believed the project was so important, he had a secret code name for it, Project Air Conditioning. The rhetorical significance of the term was the impact that air-conditioning had on the state's economy in the 1950s and 1960s. For many American migrants, air-conditioning was a necessity to make Florida's tropical climate viable to live and to do business. Governor Bush believed that the Scripps deal could have the same transformative impact on the state's economy.[19]

Bush's concept was that one major biomedical institute would act as an anchor and a spark for widespread expansion of the biomedical industry in the state. So large, he believed, were the stakes in bringing Scripps to Florida that he literally offered them a deal they could not refuse. The governor would provide more than $310 million in state funds directly to the Institute. He also urged Palm Beach County, where the Institute would be located, to offer another $200 million in incentives. The total package—more than half a billion dollars in incentives for one nonprofit entity—was about half the amount of the budgetary increase for the entire public education system in Florida the following year. The incentive money would go for land, buildings, laboratories, office space, and seven years of employee salaries.[20] Having a government entity directly pay the salaries of the nonprofit entity would be an unprecedented gamble. An unsettling aspect of this deal was that originally Scripps only committed to 545 jobs. Yet Governor Bush argued that analyses had shown that a center like this could eventually create 50,000 jobs over fifteen years.[21] The 545 jobs worked out to a state investment of more than $800,000 per job. Governor Bush countered that this type of analysis was too simple. If Scripps came to Florida, it would transform the economy of the state. "Florida stands at the threshold of opportunity that will forever change the destiny of our state," Bush declared.[22]

Because the Scripps deal was so big, it had to go before the legislature for approval. This massive deal was being considered during the same week as the Terri Schiavo bill. Some legislators wanted more controls over the vast incentives. But even though most of the details were announced only two weeks prior to a special session called by the governor, the Florida legislature passed this economic development legislation easily. Another important part of Bush's argument for the large incentive package was that it would attract other venture capitalists to start up operations in the state.

The transition to leader in the biotech industry would not be easy for Governor Bush or for Florida after approval of the package. First there was some confusion whether the Scripps group was going to pay back half the money the state of Florida invested in its recruitment to the state. Some Florida legislators thought this provision was in the package, but the governor's office later said that Scripps was not required to pay money back.[23] Then the location of the site in Palm Beach County became a source of tremendous disagreement and legal conflict. Environmental groups objected to the placement of the Scripps campus near some environmentally sensitive lands.[24] Two years after the massive incentive package was passed, the head of Scripps told a group of Florida business leaders that the Scripps facilities in Florida would not include a technology transfer office to help get research translated into products.[25]

Yet even with these setbacks, the Scripps campus was built in Palm Beach County. The Scripps name added to the cachet of Florida in trying to attract biomedical industries. A review released in 2011, eight years after ground was broken, gave a very mixed picture of the success of the public investment in Scripps. According to the funding authority that oversees the public payouts to Scripps, the presence of the Scripps Institute helped to create more than 11,000 jobs in eight years both directly and indirectly.[26] This number, while impressive, falls far short of the 50,000 figure that was cited when the Scripps project was proposed. Measuring the impact of public incentives on eventual job growth and benefit to the states is a difficult undertaking. While Scripps may not create as many direct jobs as advertised, the deal did pave the way for more biotechnical institutes to look at Florida. These groups included the Max Planck Institute, the Torrey Pines Institute for Molecular Studies, and the Burnham Institute. The Burnham Institute created a biomedical hub called Lake Nona in the center of the state. The Lake Nona site was first visualized during the competition to get Scripps to come to Orlando instead of Palm Beach County.[27] Orlando also began developing a video game industry with incentive assistance from the state. These initiatives were real successes for the Bush administration. However, the original project was not as successful. As of 2014, the Scripps Research Institute website gave the number of employees in Florida as barely 600.[28]

These types of incentives present real challenges. In an exhaustive review performed by the *New York Times* in 2012, incentives and subsidies were examined nationwide. The report called into question the direct impact these subsidies have on unemployment. Reviewing Florida's incentives from 2000 to 2010, the report found that through state and local agencies Florida spent more than $3.5 billion a year to attract and retain businesses. Most of these funds went for sales tax exemptions and refunds.[29] In a state that is always trying to catch up with its increasing population and has no income tax, the sales tax is a vital revenue generator. The hundreds of exemptions and tax breaks in the Florida sales tax code create unfair advantages for some businesses and hardships for others. The *Times* report also showed that even with Governor Bush's emphasis on biotech, most of the state incentives by 2010 went to the agricultural and film industries.[30] Neither of these industries creates many high-paying jobs. Moreover, the vast majority of incentive money goes to large research groups or big businesses. Small businesses are generally left out of the incentive and recruitment efforts of states.

There is an important ideological consideration: a true commitment to free market principles means that companies thrive or die on their own—without government assistance. The Tea Party movement in the Republican Party has advanced this argument ever since the federal bailouts of the banks and financial institutions in 2008–9. This theoretical argument is strong but not practical. As the *Times* report reveals, if a state chooses not to be part of economic recruitment through incentives, many others states are more than willing to engage in bidding even though the economic benefits may be less than clear. Jeb Bush's administration took the incentives strategy to new heights with mixed success. An entire medical industry was created in Orlando, but the results fell far short in Palm Beach County. These experiences show how daunting is the task of moving Florida's economy away from the service sector to research and development.

Privatization

With Governor Bush's philosophy that government had grown too big and tried to do too much, the concept of privatization of government services was bound to be a major undertaking of his administration. The idea that nonprofit organizations and businesses perform better than government entities or employees was the guiding principle in Jeb Bush's tenure. Bush rejected the idea of market failure—the concept that government has to perform certain services that the private sector will not do because of the lack of a profit margin. There is no economic market for taking care of the homeless, helping the poor citizens in the state, or a myriad of other issues in a society. such as providing inspections of restaurants. Because there is no market, no private businesses exist to meet these needs unless the revenue comes from the state. A major part of running government services is providing personnel to implement these services. As the public sector became more unionized in the late twentieth century, the cost of providing certain services increased. As of this writing in 2014, strong efforts are under way to combat the power of public unions in several states, including Wisconsin and Michigan. The Republican governor of Wisconsin narrowly survived a recall vote over his efforts to limit public employee unions in his state. Almost a decade before the broader pushback against public unions occurred, Governor Jeb Bush moved to reduce public union power and to draw down state government personnel. By his second year in office he was able to get legislation passed to reclassify 16,000 state workers out of the civil service with its protections and regulations. Bush argued that the legislation would "eliminate, over time, the good old boy system."[31] It also made it easier to provide bonuses for job performance.

For some of the employees whose work could not be reclassified, Bush pushed aggressively to find outside vendors to perform their work. The first major privatization effort Governor Bush looked to was an unlikely place to use a business-friendly model—the care of the most vulnerable children in the state, those in foster care. In 1998 the Florida legislature had passed a proposal to allow companies and nonprofits to bid on a whole range of child protective services including investigations of abuse, adoption, and foster care.[32] Governor Bush picked up on this plan when he came into office and implemented it aggressively. He wanted regional and community-based private companies or agencies to take over the state functions. Child protective services was a sensitive political issue for the state in 2000 with the discovery that a child in foster care had been murdered a year earlier and no caseworker had checked on her for more than fifteen months.

The plan put forward by the Department of Children and Families was to reduce fifteen service districts to seven regions of service. With this reduction, almost half of the Department's 27,000 positions would be eliminated.[33] By 2003, child protective services were handed over to local organizations and some for-profit entities. Problems continued in the agency for most of Bush's tenure. Jerry Regier, the head of DCF for two years from 2003 to 2005, had to resign after it was revealed that he and several aides had improper contacts with lobbyists for companies seeking DCF contracts.[34]

Yet Governor Bush's effort to privatize government services was just beginning. With the approval of the legislature, Bush outsourced a variety of government services, from administering state parks and identifying uninsured drivers to feeding state prisoners and providing legal counsel to death row inmates. The state's biggest privatization project was the transfer of the state's personnel services to a private bidder. The Convergys Corporation of Cincinnati won a massive contract, $280 million through the first year, to oversee all personnel administration in the state. The breadth of such activity spurred the executive director of the group in Florida that monitors government spending and taxation to announce, "We have a governor who is committed to free enterprise like no other governor in Florida history.

. . . In fact, Jeb Bush is probably the most committed governor to free enterprise of any of the fifty governors in the nation."[35] Yet the size of the incentives offered would require an oversight regime that simply was not in place in state government.

Not only was was the outsourcing of state government personnel services the most ambitious effort to privatize an essential state government function, but its effects were felt in all areas of state government that were *not* being privatized, as the state employees who remained would now fall under the personnel administration of a private entity. The organization of payment to employees and the management of the benefits that they receive is a massive undertaking for any organization, private or public. It was estimated that 850 state jobs would be eliminated when Convergys moved in to administer payment and benefits for all state workers. The challenge was that personnel administration had been spread throughout state government for years. The transition to a centralized operation under private control would be difficult. Initial estimates were that it would save more than $5 million per budget year, but the transition was long and complicated and the cost savings were not apparent. The Convergys contract would highlight some of the disadvantages of moving toward privatization.

While the initial bidding to privatize government services involves competition, once a company or nonprofit wins a contract, it in effect becomes a monopoly provider of that service. Contracts and legislative agreements are supposed to guide the work of the private entity, but real accountability and oversight is elusive, and it becomes difficult and expensive to switch providers if their services are not satisfactory. Convergys started the project months behind schedule, and when they did start, problems emerged. For example, a cabinet member, Agriculture Commissioner Charles Bronson, did not get paid. Other employees lost their insurance coverage temporarily.[36]

The Convergys contract is only one example of the challenges that the state of Florida faced under Governor Bush when it tried to privatize government services. Some that were privatized were services that did not enjoy a great deal of public support. For example, the Aramark Corporation won the contact to provide food services in 90 percent of Florida's prisons and correctional facilities. For $58 million per year, the corporation promised to provide meals to prisoners at $2.32 an inmate. This contract produced some problems throughout the system. In one facility, prison workers were directed by Aramark supervisors to serve spoiled chicken by masking its bad smell in vinegar. Inspections of the kitchen facilities managed by Aramark found some of them to be "filthy" and "horrendous." The most egregious error that Aramark committed was providing insufficient food, so that it would simply run out before all the prisoners were fed. While Florida voters cared little about how prisoners were fed, unsatisfactory food service to prisoners can result in safety threats to correctional officers. Since food is one of the only comforts that prisoners have, a corrections spokesman said, in order to keep the peace "what the first inmate eats, the last inmate eats." Aramark was not concerned about the criticism; the company spokesperson at the time said, "Making too many meals means a waste for the taxpayers." The company seemed to care little about the danger to correctional officers and the human rights implications of treating prisoners inhumanely.[37]

Another privatization effort that met with disappointing results was contracting out the legal defense of death row inmates. In the mid-1980s a state agency was formed to assist death row inmates in their appeals because not enough private attorneys were volunteering to do the work. Governor Bush's effort to eliminate the office and contract out the work to private attorneys came after the state agency had successfully appealed a death penalty case.[38] In another strange case of privatization, librarians and historians from across the state protested Governor Bush's plan to move part of Florida's library collection from Tallahassee to a private university in South Florida. They held up signs saying "Don't privatize the state's library" and "Move Jeb instead."[39] The plan was eventually dropped.

Governor Bush did not relax on his privatization campaign even during the last two years of his second term. His last major push for privatization involved the state's Medicaid program. Medicaid, the joint federal-state program that provides medical benefits to low-income citizens, is a huge expense in Florida because of the large senior citizen population. Medicare, the federal program that provides medical insurance to citizens over sixty-five, does not cover every health expense. Low-income seniors, especially those who need nursing home care, rely upon Medicaid to pay for that care. By 2005 the Medicaid program was consuming more than one-fourth of the state's budget. In a growing state like Florida with massive demands upon state government, the Medicaid program would continue to be a major challenge. Bush stated in 2005, "Florida's Medicaid program will collapse under its own weight if we do not fundamentally transform the way it operates." Rather than paying doctors and hospitals directly, Bush's proposal was to pay private insurers the money to address the cost of caring for 2.3 million people. Bush believed private insurers would want to be in the program if costs were capped.[40]

Governor Bush found the politics of health care reform as difficult as other governors, and indeed presidents, had found them to be in the 1990s. Health providers wanted to make sure that their payments would cover the cost of care, and patient advocates were concerned about any changes to their health care coverage. Eventually the Florida legislature scaled down Bush's proposal to allow for pilot programs in Broward County in South Florida and Duval County in North Florida. The results of these pilot experiments were mixed. Yet even with the tepid reaction to his Medicaid reforms in 2005 and 2006, future Republican legislatures and the state would continue to push the reforms. Governor Charlie Crist, Governor Bush's successor, vetoed most of the Medicaid reforms passed by the Republican legislature. However, Crist's successor in the governor's office, Rick Scott, signed legislation in 2012 that strongly resembled Bush's plan. In many ways, Bush's privatization push in his two terms governing Florida changed the way government operated not only during his time but in the years following his administration.

Results

Jeb Bush transformed Florida state government. These examples show the challenges that exist when transitioning from long-entrenched state entities to businesses and nonprofit organizations. Since many government functions would not exist in a private marketplace because of a lack of profit, combining private-sector and public functions can be difficult and messy. Essentially, when a private entity is awarded a state contract and thus becomes the monopoly provider for that service, this takes away some of the competitive market mechanisms that the private sector is supposed to provide. Moreover, measuring the outputs from private vendors doing public work is a daunting task. Assuming there is oversight of private vendors, it is still difficult to measure their efficiencies. Should the assessment be based on the number of citizens served? A per cost ratio for service provided? The amount of saving the privatizing entity is supposed to provide?

Unfortunately for some of these projects, Florida did not reach a high level of accountability. Governor Bush appointed an efficiency czar to monitor how well the state government was spending its money. The appointment only lasted for four months, then Ruth Sykes resigned because she felt she did not have the autonomy the position required and that privatization efforts were being rushed without enough analysis.[41] Agencies that reviewed the privatization and contracting initiatives were generally unimpressed with the accountability for these initiatives. The director of the state legislature's Office of Program Policy Analysis and Government Accountability (OPPAGA) said in 2004, "It's hard to tell how things are working and whether privatization is achieving goals the policymakers were trying to reach. In some cases it's been planned well and works well; in some cases it hasn't. There's just a lack of common business analysis." Moreover, in 2003 the inspector general for the executive office of the governor, Derry Harper, wrote a report critical of the state's contracting services in 2003, saying, "As documented in almost 500 audit findings over a three-year period, controls over contracting are in a state of disrepair."[42] Governor Bush responded to the audit by creating the Government Center for Efficient Government. Yet he made it clear that this center would work out of the governor's office. He vetoed legislation that would have given the state legislature a stronger hand in the operations of this oversight center. When a newly elected state chief financial officer took office after Governor Bush's two terms, he found large problems with the oversight of the largest privatization contract in the state—the Convergys contract that privatized personnel services.[43]

The privatization effort was similar to other Bush initiatives. He had reversed years of state policymaking and changed the direction of state government. Yet the implementation of these aggressive privatization initiatives was problematic. The savings from some of these initiatives were either never realized or never documented. Still, the seeds of innovation have been planted for some of these government services. For example, when many of the support services for families and foster children were originally privatized, implementation problems abounded, especially in Pinellas and Pasco Counties. Yet in Duval County in northern Florida, by the end of the first decade of the 2000s the private and public agencies involved in foster care had combined to streamline many different policies to allow for a record number of foster children to be adopted. Most research that examines vulnerable children shows that adopted children generally have better life outcomes than those that remain in foster care.

However, this policy area continues to highlight the challenges of taking difficult social problems and attempting to address them by privatization. The different local agencies have had some of the same problems that the Department of Children and Families experienced during and after Bush's tenure. In 2013 more than twenty children died of abuse and neglect in the Florida system. After seeing another tragic case of abuse, Judge Larry Schack of the 19th Judicial Circuit called out the entire system: "Something in the system is fundamentally wrong. I submit to you that the system in Florida does not and can't function effectively the way it's structured." The judge cited difficulties in the relationship between the department and the community-based agencies that had been created under Governor Bush. These circumstances show that public policies that focus on difficult social issues are not easy to address with a government agency or a private vendor.[44]

Yet another important consideration in with the privatization issue is the fiscal climate of states and cities after the recession of 2008. As of this writing, pension benefits for government employees are a major source of fiscal stress for many states and localities. Governor Bush's efforts to minimize some of these future costs through privatization may produce savings in the long run that will help Florida's pension fund remain one of the strongest in the nation. Finally, the culture of privatization is embedded within Florida government. Many normal government functions such as managing reservations for state parks and collecting tolls on state highways are now done by private agencies with a state contract.

Bush and the Importance of Government Functions

As detailed throughout the book, Governor Bush advanced his activist conservative agenda during his two terms. His approach to managing government was a major part of this agenda. Tax reductions and fewer regulations for businesses combined with a vigorous approach to privatization of government services showed again how Governor Bush translated conservative campaign speeches into policy realities. Yet his approach to government and public policy was (and is) not uniformly rigid. While he attempted to reduce state government, he did not dismantle it. There were policy areas where he believed government had a responsibility both to set the agenda and to protect the public. After his experiences with the Liberty City Charter School in the mid-1990s, he consistently showed a concern about inner-city issues. While critics have attacked his softening of the regulations that govern the housing industry in the state, he embarked on several historic efforts in the environmental field. One of these programs was Florida Forever, under which Governor Bush devoted hundreds of millions of dollars to land preservation in the state of Florida. These environmentally sensitive lands are now under state protection indefinitely. Governor Bush and Republican mayor John Delaney of Jacksonville advocated for the land-buying program. Bush fell in line with other traditional conservatives in the state who wanted to create a strong business climate by reducing regulations and taxes, yet he also realized that Florida's natural beauty was an economic driver in itself and needed to be protected. When he signed the Florida Forever bill, Bush said, "Out of 500 pieces of legislation that passed [in this session], this has to be the most significant in terms of legislative that impacts the citizens of Florida."[45]

Also, in opposition to his own brother's presidential administration, Governor Bush fought any expansion of oil drilling near Florida's coastlines. While his opposition softened toward the end of his administration, drilling closer to Florida shorelines never occurred. When the major BP oil spill occurred in the Gulf in 2010, Governor Bush's caution and the warnings of environmentalists regarding the expansion of drilling were justified.

The Everglades

In an unusual twist that involved politics, practicality, and bipartisan compromise, Governor Jeb Bush became a major player in getting funding from the federal government to restore the Everglades. This huge river of grass in southeastern and central Florida is adjacent to some of the most expensive real estate in the country. While to some observers the Everglades is just a large swamp, environmentalists see it as an important natural treasure that reflects Florida's original natural heritage. To assist with development, parts of the Everglades saw large dams and levees that diverted the water for use by Florida's growing population. This diversion of water was ruining the natural swamp. The intent of the restoration was to return the natural flow to the Everglades.

Governor Bush had been roundly criticized in his first gubernatorial race in 1994 for not talking about the environment. Florida's unusual politics welcomed growth and development, but at the same time citizens wanted to protect the natural treasures of the state. By 1999 Bush had learned better how to walk the tightrope between development and protecting the environment. He became an Audubon board member in Florida and, when elected, made it clear that he wanted to support a plan to help the Everglades. He told several environmental groups that if Nixon could go to China, a Miami developer could help save the swamp. Governor Bush worked diligently to support the federal Comprehensive Everglades Restoration Project. It would take serious deal-making and compromise, but the Clinton administration, U.S. senators from both political parties, environmental groups, the sugar lobby, and Governor Bush finally forged a compromise for a restoration bill in the year 2000. Both Vice President Gore, who was running for president at the time, and Governor Jeb Bush, whose brother was also running for president, believed that the Everglades restoration was both good politics and good policy in the presidential election year 2000. Accordingly, a massive $7.8 billion restoration program made its way through Congress in late 2000. As documented by journalist Michael Grunwald, the legislation to implement the restoration of the Everglades was signed at the White House with Jeb Bush in attendance at the exact time that the *Bush v. Gore* presidential voting case was being heard at the Supreme Court in December 2000.[46] Because of the national election crisis, the signing did not get much publicity. Yet the bottom line of this effort is that the biggest environmental restoration project in American history was approved during Jeb Bush's tenure. While his growth management policies were widely criticized by Florida environmentalists, this Everglades project was historic. Because of lawsuits, environmental impact studies, and a slowing economy, the restoration did not truly begin until 2009.[47] By 2012 positive impacts were being seen, but the project was way behind schedule and the ultimate outcome unclear. However, the onetime Miami developer Jeb Bush had ushered in a huge land-buying conservation program and started the Everglades restoration project. These two efforts may leave a significant environmental legacy.

7

. . . .

The Shadow Governor—
and Maybe More?

A week before the presidential election in Florida in 2012, Republican presidential candidate Mitt Romney came to the must-win state of Florida to shore up his support. Onstage in both Tampa and Miami—two of the largest cities in the state—Governor Romney introduced a Florida governor as "the education governor that all of us looked at with great admiration."[1] The unusual part of the introduction is that Romney was talking about former governor Jeb Bush and not the present governor, Republican Rick Scott. Governor Scott had not joined Romney during these visits, and they had been together infrequently in the state in the 2012 campaign. Instead, Governor Bush, who had not been in office for almost six years, was seen as the most popular politician in Florida to appear with Governor Romney during the campaign. This instance shows the lasting duration of Governor Bush's political standing in the state. As previous chapters have shown, Governor Bush became the most powerful governor in Florida history. This chapter argues that he became the most powerful ex-governor in Florida history as well. His record as governor, combined with his national profile as an educational leader, has kept Governor Bush in the spotlight. He has carefully retained tremendous power within the state's Republican Party and set a standard on how to use the post of former governor as a center of influence. After the 2012 election, he also found himself in a unique place in the Republican Party as a bridge between establishment Republicans and more conservative Tea Party Republicans. In many ways Governor Bush remains a shadow governor of the state, whose ideas and political influence hover over the political landscape unlike any former governor of Florida.

Jeb Bush's Legacy

In the political year 2013 in Washington, D.C., the federal government was locked in a continual budget struggle. The government of the supposed greatest constitutional republic in the world was careening from one budget crisis to the next. After his reelection in 2012 and before he even started his second term, President Barack Obama had to come to an agreement with a lame-duck Congress about raising the nation's debt ceiling. Two months later he was locked in another struggle to head off automatic spending cuts that had been agreed upon by both Democrats and Republicans eighteen months earlier as a way of forcing Democrats and Republicans to work together. While the United States was trying to recover from a massive recession that began in 2008, the federal government was involved in a serious budgetary leadership crisis.

Seven years earlier in the state of Florida, Governor Jeb Bush was coming to the end of his second term. He would provide a stark contrast to the paralysis in Washington that plagued the end of his brother's presidency and most of the Obama presidency as well. After Jeb Bush was elected governor, he was going to lead and he was going to get legislation passed. As detailed in these pages, the unique combination of Florida history, major changes in the structure of Florida government, and the rise of the conservative movement in the nation had come together to make Governor Jeb Bush the most powerful governor in Florida history.

It was clear from his swearing-in in 1999 that Governor Bush was going to use this power aggressively and effectively. By the time his was finished, a partial list of his major initiatives and accomplishments included

- getting approval and implementing a massive testing/accountability system in K–12 public education,
- changing the governance of the entire higher education system,
- reducing taxes by nearly $20 billion on the state level,
- leaving the state with a AAA bond rating from Wall Street due to increasing revenues,
- eliminating thousands of public jobs while expanding private contracting of state services,
- dramatically expanding the rights of gun owners in the state,
- reducing the number of abortion providers in the state,
- leading the state through preparation and recovery from multiple major hurricanes in 2004–5,
- beginning a massive restoration project for the Florida Everglades and purchasing more environmental land than any governor in history,
- giving the largest incentive package in the state's history to the Scripps Research Institute, and
- almost provoking a constitutional crisis over life issues involving the Terri Schiavo case.

The list is not even complete. Bush believes his greatest accomplishment was to bring a strong governor to a traditionally weak-governor state. He said he came to Florida with BHAGs—"big hairy audacious goals." Representative Dan Gelber, a prominent Democratic former state senator from Miami Beach, called Bush "the ubergovernor." Another state Democratic leader said, "I think things were just in line for Jeb Bush . . . he was the right person at the right time to assemble all that power." One of Bush's major advantages was a Republican-controlled legislature that allowed him to dominate policymaking in Florida for most of his two terms. Representative Gelber described it this way: "That first year, 63 lawmakers came on board ready to jump off a cliff if he asked them to. And they did it smiling, singing 'Kumbaya.'" Even with these political advantages, Bush did not cede the details of policymaking to his staff and lobbyists. His knowledge of the details of policy was another lever of power for Bush. He knew that to advance his conservative vision, he would have to define the details of his policies.[2]

The general public in Florida seemed to agree with a positive valuation of Bush's leadership. In a public opinion survey of Florida voters published by Quinnipiac University in his last month in office, 57 percent of respondents described Bush's tenure as governor as either "great" or "good."[3] These poll numbers are particularly strong given that voters tend to get weary of presidents and governors in their second terms. Bush was able to maintain positive approval ratings while he pursued a conservative and controversial agenda.

Of course, Bush's administration had some serious problems with implementing these major changes. Bush was a strong advocate of contracting out public services to the private sector, but the oversight of these privatization efforts was never strong. In particular, the management of the Department of Children and Families suffered under both state control and privatization efforts. His director of corrections was indicted and eventually found guilty of corruption. Bush believed that he could make state government smaller and more efficient, but his efficiency czar resigned shortly after she took the appointment in 2001. He almost initiated a constitutional crisis with the state judiciary when he would not let the courts decide the Terri Schiavo case. His tax cuts and incentive policies did not produce a vastly changed Florida economy that could weather the terrible recession that began in 2008. Finally, his major changes to educational policy remain controversial fifteen years after they were put into place.

Yet the mere fact that he was able to propose and implement a sweeping change in Florida government during his two terms remains

Table 8. Who has been Florida's best governor over the last 42 years?

	Percentage
1. Reubin Askew	1.4
2. Bob Graham	14.8
3. Bob Martinez	2.8
4. Lawton Chiles	9.7
5. Jeb Bush	34.4
6. Charlie Crist	12.2
7. Rick Scott	4.6
8. Don't Know	15.4
9. No Answer	4.7
Total	100.0

Source: University of North Florida public opinion survey of 790 Florida voters, October 2, 2012.

a notable achievement in state governance. It is also a notable achievement for the conservative movement, because Bush showed that conservatives could do more than offer tax cuts; they could also change government in fundamental ways.

Jeb Bush remains a prominent figure in the eyes of Floridians. As table 8 indicates, in a poll conducted in 2012, Florida voters rated Bush the clear choice as Florida's best governor since 1970. The poll, taken during the 2012 presidential election season by the University of North Florida, shows Bush to be the plurality choice of voters by a good 2–1 margin over the next most popular choice, former Democratic governor and U.S. senator Bob Graham. Bush gets nearly three times the support of the former Republican governor turned Democrat Charlie Crist (who is running again in 2014 as a Democrat). The current Republican governor Rick Scott gets only 5 percent of the responses as best governor.[4]

In his time as former governor, Bush has used this reservoir of goodwill as a springboard to a new life that combines business interests and policy leadership. Bush's public record is so large that he remains the most dominant political figure in the state with the possible exception of his protégé Marco Rubio, Florida's junior U.S. senator. As he left office, he would use the political capital that he acquired during his time as governor to make money for his family and also remain a leading conservative voice for K–12 education changes in the state and the nation.

A National Leader on Education

Governor Bush was succeeded by his attorney general, Charlie Crist. Crist had won a competitive Republican primary in 2006 by proclaiming himself a "Jeb Bush Republican" and claiming he could continue Bush's conservative legacy. When Crist won the general election in November 2006, Governor Bush said that he would back away from public life to give his successor the room to operate. Governor Bush also made it clear that he would not try to succeed his brother George W. Bush as president in 2008.

Yet he could not stay out of the political spotlight for too long. Alongside his work with several corporate boards and real estate interests, he focused his public policy attention on his signature issue from his time as Florida's governor: K–12 education. He rejoined a foundation that he had started in the 1990s, the Foundation for Florida's Future. This foundation would concentrate on maintaining the educational reforms Bush had put in place in Florida and would advocate for more change, including a renewed push for private school vouchers and expansion of online education. A year after Governor Bush left office, he moved to spread his education reform efforts nationwide. He started a second foundation, the Foundation for Excellence in Education, to be a policy and political operation that could advance his ideas of conservative educational reform. This foundation would not be merely a publicity platform for Governor Bush to advance his policies. The foundation eventually grew to nearly thirty employees with a combination of academic, political, and communication skills, continually producing policy ideas for the state of Florida and other states, and using Governor Bush and a lobbying team to advocate for these ideas with state legislators. In effect, the foundation became Governor Bush's own private Department of Education to advocate for his ideas. The foundation has been funded by a combination of individual donors, other foundations, and businesses seeking to benefit from Governor Bush's reforms, including education companies that specialize in online education and school testing. These contributions by private companies have come under criticism as a conflict of interest.[5] Most of the contributions from companies apparently sponsored conferences where state legislators and their staffs could come to hear about conservative educational reforms and also view online testing products from companies such as Pearson education. These private companies have a major financial stake in helping the foundation to push Bush's goals. For example, the Pearson company was paid nearly $250 million to administer FCAT testing in the state of Florida. Bush's efforts at fundraising for the foundation became so successful that the foundation raised more than $8 million in 2011.[6]

The foundation was not simply a speakers bureau for Governor Bush, it became a political and economic powerhouse in educational policy across the United States. Arguably, as a former governor, Jeb Bush had more success in becoming a recognized national leader in one policy area than any other former governor since Tommy Thompson of Wisconsin in the 1990s, who was known as an expert on welfare reform.

The nationwide rollout of the Foundation for Excellence in Education occurred in June 2008 in Orlando. The U.S. secretary of education in his brother's administration, Margaret Spellings, was the keynote speaker. New York mayor Michael Bloomberg and former first lady Barbara Bush also made speeches. Panels on combining technology to raise student testing scores were prominent. Bush told the conference that the educational system in America was far behind: "our education system is an eight-track system living in an iPod world." Secretary Spellings said that the testing regime that Governor Bush had started was enshrined in the federal No Child Left Behind Act. She called the high-stakes testing regime in the act both "right" and "righteous."[7]

The turnout for the kickoff of the foundation showed the political power of Jeb Bush and the potency of the education issue. Since many different sectors of society benefit from a stronger educational system, including businesses that need higher-quality workers and families that want their children to achieve economic success, the issue receives support across the American political spectrum. Bill Clinton, at the time a little-known Democratic governor, used education reforms in his state of Arkansas in the 1980s as a platform for a long-shot bid for the presidency in 1992. Jeb Bush as a former governor reveled in his reputation as a conservative reformer, and he made education his top personal and policy concern. His foundation's priorities have tremendous influence in states with Republican governors, such as Arizona and Indiana. His Foundation for Excellence in Education now grades states on whether they have implemented conservative educational reforms. The work of the foundation has gained so much attention that after Barack Obama was elected in 2008, his secretary of education, Arne Duncan, endorsed several of Jeb Bush's ideas about educational reform.[8]

Ironically, this was occurring nationally as the FCAT was coming under increasing criticism and scrutiny in the state of the Florida. In 2007, FCAT scores were miscalculated by the Florida Department of Education.[9] The FDOE was continually changing the standards by which students and schools were graded, to the point that local school districts and parents did not know how to interpret the scores. Both elected leaders and policymakers in Florida became so disenchanted with the FCAT that a new testing scheme is now being developed by American Institutes for Research under a $220 million contract.[10] Even with these changes, some type of testing will remain in Florida, and that legacy belongs to Jeb Bush. He made sure that his voice and his ideas would be heard in Florida long after he had left the governor's mansion.

Even though he is no longer governor, Bush has remained a central part of educational policymaking in Florida. In 2008, without coordination with Governor Crist's administration, Governor Bush lobbied a Budget Reform Commission in Florida to place two constitutional amendments on the state ballot. These amendments would remove several constitutional hurdles to implementing state-funded vouchers for parents of Florida's schoolchildren. The amendments were cleared by the commission to appear on the ballot in the 2008 presidential election. However, Governor Bush's old nemesis the Florida Supreme Court blocked the measures from the final ballot. Governor Bush called the ruling "heartbreaking," while the House Democratic leader hailed the ruling and said the amendments were a result of "the unseen hand of our former governor."[11]

Bush's involvement in Florida's educational system did not end with the loss on vouchers. In 2009 Bush's foundation began a strong push to end teacher tenure in K–12 education. Bush and others argued that during an economic downturn that put heavy pressure on local school districts' budgets, tenured teachers should not be protected over younger nontenured teachers. In 2010 Bush's influence in the Florida legislature reached a post-gubernatorial high when the legislature passed bills that would end teacher tenure, tie teacher promotions to test scores of students, and expand the private tuition voucher program. He also promoted an amendment to loosen class-size requirements. Bush's presence was everywhere, although he was physically invisible in the Florida legislature. One Florida columnist compared him to the Harry Potter figure Voldemort "because you can feel his presence in the room [as] his surrogates are doing the dirty work . . . and there is no Harry Potter around to match his intellect or political skills." The sitting governor at the time, Charlie Crist, had the final say with a veto pen that canceled some of Bush's initiatives, but the mere fact that Bush as a former governor had his "best legislative session" is unprecedented.[12]

Former governor Bush was able to get a Republican-led legislature to do his bidding on a number of items without having the nuisance of actually running the government. The most obvious sign that Bush remains a powerful unelected executive in the state came in 2012. The state's Board of Education filled the open state education commissioner slot with a strong ally of Jeb Bush named Tony Bennett (not the singer). Before he was hired by the state of Florida, Bennett was voted out of office as superintendent of public instruction in Indiana in 2012. In Indiana he advocated for many of former governor Bush's initiatives, including ending teacher tenure and placing heavy emphasis on high-stakes testing. The head of the teachers' union in Florida said the appointment was a victory for the "Jeb Bush educational agenda."[13] Nearly six years after he ceased to be governor of Florida, Jeb Bush was essentially able to name the executive for the policy area that has one of the largest expenditures in Florida's state budget—K–12 education. However, his handpicked leader of the Florida school system, Tony Bennett, came under heavy scrutiny and had to resign in 2013 because as superintendent in Indiana he had led the effort to change a private school's grade.

As of this writing, former governor Bush is continuing to press the legislature for conservative educational changes. One of his latest concepts is a parent trigger provision that would allow parents of public school children in schools that have low grades to vote on whether the principal and teachers can remain employed at the school. This dramatic and controversial provision would put school administrators and teachers at the mercy of parents. The legislation almost made it through the 2012 Florida state legislature, but it failed again in the 2013 legislative session. In the 2014 legislative session, Bush's ally Will Weatherford, Speaker of the Florida House, advocated for a huge increase in funding for school choice programs in Florida—more than seven years after Jeb Bush was governor.

However, even former governor Bush has found limits in pushing his agenda. The Common Core standards, the next major step in national school testing advocated by Bush, have come under heavy political pressure from some Tea Party conservatives in the state. The Common Core is a curriculum and a testing regime developed by governors and then promoted by the federal government to allow comparison of test results from state to state. It also gives national indicators of how the United States fares against international students. Governor Rick Scott announced in September 2013 that Florida would not participate in the Common Core because it would bring too much federal involvement in education.[14] Bush strongly disagreed with the decision. His support of a Common Core curriculum would bring him to direct conflict with many in the Tea Party movement. Because of this development, his national standing as educational leader may be a major source of controversy if he runs for president or is nominated as a secretary of education.

Charlie Crist, Jeb Bush, and the Tea Party

Jeb Bush remained a potent force in Florida politics after the completion of his governorship, and he found himself in the middle of an ideological fight within the state Republican Party to determine its future. His two Republican successors, Charlie Crist and Rick Scott, personify the differences in the party. Crist, who was governor from 2007 to 2011, took a decidedly more moderate approach in tone and policy as governor after eight years of Jeb Bush's aggressive leadership. Rick Scott used $73 million of his own money, and he rode a wave of conservative anger in the form of the Tea Party that was building up in the nation and in the state in 2010 to win the governor's seat. As a strong conservative who is able to put together practical political deals when necessary, Jeb Bush had to navigate the contours of the new Republican Party after the 2008 presidential election. Yet one political decision was made easy for Jeb Bush—the decision to move farther and farther away from Charlie Crist the longer Crist stayed as governor of Florida.

Governor Crist's more moderate agenda soon caught the attention of conservatives in the state and in the nation. Even though he campaigned as a Republican conservative, Charlie Crist began to call himself a "big tent" Republican who could reach out to Democrats and Independents. It was a successful political strategy in terms of public support during his first year. Most Republicans supported him because of his party identification and Democrats appreciated his outreach. His approval ratings during his first year remained in the seventies. Yet this more laid-back approach did not immediately translate into successes for his legislative agenda. He made it clear that he was not going to mandate that the legislature do his bidding. He did not see himself in the strong-governor mode that Jeb Bush had created. In a sharp turnaround from Bush's social conservatism, Charlie Crist supported state funding for stem cell research during his first legislative session. He also wanted an across-the-board pay raise for state employees. The legislature barely moved on either issue. Crist said he wasn't disappointed, "I respect their right to do it. If I get offended by everyone not doing exactly what I want to do, I would not be a very fun guy. I'm not the king. I'm just the governor." The importance of leadership characteristics cited by scholars Colburn and Scher is highlighted by the contrast between Crist and Bush. It is hard to imagine Jeb Bush during a legislative session uttering the words "I am just the governor." Bush's model of leadership had a simple premise. This episode also shows that even though Florida's governor has enhanced power under the amended state constitution, without personal leadership characteristics the Florida legislature can again take the lead. To get all that Jeb Bush wanted from the legislature, it would take a strong hand, not an affable smile. The Republican president of the Florida Senate at the time gave Crist a backhanded compliment when he said, "I don't think the word 'forceful' could be used for Charlie Crist. He generally is the nicest guy I have ever met."[15]

Crist would also have to face a strong rival in the Florida Republican Party, Marco Rubio. In the late 1990s Rubio was a little-known twenty-six-year-old Cuban American who won a West Miami City Commission seat. The night he won the seat, victorious gubernatorial candidate Jeb Bush called him to congratulate him. Since that time Bush has worked to advance Rubio's career. Most notably, he endorsed Rubio's bid to become the Speaker of the House in Florida in 2006. To burnish his conservative credentials, Rubio advocated the cancellation of all property taxes in the state. It was an idea that garnered him national attention.[16] In a state with no income tax, property taxes are a critical source of revenue for local governments. Rubio's suggested replacement was a consumption tax, but local governments fought the idea. To symbolize what Governor Bush thought of Marco Rubio, Bush gave Rubio a sword on the floor of the House and declared Rubio a "conservative warrior."[17] This relationship could take an unexpected turn if they both decide to run for president of the United States in 2016.

Crist's problems with the Florida legislature in 2007 did not cause him to change course. Crist promised action on an issue that no other Florida governor touched: climate change. With the state's hundreds of miles of coastline, climate change could have a huge impact if most scientific predictions are accurate. Crist held a two-day summit in Florida in the summer of 2007 to bring attention to the issue. He then attended a Sheryl Crow concert to underscore his focus on the issue.[18]

By the end of his second legislative session in 2008, House Speaker Rubio began to criticize Governor Crist and separate himself from Crist's agenda. Rubio had offered a large property tax cut as a main part of his leadership agenda in 2008. Governor Crist's administration never fully embraced the Rubio proposal and instead supported a tax cut package that was much less than what Rubio wanted. Crist also wanted to expand the medical coverage for uninsured children in the state. Rubio said the money was not there to do it. In 2010, when they both ran for the U.S. Senate, the Rubio-Crist rivalry would move to a much bigger stage than anyone could have imagined in 2008, and again Jeb Bush would be a key player in deciding the political futures of both men.

Charlie Crist set the stage for his own political problems in Florida in the days following the 2008 presidential election. By some accounts Crist had come close to being named John McCain's running mate. After Barack Obama's election, Crist spoke at the Republican Governors Association meeting and urged bipartisanship. He said that in Florida "we ended the tragic cycle of politicizing issues that impact real people." Was this a political slap at his predecessor Jeb Bush?[19] In any case, Charlie Crist completely misjudged the mood of the Republican Party after the loss to Barack Obama in 2008. A U.S. Senate seat from Florida unexpectedly became open, and Crist made it clear that he would run for the seat. In this climate Crist kept talking about inclusion, reaching out and forging a bipartisan consensus. But Republican voters were looking for a political warrior to take on the Obama administration, not a moderate consensus builder.

As Barack Obama entered the presidency in 2009, the Florida economy and the national economy were at the start of a severe recession. The Obama administration's answer to the recession was a massive stimulus program of nearly $800 billion. Republicans around the nation spoke out against the stimulus, but Republican (at that time) governor Charlie Crist was not among them. He made the political and policy calculation that Florida needed the stimulus money in order to balance its own budget. Otherwise the state would have to severely cut spending or raise taxes in the middle of a recession. In February 2009, President Obama came to Florida to sell the stimulus package to Florida voters. Governor Crist welcomed the president to Florida and gave him a brief hug. The visual of Governor Crist hugging President Obama would haunt Charlie Crist for the rest of his time as Florida's governor and as a candidate for the U.S. Senate.[20] Jeb Bush later called Crist's support of the stimulus package "unforgiveable," and Rubio featured "the hug" in his campaign literature to raise money from conservatives.

Crist's fortunes in 2009 did not improve. When he appointed his chief of staff, George LeMieux, to fill the U.S. Senate seat vacated by Republican Mel Martinez, the move was widely seen as using LeMieux as a placeholder until Crist himself could run for the seat in 2010. Even though Crist had a large lead in most public opinion polls in 2009 for the Senate seat, former House Speaker and Crist critic Marco Rubio announced he would challenge Crist for the Republican nomination.

All of this was occurring against the backdrop of a state and national economy in deep recession—caused by a housing crisis that hit Floridians particularly hard. When Crist took office, the unemployment rate was 3.3 percent; by 2009, the third year of his administration, it was above 10 percent. By the end of that year, Crist was in political trouble and Marco Rubio was rising in the polls. One national pollster summed up Crist's fate in the Senate race like this: "Crist may have appointed the last US Senator, but Bush has it in his hands to appoint the next one."[21] At the end of 2009, 71 percent of Florida Republicans surveyed by the polling company Schroth and Associates would rather have had Bush as governor than Charlie Crist. Among all voters, Bush was also the favorite, 46 percent to 41 percent. Crist's support was collapsing, and only an endorsement by Jeb Bush could save him. There would be no endorsement for Crist. While Bush would not publicly endorse Marco Rubio in a competitive primary, it was clear whom he favored in the 2010 Republican Senate race.

The Tea Party movement both within the state and across the nation rallied behind Marco Rubio's Senate candidacy. The movement had its stirrings during the waning days of George W. Bush's presidential administration. In late September 2008 the U.S. treasury secretary asked Congress to pass a $700 billion Troubled Asset Relief Program. The Federal Reserve and the Bush administration argued that without the program, the U.S. economy would essentially collapse. The first iteration of the legislation failed in the House of Representatives amid the outcry the bailout produced.[22] The legislation eventually passed, but fiscal conservatives across the country now had a cause to rally around. The movement would be a mixture of libertarians, fiscal conservatives, and antiestablishment Republicans. The movement gained more momentum with the election of Barack Obama and the passage of his health care reform.

Conservative U.S. senator Jim DeMint of South Carolina offered early support for Rubio, and the Club for Growth, a libertarian group, publicly backed Rubio's campaign. When Rubio appeared on the cover of the conservative publication *National Review*, his campaign gained national notice and took off.[23] Jeb Bush was caught between the establishment Republican Crist and the new Tea Party favorite Rubio.

As Crist sank in the polls, Bush and Crist drew further apart. The final act in their separation came in April 2010 when Crist vetoed a bill that would tie any public school teacher raises to student learning gains on standardized tests. The legislation was essentially written by Bush's education foundation, and the former governor had lobbied hard for the legislation. Florida's teachers' union fought a sustained campaign to defeat the bill. Governor Charlie Crist, who was then contemplating leaving the Republican Party to run as an independent in the U.S. Senate race, was courting the teachers' union for political support. When he decided to veto the Jeb-Bush-sponsored legislation, he signaled that he was completely breaking with Bush and the Republican Party. The man who was nearly the Republican vice-presidential nominee less than two years earlier would no longer be a Republican. Jeb Bush would endorse Marco Rubio for U.S. Senate soon after, and Charlie Crist would struggle for the rest of his campaign. Bush had helped to push the moderate Charlie Crist out of the Republican Party and keep him out of the U.S. Senate.

The Crist-Rubio drama had an important if unintended consequence. Crist left the governor's office open with no natural successor in place. Since Crist had left the Republican Party, he had no influence on who would succeed him as governor. On the Republican side, Bill McCollum, the Florida attorney general and former congressman, was the early favorite to win the nomination. Democratic nominee Alex

Sink was a banking executive and the chief financial officer for the state. She was seen as a real threat to return the governor's office to the Democrats for the first time in twelve years. Sink's husband, Bill McBride, had run for governor against Jeb Bush in 2002 and lost decisively. This predictable race between two cabinet members was completely scrambled when Rick Scott, a former health care executive, entered the Republican race.

Scott's campaign picked up on the Tea Party movement that was capturing the imagination of Republicans across the nation. After President Obama's election, the political movement picked up even more steam out of frustration with his domestic agenda. This aggressive agenda included a record federal stimulus bill and a health care reform bill that would make a wide variety of government-mandated changes to the health care system in the United States in order to offer medical coverage to the uninsured. Rick Scott was a natural part of the Tea Party movement. As soon as the health care legislation was proposed in 2009, he started an organization to fight the legislation from ever being implemented.

Simply put, Scott had become rich from the health care system as it was before the Affordable Care Act. As a young lawyer in Texas, he invested in a hospital chain and soon owned a network of hospitals. His hospital chain, Columbia/HCA, became controversial for its cost-cutting practices and its relentless drive for bigger profits. While Scott became enormously wealthy as a health care executive, Columbia/HCA also came under serious legal scrutiny in the 1990s. After an FBI investigation, the board of directors of HCA asked Scott to resign, and the company paid the largest fine for Medicare fraud in American history.[24] Scott was not personally charged, even though he was CEO at the time of the fraud. He left the company with a payout exceeding $300 million in stocks.

It would seem unlikely that a disgraced former executive whose company was accused of extensive Medicare fraud could be a viable candidate for governor in a state where seniors make up more than 25 percent of the vote. Yet Scott had a great deal of money and was not afraid to use it in his campaign. Because he was not well known in Florida (he had lived in the state for only seven years), he could not raise enough money from contributors, so he used his own. He spent a record $73 million on the campaign—a staggering amount even by Florida standards. In the primary, he used the nationwide momentum of the Tea Party to great effect. He blasted President Obama in commercial after commercial and said Republicans had to stand up to him. The economy in the state and the nation was still in a deep recession. The Scott campaign played commercial after commercial saying the state needed to "Get to Work."

However, Scott adopted several campaign themes in the primary that put him on a collision course with Jeb Bush. He said the Floridians wanted change in Tallahassee that was dominated by Republicans. A fundamental difference with Jeb Bush was on an issue that Bush had been a part of his whole adult life: immigration reform. Copying other Republicans across the nation, Rick Scott's campaign used the issue of immigration to further set himself up to the right of Bill McCollum and even Jeb Bush. Scott endorsed a controversial Arizona law that allowed the police to use their discretion to ask anyone they stopped for citizenship papers. Moreover, Scott wanted to make employers more accountable for hiring undocumented workers. These policies may be good politics in a Republican primary in an off-year election, but in a state like Florida they made no sense as public policy. Florida's population is 23 percent Hispanic with a wide diversity of national origins. Giving the police in Florida the discretion to ask anyone they deem suspicious for their citizenship identification would be an implementation nightmare. Moreover, making employers more liable for hiring undocumented workers would severely harm the two major industries in Florida, tourism and agriculture, both of which hire large numbers of Hispanic immigrants. The theme parks, the hotels, and other tourist venues depend upon low-cost workers to serve in restaurants and perform other maintenance functions. The Florida agriculture industry is still a major driver of the Florida economy, and it depends on seasonal workers who are mostly immigrants, many of them undocumented.

The even bigger problem that this issue brought between Scott and Bush is how the Florida Republican Party is branded. Jeb Bush has worked his whole political life to make the Republican Party more open to Hispanic voters. He was born in Texas as the number of Hispanic residents in the state dramatically increased. His father George H. W. Bush, before being elected to Congress, was a leader of the Republican Party in Texas and saw the importance of the rising Hispanic vote. Jeb Bush attended the University of Texas, with a larger Hispanic student population than most universities, and he graduated with a degree in Latin American studies. His met his wife, Columba, in Mexico on a student exchange trip. They married in 1974, which allowed her to become a U.S. citizen. Jeb Bush worked in banking in Latin America for a short time before he returned to help his father in his 1980 presidential campaign.

After his father became vice president, Jeb Bush moved his family to Florida. They did not settle in the conservative northern part of the state; instead he brought his family to cosmopolitan Miami with its high Cuban and other Latin population. Bush partnered with a Cuban American in business and served under the first Hispanic governor in Florida history as commerce secretary. During his political career, outreach to Hispanics was a crucial part of his strategy. In his two victories, he won the both the Cuban and the non-Cuban Hispanic vote in the state. He also helped his brother win the Hispanic vote in close Florida elections in 2000 and 2004. He was a leading voice on immigration reform in his party long before others in the party paid attention to the issue.

Accordingly, Bush did not support Scott in the primary. Yet with a low turnout in a midterm primary and Scott's millions of dollars in television ads, Scott beat Bill McCollum for the Republican nomination. It was a rare defeat for Jeb Bush. The candidates he endorsed in the state usually won their elections. After the primary, Jeb Bush did endorse Rick Scott in the general election in Florida in 2010. He called him a principled conservative. However, they were not close personally or politically.

Bush's first doubts about Governor Scott may prove to be correct. As of this writing, Governor Scott is struggling politically. He presented his first budget in front of a Tea Party crowd in Eustis, Florida, to much statewide criticism. The budget slashed education spending in the state. He came to regret this first budget, because he then was branded as anti-education. When observers commented that he moved too far to the right, he tried to move back to the middle ground. Two years later he endorsed an across-the-board pay raise for teachers in the state without regard to their performance and student achievement. This violated a core principle of Jeb Bush's education reforms—tying raises for teachers to student performance. In 2013, after President Obama's reelection, Scott shocked the Republican Party in Florida by agreeing to expand Medicaid as part of the Obama administration's Affordable Care Act. This was a huge turnaround for Scott, who had entered the political realm to fight the Obamacare legislation. Jeb Bush opposed the Medicaid expansion and told state legislators that they should oppose it as well. Many Republican legislators followed Bush's lead. Scott had ridden a wave of voter anger to the Florida governor's office. However, when he got there, he soon found out that it was not wise to cross Jeb Bush in Florida politics.

Jeb Bush's Future: White House or Party Elder?

As of this writing in 2014, Jeb Bush is actively considering running for president in 2016. In a host of interviews in 2013 during a book tour, Bush made it clear he had not ruled out the possibility. One of his long-time aides said he will "seriously think about it."[25] These comments made news because, ever since his time as Florida's governor, he had said no to a possible presidential bid. Why would Jeb Bush consider this?

First, Jeb Bush has a political pedigree that no other American has ever possessed. He has been a successful two-term governor of a state that Republicans need in order to win the presidency but have lost in the last two presidential elections. He has unprecedented name recognition as the son of a former president and brother of a former president. He would be able to raise the money for a presidential run from both his own sources and his family's political connections. He is a recognized leader on education reform—an issue area that can cut across party and ideological lines like few others. He is a longtime advocate for his party to reach out to Hispanics and embrace immigration reform. Even though, during his 2013 tour for his book about immigration reform, he muddled his message on whether he would

Table 9. (Among Hispanic voters in Florida): Who has been Florida's best governor over the last 42 years?

	Percentage
1. Reubin Askew	0.8
2. Bob Graham	8.5
3. Bob Martinez	10.1
4. Lawton Chiles	5.4
5. Jeb Bush	32.6
6. Charlie Crist	9.3
7. Rick Scott	6.2
8. Don't Know	20.2
9. No Answer	7.0
Total	100.1[a]

Source: University of North Florida public opinion survey, October 2, 2012, subsample of 129 Hispanic voters.

Note: a. Total diverges from 100.0 owing to rounding.

support a path to citizenship, he still remains a leader in the party on the issue. Moreover, his broader appeal to Hispanics is real in the state of Florida. In a poll taken by the University of North Florida during the 2012 presidential race (table 9), among Hispanics in the state Jeb Bush was the choice for the state's best governor in the state since 1970—even decisively beating out Republican Bob Martinez, the first Hispanic governor in state history! This Spanish-speaking governor with a wife who is a Mexican immigrant would appeal to Hispanic voters in a way other Republican candidates, with the exception of Senator Marco Rubio and possibly Senator Ted Cruz of Texas, cannot. This is a priority for a party that lost the Hispanic vote nationwide by 40 percentage points.

Of course, his family political lineage also brings many negatives. His father lost reelection. His brother George left office in the middle of an unpopular war in Iraq and at the beginning of the worst recession since World War II. Moreover, even though Jeb Bush has a solidly conservative record as governor, his brother's policy on assisting the financial institutions during the last months of his presidency in 2008 helped to begin the Tea Party movement. The movement, which started when the Wall Street bailouts were passed in 2008, is staunchly antigovernment. This fact puts Bush in a difficult place with the movement, because he has practiced government activism in the areas of education reform and economic incentives for businesses. He also spoke out against the federal government shutdown in 2013 begun by Tea Party Republicans. Moreover, many Tea Party adherents do not like political veterans and certainly do not like political dynasties. Bush most recently clashed with Tea Party activists over the Common Core standards for education. Bush and his foundation have been pushing for these standards to be adopted in the state. Although they were endorsed by a national organization of governors, Tea Party groups see the Common Core standards as federal intrusion into local education. Mark Meckler, president of a national Tea Party group, said that Bush's support for these standards is problematic for any future political plans, as "the Common Core issue will probably be a deal killer for the tea party at large."[26]

Yet Bush has not totally distanced himself from the movement. He helped to start the political career of Senator Rubio, who became a Tea Party stalwart. He has strongly supported Tea Party governors such as Paul LePage in Maine.[27] He also maintained contacts with Tea Party groups during the immigration reform debate in 2013 even though he disagreed with most of their views on the issue.[28] These meetings may have caused him to soften his support for citizenship for undocumented workers.

However, a Tea Party candidate did not win the Republican presidential nomination in 2012, which went to Mitt Romney. Many potential candidates including Senators Ted Cruz of Texas, Rand Paul of Kentucky, and Marco Rubio of Florida could split the Tea Party vote if they decided to run for the White House in 2016, leaving an opening for a more establishment candidate like Jeb Bush. Wall Street Republicans and other traditional Republican financial donors have been encouraging him to run.

Yet, after dominating Florida politics, does he want to submit himself to the criticism and attacks from the left and the right that come with a presidential campaign? His wife, Columba, is said not to enjoy political campaigning. His daughter, Noelle, had a well-publicized struggle with drug addiction during his years as governor. Moreover,

Jeb Bush likes to control his message and surroundings. The unpredictability and chaos of a national presidential campaign may prove to be too uninviting for another member of the Bush family to run. His mother, Barbara, has openly encouraged him *not* to run. He will decide sometime close to the November 2014 midterm elections.

Agree with him or not, as governor and former governor, Jeb Bush changed Florida. The state surged to the forefront of the conservative educational reform movement. Social issues that most politicians had shied away from became normal parts of the legislative process under Jeb Bush. Bush also implemented record tax cuts, privatized a good portion of state government, and gave large incentives to private businesses. The question now becomes: Will Jeb Bush try to change America?

Acknowledgments

First I would like to thank the four reviewers who read this work and offered important guidance. In particular Martin Dyckman and Aubrey Jewett performed multiple thorough reviews and helped to bring this book from concept to printed reality. Of course, all errors are my responsibility.

Thanks are due also to the professionals of the Florida press corps, whose observations and writings during Governor Bush's two terms were invaluable, and to my fellow scholars who have written about Florida politics and gubernatorial politics.

Abundant appreciation goes to Meredith Babb and the professionals at the University Press of Florida. Meredith is a patient but firm editor who has taken a benign interest in my work and career.

Thanks go too to Michael Binder and the students in the Public Opinion Laboratory at the University of North Florida. Collecting survey data is a challenging endeavor these days, and they do it very well.

I owe a great debt to Dean Barbara Hetrick and my departmental colleagues at UNF for their support as I completed this research while also serving as department chair. Our office professionals in the department, Magdeline Steinbrecher and Wendy Rahman, assisted greatly in preparing the manuscript.

My wife, Mary, has endured countless weekends and nights without my help at home. I thank her for her love and support.

Finally, it is appropriate to thank former governor Jeb Bush. While he declined to be interviewed for this work, he has had a political career in Florida that is worth examining—a claim not all former elected officials can make.

Notes

Chapter 1. Introduction

1. Mary Jo Melone, "In English and Spanish, Bush Spoke Over the Gale," *St. Petersburg Times*, September 29, 2004.

2. Jamie Dettmer, "In Hurricanes' Wake, Jeb Bush Is Seen as a Powerful Asset for His Brother," *New York Sun*, October 18, 2004.

3. "Gubernatorial Power: The Institutional Power Ratings for the 50 Governors of the United States," website of Professor Thad Beyle, http://www.unc.edu/~beyle/gubnewpwr.html.

4. Jerome Stockfisch, "The Jeb Bush Legacy," *Tampa Tribune*, January 1, 2007.

Chapter 2. Gubernatorial Power in Florida History

1. Schafer, "U.S. Territory and State," 207.

2. S. V. Dáte also made this comparison.

3. Colburn and Scher, *Florida's Gubernatorial Politics*.

4. Schafer, "U.S. Territory and State," 212, 216, 222.

5. Meacham, *American Lion*, 52–53.

6. Schafer, "U.S. Territory and State," 220.

7. Ibid., 245.

8. C. Brown, "The Civil War," 231, 234, 239, 244, 245.

9. Shofner, "Reconstruction and Renewal," 255.

10. Ibid., 262.

11. Colburn and Scher, *Florida's Gubernatorial Politics*, 101–5.

12. Pavlovsky, "'We Busted Because We Failed.'"

13. Ibid., 5.

14. Dyckman, *Floridian of His Century*, 29.

15. Proctor, "Prelude to the New Florida," 275.

16. Colburn and Scher, *Florida's Gubernatorial Politics*, 33.

17. Ibid., 278.

18. Sabato, *Goodbye to Good-time Charlie*; Beyle and Muchmore, *Being Governor*.

19. Proctor, "Prelude to the New Florida," 270.

20. Bramson, *Miami: The Magic City*.

21. Rogers, "Fortune and Misfortune," 291.

22. Ibid., 294.

23. Ibid., 291.

24. Dunn, "New Deal and Florida Politics," 5.

25. Ibid., 37.

26. Ibid., 45.

27. Rogers, "Great Depression," 305.

28. Dunn, "New Deal and Florida Politics," 123, 145–49, 258.

29. Colburn and Scher, *Florida's Gubernatorial Politics*, 356.

30. Dyckman, *Floridian of His Century*, 70.

31. Ibid., 80.

32. Colburn, *From Yellow Dog*, 32.

33. Dyckman, *Floridian of His Century*, 98.

34. Ibid., 114.

35. Carter, *The Politics of Rage*.

36. Colburn, *From Yellow Dog*, 33–34, 37.

37. Kernell, *Going Public*.

38. Colburn, *From Yellow Dog*, 52–53, 54, 59.

39. Ibid., 60.

40. Gannon, *Florida: A Short History*, 134.

41. Colburn and Scher, *Florida's Gubernatorial Politics*, 112.

42. Ibid., 111.

43. Colburn, *From Yellow Dog*, 70.

44. Ibid., 72.

45. Ibid., 91.

46. Dyckman, *Reubin O'D. Askew and the Golden Age of Florida Politics*.

47. Colburn, *From Yellow Dog*, 107.

Chapter 3. The Conservative Movement and Jeb Bush

1. Parmet, *George Bush*, 19.
2. Allitt, *The Conservatives*, 2.
3. Bowen, *Miracle at Philadelphia*, 304.
4. Ibid., 67.
5. Oakes, *The Radical and the Republican*, 108.
6. Ibid.
7. Gould, *Grand Old Party*, 29.
8. Bush and Yablonski, *Profiles in Character*, 173.
9. Leuchtenburg, *Roosevelt and the New Deal*, 11; also 15, 19, 20, 36, for this and the following two paragraphs.
10. Ibid., 41–166 passim.
11. Cardozier, *Mobilization*, 3, 104, 129.
12. Edwards, *The Conservative Revolution*, 21.
13. Allitt, *The Conservatives*, 174.
14. Buckley, "*National Review*: Statement of Intentions," 196.
15. Allitt, *The Conservatives*, 170.
16. Friedman, *There's No Such Thing as a Free Lunch*, 6.
17. Ibid.
18. Bush and Bolick, *Immigration Wars*, 74.
19. Allitt, *The Conservatives*, 188.
20. Goldwater, *Conscience of a Conservative*, in Schneider, *Conservatism in America*, 211 (Eisenhower quote), 213.
21. Middendorf, *A Glorious Disaster*, 59.
22. Ibid., 131.
23. Ibid., 138.
24. Edwards, *The Conservative Revolution*, 132.
25. Corrigan, *American Royalty*, 58.
26. Ibid., 59.
27. Black and Black, *Politics and Society in the South*, 215.
28. Ibid., 216.
29. Boller, *Presidential Campaigns*, 358.
30. Parmet, *George Bush*, 233.
31. Crew, *Jeb Bush*, 7.
32. Ibid., 12.
33. Jodi Mailander, "Dade's First Charter School Wins OK," *St. Petersburg Times*, July 30, 1996.
34. Bush and Yablonski, *Profiles in Character*.
35. William March, "The Governor's Race: Bush vs. MacKay; Democrat Buddy

MacKay Makes His Play for the Job He Has Pondered for More Than a Decade," *Tampa Tribune*, October 18, 1998.

36. Alisa Ulferts, "Governor Gains Influence in Judge Selection," *St. Petersburg Times*, June 20, 2001.

37. Dáte, *Jeb*, 321.

38. Bush First Inaugural Address, January 4, 1999, http://lpca.us/inaugural_address%20jeb.htm.

39. Dáte, *Jeb*, 300.

40. Ibid.

Chapter 4. Jeb Bush, Culture Warrior

1. Bush and Yablonski, *Profiles in Character*.

2. Ibid., 21, 22, 33, 35, 41, 128, for this and the next three paragraphs.

3. See Corrigan, *Race, Religion, and Economic Change,* 59.

4. Department of Child and Family Studies, College of Behavioral and Community Sciences, University of South Florida, *Florida KIDS COUNT*, http://www.floridakidscount.org.

5. Andrew Coulton, "Jeb Bush's Daughter Jailed," ABC News, July 17, 2002, http://abcnews.go.com/US/story?id=91454.

6. Corrigan, *Race, Religion, and Economic Change*, 59.

7. Howell Raines, "Reagan Backs Evangelicals in Their Political Activities," *New York Times*, August 23, 1980.

8. Julie Hauserman, "Political Shift May Restrict Abortion," *St. Petersburg Times*, March 20, 1999.

9. "'Morality Agenda' Will Be Before Legislature Again," *Florida Times-Union*, February 23, 1999.

10. Beth Kassab, "Senate Panel OKs 'Choose Life': Plate 'Adopt a Child' Alternative Defeated," *Florida Times-Union*, March 18, 1999.

11. Antigone Barton and John Pacenti, "Judge Says 'Choose Life' Plates Can Stay on Cars," *Palm Beach Post*, June 9, 2001.

12. Diane Rado, "Judge Blocks State on Abortion," *St. Petersburg Times*, July 27, 1999.

13. Jackie Hallifax, "Gov. Bush Signs Florida Bill Requiring Parents Be Told of Minor Daughter's Abortion Plan," Associated Press, May 25, 2005.

14. Jo Becker, "Governor Signs Ban on 'Partial Birth' Abortions," *St. Petersburg Times*, May 26, 2000.

15. Kathleen Chapman, "DCF Out to Block Teen's Abortion," *Palm Beach Post*, April 28, 2005; Jill Barton, "Florida Judge Approves Abortion for 13-Year-Old: Gov. Bush Says No Further Appeal Planned," Associated Press, May 3, 2005.

16. Jill Barton, "ACLU Appeals State Decision Barring Abortion for 13-Year-Old," Associated Press, April 27, 2005.

17. Russ Bynum, "Gov. Jeb Bush Strikes Moral Tone at Ga. Republican Convention," Associated Press, May 7, 2005.

18. Alan Gomez, "After 5 years, Criticism of 10-20-Life Continues," *Palm Beach Post*, February 23, 2004.

19. "Concealed Gun Rights Expanded," *St. Petersburg Times*, April 21, 1999.

20. Martin Dyckman, "The NRA's Investment Pays Off," *St. Petersburg Times*, April 8, 1999.

21. See note 19.

22. David Royse, "Bush Signs Bills Nixing Gun Range Lawsuits and Gun Owner Lists," Associated Press, May 13, 2004.

23. David Royse, "Bill Allowing People to 'Meet Force with Force' Heads to Governor," Associated Press, April 5, 2005.

24. Jacqui Goddard, "Florida Boosts Gun Rights, Igniting a Debate," *Christian Science Monitor*, May 10, 2005.

25. Alan Gomez, "Florida Democrats Support Pro-Gun Law," Cox News Service, April 5, 2005.

26. Kameel Stanley and Connie Humburg, "Many Killers Who Go Free with Florida 'Stand Your Ground Law' Have History of Violence," *Tampa Bay Times*, July 21, 2012.

27. Alex Leary, "Six NRA-Backed Bills Signed into Law by Bush," *St. Petersburg Times*, June 8, 2006.

28. Sue Anne Pressley, "Florida Plan Aims to End Race-Based Preferences," *Washington Post*, November 11, 1999.

29. Janet Marshall, "Attacks on Bush Initiative Mount: A State Senator Retracts His Support and Resigns as Chair of the Governor's Task Force; Affirmative Action," *Lakeland Ledger*, November 17, 1999.

30. "Interim UF President Predicts Bush Plan Will Drain Minority Students," Associated Press, November 23, 1999.

31. William Yardley, "Two State Legislators Sit-In in Bush's Office," *St. Petersburg Times*, January 19, 2000.

32. Paul Pinkham, "Lawtey to House Nation's First Faith-Based Prison: Critics Say Program for Inmates at the End of Their Sentences Is Unconstitutional," *Florida Times-Union*, December 6, 2003.

33. Jeff Brumley, "Governor Shepherding Faith Groups into State Service," *Florida Times-Union*, March 21, 2005.

34. *In Re: The Guardianship of Theresa Schiavo . . .*

35. *Cruzan et Ux. v. Director, Missouri Department of Health.*

36. Caplan, McCartney, and Sisti, *Case of Terri Schiavo*, 20, 71, 72. This section offers extensive explanation of Florida law.

37. Anita Kumar, "Deciding the Fate of Terri," *St. Petersburg Times*, January 25, 2000

38. Caplan, McCartney, and Sisti, *Case of Terri Schiavo*, 333.

39. William R. Levesque, "Governor Has a Suggestion in Schiavo Case," *St. Petersburg Times*, August 27, 2003.

40. Ibid.

41. Abby Goodnough, "Feeding Tube Is Removed in Florida Right-to-Die Case," *New York Times*, October 16, 2003.

42. Alisa Ulferts, William R. Levesque, and Steve Bousquet, "House Votes to Save Schiavo," *St. Petersburg Times*, October 21, 2003.

43. William R. Levesque, Lucy Morgan, Jamie Jones, and Craig Pittman, "Gov. Bush's Order Puts Schiavo Back on Fluids," *St. Petersburg Times*, October 22, 2003.

44. Ibid.

45. "Political Theater," editorial, *St. Petersburg Times*, July 11, 2002.

46. See note 43.

47. William R. Levesque, "Justices Skeptical of Bush Team's Defense of 'Terri's Law,'" *St. Petersburg Times*, September 1, 2004.

48. Dara Kam, "Bush Vows to Keep Fighting for Schiavo," Cox News Service, January 25, 2005.

49. Catholic Bishops of Florida, "Continued Concerns."

50. Larry Fish and Tom Infield, "Terri Schiavo Stay Extended by 48 Hours," *Philadelphia Inquirer*, February 24, 2005.

51. Caplan, McCartney, and Sisti, *Case of Terri Schiavo*, 124.

52. Cheshire, "Affidavit."

53. Caplan, McCartney, and Sisti, *Case of Terri Schiavo*, 125.

54. Ibid., 343.

55. Adam Nagourney, "Jeb Bush's Credentials Cohere in Schiavo Case," *New York Times*, March 26, 2005.

56. Abby Goodnough, "Schiavo Autopsy Says Brain, Withered, Was Untreatable," *New York Times*, June 16, 2005.

57. Caplan, McCartney, and Sisti, *Case of Terri Schiavo*, 345.

58. Guttmacher Institute, "Abortion."

59. Tim Stanley, "US Court Saves Mississippi's Last Abortion Clinic: But It's the Pro-Lifers Who Enjoy Political Momentum," *London Telegraph*, July 2, 2012.

60. Florida Department of Law Enforcement, "Firearm Involved Violent Crimes."

61. PolitiFact.com, "Self-Defense Deaths."

62. Scott Powers and Luis Zaragoza, "10 Years In, 'One Florida' Posts Results for Minorities at Universities," *Orlando Sentinel*, April 10, 2010.

63. Matt Sedensky, "5 years after Schiavo, Few Make End-of-Life Plans," Associated Press, March 30, 2010.

Chapter 5. Jeb Bush's Education Revolution

1. Crew, *Jeb Bush*, 7.

2. For Florida's annual state budget by program area, see http://transparency florida.gov/OBReportPA.aspx.

3. Valerie Strauss, "E-mails Link Bush Foundation, Companies and Educational Officials," *Washington Post*, January 30, 2013.

4. Reese, *America's Public Schools*, 11, 13.

5. Ibid., 22.

6. Ibid., 28. For this section, see chap. 1, "The Origins of the Common School," passim.

7. Kimbrough, Alexander, and Wattenbarger, "Government and Education," 423.

8. Cobb-Roberts and Shircliffe, "Legacy of Desegregation," 19–35.

9. Dorn and Michael, "Education Finance Reform," 56.

10. Dyckman, *Floridian of His Century*, 59, 63, 74, 94, 96.

11. U.S. Census Bureau, http://www.census.gov/prod/2002pubs/censr-4.pdf.

12. Florida Department of Education, 2002, http://schoolgrades.fldoe.org/pdf/0203/158clp-combined.pdf.

13. Eitle, "Diversity, Desegregation, and Accountability," 123.

14. Kit Troyer and Stephen Hegarty, "Florida's First Charter Schools May Open in Fall," *St. Petersburg Times*, May 1, 1996.

15. Schweizer and Schweizer, *The Bushes*, 454.

16. Jodi Mailander, "Dade's First Charter School Wins OK," *Miami Herald*, July 30, 1996.

17. Bill Maxwell, "Bush and the Black Activist," *St. Petersburg Times*, October 26, 1997.

18. Borman and Dorn, *Education Reform in Florida*, 3.

19. Shelby Oppel, "Bush Signs Law Abolishing Board of Regents," *St. Petersburg Times*, June 20, 2000.

20. Jacqueline Charles, "Grading of Schools Opposed," *Miami Herald*, December 9, 1998.

21. Diane Rado, "Graduate Rate Dismays Top Leaders," *St. Petersburg Times*, February 10, 1999.

22. Ibid.

23. Sonya Ross, "Clinton Pushes Education Reform," Associated Press, February 22, 1999.

24. Jackie Hallifax, "Bush's $46.8 Billion Budget Plan Has It All: Tax Cuts, Spending Increases," Associated Press, February 2, 1999.

25. S. V. Dáte, "House Passes School Voucher Plan: Approval Predicted Today in Senate," *Palm Beach Post*, April 29, 1999.

26. Marilyn Brown, "Educators Question How A+ Will Work," *Tampa Tribune*, May 2, 1999.

27. Alan Judd, "Will A-Plus Pass the Test? Bush's Plan Gets Tough on Schools," *Sarasota Herald-Tribune*, February 28, 1999.

28. Analisa Nazareno, "Tests Keep Schools on Edge," *Miami Herald*, February 14, 2000.

29. Walter Shapiro, "Florida School Plan Watched Closely," *USA Today*, March 17, 2000.

30. Sarah Schweitzer, "Grade-D Schools Winning Notice," *St. Petersburg Times*, April 15, 2000.

31. Ibid.

32. Michael and Dorn, "Accountability," 103.

33. See note 32.

34. Henig and Sugarman, "Nature and Extent of School Choice," 14.

35. Ibid.

36. Tonyaa Weathersbee, "Budget Cuts Threaten School Equality," *Florida Times-Union*, August 2, 2011.

37. Walberg, *School Choice: The Findings*, 21.

38. Jo Becker, "Bush's Liberty City Charter School Scores a D: A Spokesman for the Governor, Who Is No Longer Directly Connected to the School, Says the Grade Isn't Unexpected." *St. Petersburg Times*, June 26, 1999.

39. "Jeb's School Could Close," Gradebook (education blog), *St. Petersburg Times*, March 12, 2008.

40. John O'Connor, "From Minnesota to Miami: The History of Florida Charter Schools," NPR, StateImpact Florida, September 28, 2011, http://stateimpact. npr.org/florida/2011/09/28/.

41. Bulman and Kirp, "Shifting Politics of School Choice," 38, 42, 44, 48.

42. Sugarman, "School Choice and Public Funding," 128.

43. Choper, "Federal Constitutional Issues," 236.

44. Henig and Sugarman, "Nature and Extent of School Choice," 25.

45. Mike Clary, "Judge Rules Florida School Vouchers Unconstitutional," *Los Angeles Times*, March 15, 2000.

46. Bill Kaczor, "Fla. Court Strikes Down School Vouchers," Associated Press, January 5, 2006.

47. Florida Department of Education, "School Choice," http://www.florida schoolchoice.org, as in table 5.1.

48. Martin A. Dyckman, "Disabled Students Can't Work Within Demands of FCAT," *St. Petersburg Times*, January 5, 2003.

49. Stephen Hegarty, "Backlash May Be Looming on State's School Reforms," *St. Petersburg Times*, April 14, 2003.

50. Ibid.

51. Melanie Ave, "Journal of an F Year," *St. Petersburg Times*, August 24, 2003.

52. Adam Emerson, "About 250 Local Schools Bag Bonuses," *Tampa Tribune*, September 1, 2005.

53. Bill Kaczor, "Bush Leaves Tumultuous Mark on Florida's Schools," Associated Press, December 14, 2006.

54. OPPAGA, *Third Grade Retention Policy*, 3.

55. Florida Department of Education, "Governor Bush and Lt. Governor Jennings Announce New Middle and High School Reform Measures."

56. Beth Kormanik, "State, Feds Differ on the Tale of the FCAT; A School Can Meet Florida's Standards and Fail Under No Child Left Behind Provisions," *Florida Times-Union*, June 17, 2004.

57. Greene and Winters, "Public School Graduation Rates,"

58. *Education Week*, "Diplomas Count 2011."

59. Florida Department of Education, "Florida's Federal High School Graduation Rates and Dropout Rates, 2011–12."

60. CBS Miami, "Florida ACT Scores Better Than 2011, But Still Lag Behind Nation," August 23, 2012.

61. Florida Department of Education, *ACT Trends*.

62. OPPAGA, *Half of College Students Needing Remediation Drop Out*.

63. Matt Coleman, "Too Many Duval Students Not College-Ready," *Florida Times-Union*, June 4, 2010.

64. Quinnipiac University, "Florida Voters Give Gov. Bush a 'C' Grade."

65. Thomas C. Tobin, "Most Voters Dislike FCAT Use," *Tampa Bay Times*, October 30, 2006.

66. Lloyd Dunkelberger, "Survey Reveals FCAT Discontent; 80 Percent of School Leaders Asked Say Test Should Not Be Used to Give Bonus Money; Changes Wanted," *Lakeland Ledger*, February 3, 2006.

67. Mike Gimignani and Raquel Manning, "Education on Minds of State Voters: In a Statewide Poll, 27 Percent Named It as Florida's Most Immediate Issue," *Florida Times-Union*, March 5, 2006.

Chapter 6. Jeb Bush versus State Government

1. Mark Hollis, "Bush Proposes $1.2 Billion in Tax Cuts: Both Parties Say the Plan Would Offer Relief to Individuals and Businesses," *Lakeland Ledger*, January 28, 1999.

2. Charles Elmore, "Floridians Could Get $96 Back in Tax Cut," *Palm Beach Post*, January 28, 1999.

3. Mary Ellen Klas, "Battle for Bucks," *Palm Beach Post*, March 1, 1999.

4. Tim Nickens, "In State of State Address, Bush Is Clearly Bush," *St. Petersburg Times*, March 3, 1999.

5. Ryan Thornburg, "Governors Use Line-Item Vetos to Cut Budgets," *Washington Post*, May 28, 1999.

6. Ibid.

7. Susan Spencer-Wendel, "Businesses in State Asked, and Received: Lobbyists Hail Legislative Session as 'Best Ever' for Commercial Interests," *Palm Beach Post*, May 2, 1999.

8. Linda Kleindienst, "The Jeb Bush Era Ends in Florida: Outgoing Governor Did Things His Way," *South Florida Sentinel*, January 7, 2007.

9. "As His Spending Went Up, Bush's Grade Dropped," *St. Petersburg Times*, December 14, 2006.

10. See note 8.

11. Stephen Hegarty and Steve Bousquet, "Bush Peppered on School Spending," *St. Petersburg Times*, February 19, 2002.

12. William Yardley and Stephen Hegarty, "Bush Plans Rewards for Standout Teachers," *St. Petersburg Times*, January 12, 2000.

13. Jim Stratton, "10 Years after 9-11, Central Florida Leans Heavily on Tourism," *Orlando Sentinel*, September 10, 2011.

14. Lloyd Dunkelberger, "Deal Reached on $1 billion in Budget Cuts: A Budget Bill Will Be Printed by Today and Voted on Thursday," *Lakeland Ledger*, December 3, 2001.

15. Ibid.

16. Kyle Parks, "Florida Bill Sets Aside Big Bucks to Lure Businesses," *St. Petersburg Times*, April 10, 1999.

17. John Hielscher, "Sarasota Not Sweet on Outcome: In the End, the Demands—Including Impact Fee Exemptions and Favorable Water and Sewer Rates—Were Too High for City and County Leaders," *Sarasota Herald-Tribune*, August 14, 1999.

18. Stephen Pounds, "Pratt Rocket Engines Stay in Palm Beach County: Decision Not to Move to Mississippi Keeps 800 Jobs, May Cost State, County $510,000 in Incentives," *Palm Beach Post*, December 22, 1999.

19. Lucy Morgan, Steve Bousquet, and Alisa Ulferts, "The Florida Experiment: Testing Bush's Theory," *St. Petersburg Times*, October 19, 2003.

20. Ibid.

21. Guy Boulton, "Some Doubt Scripps Deal Job Outlook," *Tampa Tribune*, October 22, 2003.

22. See note 19.

23. Mike Salinero, "Senator Says Bush Misled Lawmakers on Biomed Benefit," *Tampa Tribune*, October 22, 2005.

24. "Groups Sue over Proposed Site of Palm Beach County, Florida Biotech Park," *South Florida Sentinel*, November 23, 2004.

25. Robert Trigaux, "Will Scripps' Bang Match Our Bucks?" *St. Petersburg Times*, February 2, 2005.

26. Lilly Rockwell, "Scripps Research Institute: Scientific Discoveries? Yes. Jobs? Not So Much," News Service of Florida, December 7, 2011.

27. Robert Trigaux, "Can State Learn a Better Way to Grow?" *Tampa Bay Times*, May 26, 2012.

28. http://www.scripps.edu/florida/about/facts.html.

29. Louise Story, "As Companies Seek Tax Deals, Governments Pay High Price," *New York Times*, December 1, 2012.

30. Ibid.

31. Alisa Ulferts, "Bush Gains More Power to Hire, Fire State Workers," *St. Petersburg Times*, May 15, 2001.

32. Ryan Davis, "Shift to Privatized Foster Care Delayed," *St. Petersburg Times*, November 16, 2000.

33. Elizabeth Bettendorf, "Florida's Social Services Localized," *Tampa Tribune*, January 10, 2000.

34. Joni James, "Bush's Privatization Legacy," *St. Petersburg Times*, December 29, 2006.

35. David Wasson, "Governor Leads Privatization Push," *Tampa Tribune*, February 25, 2001.

36. Joni James, "Debut of Privatized Payroll System Ugly," *St. Petersburg Times*, November 11, 2004.

37. Thomas C. Tobin, "Prison Food Costs Less, but at a Price," *St. Petersburg Times*, June 17, 2002.

38. Joe Follick, "State-Funded Counsel for Death Row Reviewed," *Tampa Tribune*, March 28, 2003.

39. Randolph Pendleton, "Hundreds Protest Bush's Plan to Move State Library," Associated Press, March 4, 2003.

40. Alisa Ulferts, "Gov. Bush Proposes Medicaid Revamp," *St. Petersburg Times*, January 12, 2005.

41. Mark Hollis, "Governor's Clout Grows and Grows," *Sun Sentinel*, May 28, 2001.

42. Joni James, "Free Market Fever," *St. Petersburg Times*, February 22, 2004.

43. Crew, *Jeb Bush*, 120–22.

44. "Critics Put Florida's Child Welfare System Under Microscope," News Service of Florida, September 25, 2013.

45. David Bauerlein, "Bush Signs Florida Forever," *Florida Times-Union*, June 8, 1999.

46. Grunwald, *The Swamp*, 2, 3, 330.

47. Grunwald, "Postcard from the Everglades."

Chapter 7. The Shadow Governor—and Maybe More?

1. Steve Bousquet, "Noticeably Absent from Mitt Romney's Florida Campaign: Gov. Rick Scott," *Tampa Bay Times*, November 1, 2012.

2. Frank Cerabino, "Executive Power: Jeb Bush's Assertive Style Has Earned Him a Love-Hate Place in Floridians' Hearts," *Palm Beach Post*, December 24, 2006.

3. Lloyd Dunkelberger, "Jeb Bush Leaves Behind Record of Forcefulness: Ambitious Governor's Aggressive Style Reshaped Role of Florida's Chief Executive," *Sarasota Herald-Tribune*, December 24, 2006.

4. Statewide poll taken in the University of North Florida Public Opinion Lab, October 4–12, 2012.

5. William March, "Jeb Bush's Education Foundation under Fire for Lobbying for Laws That Benefit Corporate Donors," *Tampa Tribune*, March 3, 2013.

6. Beckel, "Jeb Bush's Education Nonprofit Rakes in Cash."

7. Ron Matus, "Bush: Education System 8-Track in an iPod World," *St. Petersburg Times*, June 20, 2008.

8. John D. Podesta, "How Obama Got It Right on School Reform," *Washington Post*, August 20, 2010.

9. "FCAT Mistakes Go Beyond Score," *St. Petersburg Times*, May 30, 2007.

10. Brandon Larrabee, "State Adds New Test to Replace FCAT," News Service of Florida, March 18, 2014.

11. Gary Fineout, "Court Blocks Florida Ballot Measures Intended to Help School Vouchers," *New York Times*, September 4, 2008.

12. See note 7.

13. Jeffrey S. Solochek, "Former Indiana Superintendent Is Florida's New Education Commissioner," *Tampa Bay Times*, December 12, 2012.

14. Gary Fineout, "Gov. Scott Makes Changes to Common Core Plan." Associated Press, September 23, 2013.

15. Steve Bousquet, "Crist Agenda Takes a Hit," *St. Petersburg Times*, May 6, 2007.

16. Alex Leary, "Rubio's Style Is Dream Big," *St. Petersburg Times*, October 10, 2010.

17. Adam C. Smith, "Ex-Gov. Bush Key to Crist's Senate Odds," *St. Petersburg Times*, November 2, 2009.

18. Craig Pittman and David Adams, "How Gov. Crist Became Gov. Climate," *St. Petersburg Times*, July 21, 2007.

19. Steve Bousquet, "Crist Calls Florida a Model for the Future of the GOP," *St. Petersburg Times*, November 11, 2008. Political reporter Steve Bousquet first highlighted this comparison.

20. Steve Bousquet and Marc Caputo, "For Gov. Charlie Crist, A Battered Image and Uncertain Future," *St. Petersburg Times*, December 31, 2009.

21. See note 18.

22. Armey and Kibbe, *Give Us Liberty*.

23. Libby, *Purging the Republican Party*, 113.

24. PolitiFact.com, "Mitt Romney and Rick Scott."

25. Peter Wallsten and David Nakamura, "Jeb Bush Is Back in the Spotlight—and Thinking about 2016," *Washington Post*, March 6, 2013.

26. Jamie Weinstein, "Jeb Bush's Tea Party Problem," *Daily Caller*, March 3, 2013.

27. Miller, "Turning LePage."

28. Tarini Parti, "Jeb Bush Met with Tea Party on Immigration," *Politico*, May 17, 2013.

References

Allitt, Patrick. *The Conservatives: Ideas and Personalities Throughout American History*. New Haven, Conn.: Yale University Press, 2009.

Armey, Dick, and Matt Kibbe. *Give Us Liberty: A Tea Party Manifesto*. New York: William Morrow, 2010.

Beckel, Michael. "Jeb Bush's Education Nonprofit Rakes in Cash." Center for Public Integrity, March 7, 2013. http://www.publicintegrity.org/2013/03/07 /12284/jeb-bushs-education-nonprofit-rakes-cash.

Beyle, Thad L., and Lynn R. Muchmore. *Being Governor: The View from the Office*. Durham, N.C.: Duke University Press, 1983.

Black, Earl, and Merle Black. *Politics and Society in the South*. Cambridge, Mass.: Harvard University Press, 1987.

Boller, Paul F., Jr. *Presidential Campaigns: From George Washington to George W. Bush*. New York: Oxford University Press, 2004.

Borman, Kathryn M., and Sherman Dorn, eds. *Education Reform in Florida*. Albany: State University of New York Press, 2007.

Bowen, Catherine Drinker. *Miracle at Philadelphia: The Story of the Constitutional Convention, May to September 1787*. Boston: Little, Brown, 1966.

Bramson, Seth H. *Miami: The Magic City*. Charleston, S.C.: Arcadia, 2007.

Brown, Canter, Jr. "The Civil War, 1861–1865." In Gannon, *New History of Florida*, 231–48.

Buckley, William F., Jr. "*National Review*: Statement of Intentions." In Schneider, *Conservatism in America*, 195–200.

Bulman, Robert C., and David L. Kirp. "The Shifting Politics of School Choice." In Sugarman and Kemerer, *School Choice and Social Controversy*, 36–67.

Bush, Jeb, and Clint Bolick. *Immigration Wars: Forging an American Solution*. New York: Threshold, 2013.

Bush, Jeb, and Brian Yablonski. *Profiles in Character*. Miami: Foundation for Florida's Future, 1995.

Caplan, Arthur L., James J. McCartney, and Dominic A. Sisti, eds. *The Case of Terri Schiavo: Ethics at the End of Life*. Amherst, N.Y.: Prometheus, 2006.

Cardozier, V. R. *The Mobilization of the United States in World War II: How the Government, Military and Industry Prepared for War*. Jefferson, N.C.: McFarland, 1995.

Carter, Dan T. *The Politics of Rage: George Wallace, the Origins of the New Conservatism, and the Transformation of American Politics*. 2nd ed. Baton Rouge: Louisiana State University Press, 2000.

Catholic Bishops of Florida. "Continued Concerns for Terri Schiavo." In Caplan, McCartney, and Sisti, *Case of Terri Schiavo*, 96–97.

Cheshire, William P. "Affidavit." In Caplan, McCartney, and Sisti, *Case of Terri Schiavo*, 163–71.

Choper, Jesse H. "Federal Constitutional Issues." In Sugarman and Kemerer, *School Choice and Social Controversy*, 235–65.

Chubb, John E., and Terry M. Moe. *Politics, Markets, and America's Schools*. Washington, D.C.: Brookings Institution, 1990.

Cobb-Roberts, Deirdre, and Barbara Shircliffe. "The Legacy of Desegregation in Florida." In Borman and Dorn, *Education Reform in Florida*, 19–52.

Colburn, David R. *From Yellow Dog Democrats to Red State Republicans: Florida and Its Politics since 1940*. Gainesville: University Press of Florida, 2007.

Colburn, David R., and Richard K. Scher. *Florida's Gubernatorial Politics in the Twentieth Century*. Tallahassee: University Presses of Florida, 1980.

Corrigan, Matthew T. *American Royalty: The Bush and Clinton Families and the Danger to the American Presidency*. New York: Palgrave Macmillan, 2008.

———. *Race, Religion, and Economic Change in the Republican South: A Study of a Southern City*. Gainesville: University Press of Florida, 2007.

Crew, Robert E., Jr. *Jeb Bush: Aggressive Conservatism in Florida*. Lanham, Md.: University Press of America, 2010.

Cruzan et Ux. v. Director, Missouri Department of Health, et al. In Caplan, McCartney, and Sisti, *Case of Terri Schiavo*, 43–54.

Dáte, S. V. *Jeb: America's Next Bush*. New York: Penguin, 2007.

Dorn, Sherman, and Deanna L. Michael. "Education Finance Reform in Florida." In Borman and Dorn, *Education Reform in Florida*, 53–82.

Dunn, William James. "The New Deal and Florida Politics." Ph.D. diss., Florida State University, 1971.

Dyckman, Martin A. *Floridian of His Century: The Courage of Governor LeRoy Collins*. Gainesville: University Press of Florida, 2006.

————. *Reubin O'D. Askew and the Golden Age of Florida Politics*. Gainesville: University Press of Florida, 2011.

Education Week. "Diplomas Count: National Graduation Rate Rebounds; 1.2 Million Students Still Fail to Earn Diplomas; Report Investigates Options Between Diploma and Four-Year Degree; Explores Multiple Pathways to College and Career." June 7, 2011. http://www.edweek.org/media/diplomas count2011_pressrelease.pdf.

Edwards, Lee. *The Conservative Revolution: The Movement That Remade America*. New York: Free Press, 1999.

Eitle, Tamela McNulty. "Diversity, Desegregation, and Accountability in Florida Districts." In Borman and Dorn, *Education Reform in Florida*, 117–52.

Florida Department of Education. *ACT Trends: Florida and the Nation*. August 2009. http://www.fldoe.org/evaluation/pdf/ACT2009.pdf.

————. "Florida's Federal High School Graduation Rates and Dropout Rates, 2011–12." Data report, November 2012. http://www.fldoe.org/eias/eiaspubs/word/FedGradRate_1112.doc.

————. "Governor Bush and Lt. Governor Jennings Announce New Middle and High School Reform Measures: New Reforms Better Prepare Students for Postsecondary Education and the Workforce." Press release, February 14, 2006. http://www.fldoe.org/news/2006/2006_02_14-2.asp.

Florida Department of Law Enforcement. "Firearm Involved Violent Crimes." Florida Statistical Analysis Center, 2008. http://www.fdle.state.fl.us/Content /getdoc/6dcf8a34-8940-4738-b8ac-5923642d32af/firearms_2008.aspx.

Friedman, Milton. *There's No Such Thing as a Free Lunch*. LaSalle, Ill.: Open Court, 1975.

Gannon, Michael. *Florida: A Short History*. Rev. ed. Gainesville: University Press of Florida, 2003.

————, ed. *The New History of Florida*. Gainesville: University Press of Florida, 1996.

Goldwater, Barry M. *The Conscience of a Conservative*. Shepherdsville, Ky.: Victor, 1960. Excerpted in Schneider, *Conservatism in America*, 211–25.

Gould, Lewis L. *Grand Old Party: A History of the Republicans*. New York: Random House, 2003.

Greene, Jay P., and Marcus A. Winters. "Public School Graduation Rates in the United States." Manhattan Institute for Policy Research, November 2002. http://www.manhattan-institute.org/html/cr_31.htm.

Grunwald, Michael. "Postcard from the Everglades." *Time*, December 11, 2011.
————. *The Swamp: The Everglades, Florida, and the Politics of Paradise*. New York: Simon & Schuster, 2006.

Guttmacher Institute. "Abortion." In "State Data Center," http://www.guttmacher .org/datacenter/trend.jsp#.

Henig, Jeffrey R., and Stephen D. Sugarman. "The Nature and Extent of School Choice." In Sugarman and Kemerer, *School Choice and Social Controversy*, 13–35.

In Re: The Guardianship of Theresa Schiavo . . . Case Number 90-2908GD-003. In Caplan, McCartney, and Sisti, *Case of Terri Schiavo*, 86–93.

Jeb Bush, Governor of Florida, et al., Appellants, v. Michael Schiavo, Guardian of Theresa Schiavo, Appellee, 885 So. 2d 321 (Fla. 2004). In Caplan, McCartney, and Sisti, *Case of Terri Schiavo*, 103–22.

Kernell, Samuel. *Going Public: New Strategies of Presidential Leadership*. 4th ed. Washington, D.C.: CQ Press, 2007.

Kimbrough, Ralph, Kern Alexander, and James Wattenbarger. "Government and Education." In *Florida's Politics and Government*, edited by Manning J. Dauer, 422–47. Gainesville: University Presses of Florida, 1980.

Leuchtenburg, William E. *Franklin D. Roosevelt and the New Deal, 1932–1940*. New York: Harper & Row, 1963.

Libby, Ronald T. *Purging the Republican Party: Tea Party Campaigns and Elections*. Lanham, Md.: Lexington, 2014.

Meacham, Jon. *American Lion: Andrew Jackson in the White House*. New York: Random House, 2008.

Michael, Deanna, and Sherman Dorn. "Accountability as a Means of Improvement: A Continuity of Themes." In Borman and Dorn, *Education Reform in Florida*, 83–116.

Middendorf, J. William, II. *A Glorious Disaster: Barry Goldwater's Presidential Campaign and the Origins of the Conservative Movement*. New York: Basic Books, 2006.

Miller, Zeke. "Turning LePage: Jeb Bush Fundraises for Tea Party Governor in Maine." Swampland. *Time*, September 25, 2013.

Oakes, James. *The Radical and the Republican: Frederick Douglass, Abraham Lincoln, and the Triumph of Antislavery Politics*. New York: W. W. Norton, 2007.

O'Connor, John. "From Minnesota to Miami: The History of Florida Charter Schools." NPR, StateImpact Florida, September 28, 2011. http://stateimpact. npr.org/florida/2011/09/28/.

OPPAGA (Office of Program Policy Analysis and Government Accountability), Florida Legislature. *Half of College Students Needing Remediation Drop Out:*

Remediation Completers Do Almost as Well as Other Students. Report 07-37. May 2007.

———. *Third Grade Retention Policy Leading to Better Student Performance Statewide.* Report 06-66. October 2006.

Parmet, Herbert S. *George Bush: The Life of a Lone Star Yankee.* 1997. Piscataway, N.J.: Transaction, 2000.

Pavlovsky, Arnold Marc. "'We Busted Because We Failed': Florida Politics, 1880–1908." Ph.D. diss., University of Florida, 1973.

PolitiFact.com (*Tampa Bay Times* website). "Mitt Romney and Rick Scott Both Have Medicare Fraud in Their Background, Super PAC Ad Claims." October 31, 2012. http://www.politifact.com/truth-o-meter/statements/2012/nov/02/priorities-usa-action/mitt-romney-and-rick-scott-both-have-medicare-frau/.

———. "Self-Defense Deaths in Florida Have Increased Dramatically Since 'Stand Your Ground' Became Law in 2005, Lawmaker Claims." March 26, 2012. http://www.politifact.com/florida/statements/2012/mar/26/christopher-l-smith/sen-chris-smith-claimed-deaths-due-self-defense-fl.

Proctor, Samuel. "Prelude to the New Florida, 1877–1919." In Gannon, *New History of Florida*, 266–86.

Quinnipiac University. "Florida Voters Give Gov. Bush a 'C' Grade, Quinnipiac University Poll Finds; Schools Need Work, Voters Say, So Spend More." February 24, 2005. http://www.quinnipiac.edu/news-and-events/quinnipiac-university-poll/florida/release-detail?ReleaseID=652.

Reese, William J. *America's Public Schools: From Common School to "No Child Left Behind."* Baltimore: Johns Hopkins University Press, 2005.

Rogers, William W. "Fortune and Misfortune: The Paradoxical Twenties." In Gannon, *New History of Florida*, 287–303.

———. "The Great Depression." In Gannon, *New History of Florida*, 304–22.

Sabato, Larry. *Goodbye to Good-time Charlie: The American Governorship Transformed.* 2nd ed. Washington, D.C.: CQ Press, 1983.

Schafer, Daniel L. "U.S. Territory and State." In Gannon, *New History of Florida*, 207–30.

Schneider, Gregory L., ed. *Conservatism in America since 1930: A Reader.* New York: New York University Press, 2003.

Schweizer, Peter, and Rochelle Schweizer. *The Bushes: Portrait of a Dynasty.* New York: Doubleday, 2004.

Shofner, Jerrell H. "Reconstruction and Renewal, 1865–1877." In Gannon, *New History of Florida*, 249–65.

Sugarman, Stephen D. "School Choice and Public Funding." In Sugarman and Kemerer, *School Choice and Social Controversy*, 111–39.

Sugarman, Stephen D., and Frank R. Kemerer, eds. *School Choice and Social Controversy: Politics, Policy, and Law*. Washington, D.C.: Brookings Institution Press, 1999.

Walberg, Herbert J. *School Choice: The Findings*. Washington, D.C.: Cato Institute, 2007.

Index

Page numbers in *italics* refer to tables.

Ball, Ed, 25
Banks, closure of, 49
Barron, Dempsey, 38
Baxley, Dennis, 85
Bennett, Tony, 182–83
Bentsen, Lloyd, 60
Beyle, Thad, 22
Bill of Rights, 44
Biotech industry, 162–63
Black, Earl, 61
Black, Merle, 61
Bloomberg, Michael, 180
Blueprint 2000, 120, 129
Board of Regents, 124
Bonus Army incident, 48
Bourbon Democrats, 19
Bozell, Brent, 56
Brady, Sarah, 85
Brain denied oxygen, 93
Breckenridge, John, 13
Brogan, Frank, 121
Bronson, Charles, 84, 166
Brown, Corrine, 89
Brown v. Board of Education, 30, 67, 118
Bryant, Farris, 32
Buckley, William F., Jr., 53, 55
Budgetary leadership crisis, 175
Burke, Edmund, 54
Burnham Institute, 163
Burns, Haydon, 32
Bush, Barbara, 59, 180
Bush, Columba, 63, 191, 194
Bush, George H. W., 1, 59–60, 62, 191
Bush, George Prescott, 42
Bush, George W., 1, 104; as evangelical Christian, 77; faith-based public policy of, 90–91; Florida won by, 3; Hurricane Katrina response of, 3; as Texas governor, 64; Texas oil career and, 63
Bush, Jeb: abortion issue of, 77–82; accountability policies of, 124–25; activist conservative government of, 40, 65–70; affirmative action ended by, 88–90; African Americans strained relations with, 69; Askew compared to, 39–40; Chiles election victory over, 64; conservative direction of, 10, 69–70; conservative domestic policies of, 4, 5; constitutional crisis and, 177; courts barrier to power of, 78; cultural activism impact of, 107–10; education reforms from, 68, 121–27, 179–83; executive-driven governorship of, 5; executive power beliefs of, 66–67; Florida economy diversification by, 24; forceful personality of, 21; Foundation for Florida's Future founded by, 111–12; free enterprise commitment of, 166; friendly state legislature for, 66, 177; health care reform and, 168; high-profile challenges faced by, xii–xiii; Hispanics relations with, 68–69; implementing education reforms from, 127–29; inaugural address of, 67–68; incentives offered by, 161–62; individual moral behavior focus of, 71–72; initiatives and accomplishments of, 176; k-12 education leader appointed by, 65–66; legacy of, 175–79, 195; as most powerful Florida governor, xi, 5, 6, 37, 175, 176; oil drilling expansion fought by, 171–72; online petition requesting intervention from, 98; philosophy on government of, 72–77; possible presidential bid of, 192–95; *Profiles in Character* by, 41; progressive leadership stopped by, 19; public opinion poll about, 107; reckless accusations by, 106–7; right-to-life issues and, 81–82; as Roman Catholic, 77; Romney's introduction of, 174–75; Rubio endorsed by, 188; run for governor of, 63–65; Schiavo, T., case intervention of, 97–98, 105–6; Schindler's meeting with, 98;

Conservative movement, xii, 7; Bush, J., shifting toward, 10, 69–70; of Goldwater, 58–59; government activism and, 53–54; major issues of, 51; Reagan and, 62–63; after World War II, 50

Conservatives, 11; capitalist, 46–51, 68; conflict between, 46; cultural, 68; Democratic Party as, 14–15; forming after American Revolution, 43–44; free-market, 54; government with activist, 40, 65–70; intellectual, 51–55; religious, 77; southern, 46; state courts distrust from, 136; tradition and class-based society of, 54

Constitutional amendments, xii, 23, 122–23, 181–82

Constitutional convention, 16–17, 44

Constitutional crisis, 177

Constitution of 1885, x; constitutional convention producing, 16–17; Florida government approaches from, 18–19; governorship limits placed by, 17–18; weak-governor system from, 4, 156

Constitution of 1968, 33–35

Containment policy, 56

Convergys Corporation, 165–66, 169

Corporate income tax, 21, 36–37, 40

Corporate Tax Credit Scholarship, 123, 136

Court system, 92–93; Bush, J., power barrier from, 78; conservatives distrusting, 136; governors conflict with, 99–100; of Schiavo, M., 95–96; of Schiavo, T., 96–97; social issues in, 78; student assessment tests blocked by, 120. *See also* Supreme Court

Crane, James, 81

Crew, Robert, 6

Crime-fighting strategy, 33

Crime rate, 108–9

Criminal activities, 84

Crisis management skills, xii

Crist, Charlie, 97, 148, 168, 178–79, 182; climate change issue of, 185–86;

Obama hugged by, 186–87; out of Republican Party, 188; political problems of, 186; Rubio challenger to, 185, 187–88; stem cell funding from, 184; support collapsing for, 187

Critical thinking, 129–30

Cruz, Ted, 193–94

Cruzan, Nancy, 92–93

Cruzan et Ux v. Director, Missouri Department of Health, 92–94

Cuban community, 63

Cultural activism, 107–10

Cultural conservatism, 68

Curriculum standardization, 113–15

Dáte, S. V., 6

Davis, Jim, 148

Davis, Jordan, 86

DCF. *See* Department of Children and Families

Death row inmates, 167

Defense of Marriage Act, 110

Delaney, John, 171

DeMint, Jim, 188

Democratic clubs, 15–16

Democratic Party, x, 34–35, 60; as conservative political party, 14–15; as only real political party, 19; as private club, 18; progressives in, 47; public opinion shifting against, 32–33; secessionist views in, 12–13

Department of Children and Families (DCF), 81, 103–4, 165, 177

Desegregation issue, 118

Dewey, Thomas E., 52, 56

Disabled students, 137

Disney World, 35

Drug testing, 139

Dukakis, Michael, 62

Duncan, Arne, 181

Dunn, Michael, 86

duPont, Alfred I., 25

Dyckman, Martin, 18, 37, 84

Dyslexic students, 137

MATTHEW CORRIGAN is professor and chair of the Department of Political Science and Public Administration at the University of North Florida. His previous books are *Race, Religion, and Economic Change* and *American Royalty*, which focuses on the Clinton and Bush families. During the aftermath of the 2000 presidential election, he was a consultant to Duval County, Florida, and assisted county leaders in reforming the county's voting system. During presidential and gubernatorial election nights, he works as a consultant for the Associated Press analyzing exit polls and turnout data for the state of Florida. He lives in Jacksonville with his wife, Mary, and children, John and Jane.

FLORIDA GOVERNMENT AND POLITICS

Series editors, David R. Colburn and Susan A. MacManus

Florida has emerged today as a microcosm of the nation and has become a political bellwether in national elections. The impact of Florida on the presidential elections of 2000, 2004, and 2008 suggests the magnitude of the state's influence. Of the four most populous states in the nation, Florida is the only one that has moved from one political column to the other in the last three national elections. These developments suggest the vital need to explore the politics of the Sunshine State in greater detail. Books in this series will explore the myriad aspects of politics, political science, public policy, history, and government in Florida.

The 57 Club: My Four Decades in Florida Politics, by Frederick B. Karl (2010)

The Political Education of Buddy MacKay, by Buddy MacKay, with Rick Edmonds (2010)

Immigrant Prince: Mel Martinez and The American Dream, by Richard E. Fogelsong (2011)

Reubin O'D. Askew and the Golden Age of Florida Politics, by Martin A. Dyckman (2011)

Red Pepper and Gorgeous George: Claude Pepper's Epic Defeat in the 1950 Democratic Primary, by James C. Clark (2011)

Inside Bush v. Gore, by Charley Wells (2013)

Conservative Hurricane: How Jeb Bush Remade Florida, by Matthew T. Corrigan (2014)

www.ingramcontent.com/pod-product-compliance
Lightning Source LLC
Chambersburg PA
CBHW020454100426

42813CB00031B/3360/J